# THE
# SONG OF SONGS

*A Twelfth-Century French Version*

UNIVERSITY OF HULL PUBLICATIONS

Car mes chevals dautre part tire
Ordains sone descendement
ki uuelt auoir aprochement
A deu e uuelt de seufk soi tendre
primes apregne en soi descendre
Je puet sauoir cele hautesce
ki ne conoist sa petitesce

a matere de cest saint liure
vuelt tot le cuer auoir deliure
uil nait al siecle baerie
e tot soit uuiz de legerie
el le requiert quar altrement
flauroit pas sein entendement
uar damor est li liures faiz
e par grant sens en fu estraiz
isages salemons le fist
Cui deus a cest honor eslist
amor dont il ici parole
flest pas del siecle nest pas fole

THE BRIDEGROOM AND HIS BRIDE

*Ms. Le Mans Bibliothèque Municipale 173  o. 33 verso*

# THE
# SONG OF SONGS

*A Twelfth-Century French Version*

━━━━

EDITED FROM MS. 173 OF THE
BIBLIOTHÈQUE MUNICIPALE OF LE MANS

BY

CEDRIC E. PICKFORD

*Published for the* UNIVERSITY OF HULL *by*
OXFORD UNIVERSITY PRESS
LONDON   NEW YORK   TORONTO
1974

*Oxford University Press, Ely House, London W. 1*

GLASGOW  NEW YORK  TORONTO  MELBOURNE  WELLINGTON
CAPE TOWN  IBADAN  NAIROBI  DAR ES SALAAM  LUSAKA  ADDIS ABABA
DELHI  BOMBAY  CALCUTTA  MADRAS  KARACHI  LAHORE  DACCA
KUALA LUMPUR  SINGAPORE  HONG KONG  TOKYO

ISBN 0 19 713418 1

*Printed in Great Britain
at the University Press, Oxford
by Vivian Ridler
Printer to the University*

# PREFACE

In the course of the preparation of this edition, I have not lacked guidance and advice from my predecessors, as well as from some quite unconventional quarters. To the Librarian of the Bibliothèque Municipale du Mans, and to Mademoiselle Edith Brayer of the Institut de Recherche et d'Histoire des Textes, I am grateful for permission to work on the photographs of MS. 173 of Le Mans. From colleagues in Hull I have received much kindly guidance. I mention especially Mr. R. W. Last of the German Department and Dr. D. W. Beard of the Centre for Computer Studies in Hull who have provided a computer-generated concordance of the text—of which copies may be purchased from the University of Hull. Above all, however, I must express my sense of the deep debt of gratitude which I owe to Professor E. Vinaver, who not only guided my first steps in the field of Medieval French Studies, but also drew my attention to the interest and importance of the present text. His example has been a continuous encouragement to me so I would like to think that whatever merits this edition may have may be attributed to him: its deficiencies are my own responsibility.

# CONTENTS

# INTRODUCTION

## 1. *The Old Testament Song of Songs*

THE Song of Songs, or as it is often called, the Song of Solomon, although a comparatively short book, has enjoyed a greater range of varying interpretations than any other book of the Old Testament. The very title arouses inquiry. What is meant by Song of Songs, or, to give the work the name by which it was known throughout the Middle Ages and beyond, Canticum Canticorum? Is this expression a form of superlative which is not uncommon in the Bible where phrases like 'King of Kings', 'Lord of Lords' convey clearly a sense of supreme omnipotence? Understood in this way, the title would mean the Supreme Song, or the most perfect of lyrics. On the other hand, it could mean little more than the fact that the book is a song made by putting together other already existing songs; that is, an anthology of Canticles or Songs. Lyric Canticles are not unknown in the Old Testament, examples include the Prophetic Blessing of Jacob (Genesis 49), or the Song of Deborah (Judges 5).[1] In the New Testament, the *Nunc Dimittis* or the Song of Simeon (Luke 2: 29–23) and the *Magnificat* (Luke 1: 46–55) or the Song of Mary are familiar examples of lyric passages which are incorporated in the Gospel narrative. The Song of Songs is not composed of lyric passages of the kind which are to be found elsewhere in the Old Testament: it is a composition of a unique kind.

The attribution to Solomon stressed in the title of the work was widely accepted from the earliest times, and it is stated as an undisputed fact on many occasions. For medieval French readers, it is almost a commonplace to observe

Li sages Salemons le fist. (v. 9)

Old Testament scholars no longer take this attribution seriously. It was, however, the name of Solomon which gave the book an air of authenticity and led to its being included in the Canon of Scripture, though not without some discussion and dispute among the rabbis in the first century A.D. Despite the arguments advanced against

---

[1] Other examples include the *Song of Moses* (Deuteronomy 32) and the *Song of Jonas* (Jonas 2), and the *Benedictus*, the Song of Ananias, Misael, and Azarias when cast into the burning fiery furnace (Daniel 3: 52–6) followed by their *Benedicite* (Daniel 3: 57–90).

including the work in the Jewish Canon of Scripture, it was seen as having an important part to play. The love depicted in the Song of Songs was understood as an allegory of the love of God for Israel, and so the work was read in the Synagogue at the time of the Passover to mark the Exodus of the children of Israel from Egypt.

A book of such rich quality naturally inspired throughout the centuries many different interpretations. It is legitimate to consider it as a work of literature, and it was of course the purely literary and erotic value of the text which caused the rabbis of the first century to question its place in the canon. When E. Reuss discussed the text as recently as 1879, he declared 'Ce n'est qu'avec une certaine hésitation que nous abordons le Cantique, pour le joindre aux autres livres bibliques . . . Nous avons maintenant affaire à une poésie profane'.[1] This interpretation is not an exclusively modern phenomenon. During the twelfth century a French rabbi, whose name has not been preserved, declared that the Song of Songs was composed by Solomon to immortalize his love for his favourite wife.[2] Modern scholars have repeatedly treated the Song of Songs as pure love poetry, and Ernest Renan commented on the possible comparisons that could be made with more recent Syrian epithalamia.[3]

The song is presented in the form of a dialogue, or of corresponding monologues. Origen, in the third century A.D., considered the possibility that it was a love drama:

> Epithalamium libellus hic . . . dramatis in modum
> mihi videt a Salamone conscriptus.[4]

If it is a drama, who then are the dramatis personae? Solomon, presumably, would be one of them, a second would be the bride, and the third could be a shepherd lover. Nineteenth-century scholars[5] who developed this theory none the less encountered many difficulties of detail in adjusting it to the text in a precise manner. It is noteworthy that although some argued that the Song of Songs is a pastoral love tale in which the Shulamite bride remains loyal to her bucolic lover despite the advances made by Solomon, this interpretation is not to be found in medieval French texts despite the fact that in lyric poetry,

---

[1] E. Reuss, *Le Cantique des Cantiques*, 1879, p. 3.
[2] The text is preserved in Bodleian, MS. Opp. 625, and was edited by H. J. Matthews, *Festschrift, zum 80en Geburtstag Moritz Steinschneider's*, 1896, pp. 164–85 and 238–40.
[3] Ernest Renan, *Le Cantique des Cantiques*, Paris, 1860, p. 86.
[4] Migne, *Patrologia Latina*, xiii (1862), col. 61.
[5] H. H. Rowley, 'The Interpretation of the Song of Songs' in *The Servant of the Lord* London, 1952, pp. 203–4.

pastoral themes of this kind were a widely practised literary genre. The medieval French *pastourelle*, a genre in which a knight or nobleman asked a shepherdess for her love—a theme to which writers returned on very many occasions in a variety of ways—does not seem to have any link at all with the Song of Songs.

When one considers possible non-literary evaluations and interpretations of the Song of Songs, a rich diversity of possibilities is revealed. In relatively recent times it has been increasingly usual to seek for and discover in the Old Testament traces of pre-Judaic or at least non-Judaic rituals. As one example of the approach, let it be sufficient to mention that W. Wittekindt in his very full commentary declared that the Song of Songs is a liturgy to be used in Jerusalem to celebrate the wedding of Ishtar and Tammuz at the Spring New Moon.[1] Interpretations of this kind are very recent, and medieval writers never reacted in this way to a book of the Old Testament.

Of much greater antiquity, however, is the interpretation of the book in terms of the history of Judah. Nicolas de Lyra in the fourteenth century argued that the history of Israel is recounted in the first four chapters, and that the last two chapters refer, prophetically, to the weakness of the Christian Church during the pre-Constantinian Roman Empire.[2] The historical interpretation never enjoyed as much popularity as that to which Nicolas de Lyra refers when discussing the last two chapters. Church fathers, saints, and scholars throughout the centuries of the Christian era felt that the marriage of Solomon and his bride as told in the Song of Songs symbolized and foretold the union of Christ with his Church, as well as symbolizing on occasion the relationship of the soul with God. This interpretation became widely accepted throughout Western Europe. The extent to which it was regarded as the only possible meaning of the book can be judged by the fact that the page and chapter headings in the Authorized Version of the English Bible form explanatory notes which reinforce this interpretation.

## II. *The Interpretation of the Song of Songs in the Middle Ages*

To explain the meaning of a work of literature was a task which writers of the twelfth century relished. The attitude of the monastic

[1] W. Wittekindt, *Das Hohe Lied und seine Beziehungen zum Istarkult*, 1926, quoted by H. H. Rowley, op. cit., pp. 217–19.          [2] Rowley, op. cit., p. 194.

exegete is well expressed by Hervé de Bourgdieu, who, in the second
half of the twelfth century, has no hesitation in declaring that the
'interpretation surpasses the narrative just as the fruit surpasses the
leaves of the tree on which it grows'.[1] A similar view was expressed
by the author of the *Livre des Rois* when he wrote 'L'estoire est paille,
le sen est grains: le sen est fruit, l'estoire raims' (the story is chaff,
the meaning is wheat, the meaning is the fruit, the story is the branch).[2]
In the domain of secular literature in twelfth-century France, perhaps
the best known comment is that made by Marie de France in the
*Prologue* to her *Lais*:

> Costume fu as anciens
> Ce testemoine Preciens
> Es livres que jadis faisoient
> Assez oscurement disoient
> Por ceus qui a venir estoient
> Et qui aprendre les devoient,
> Qu'il peussent gloser la lettre
> Et de lor sen le surplus mettre.[3]

This observation is to be found in the *Prologue* to a purely secular
work: a collection of a dozen *Lais*, stories of human love, some of
which are set at the court of King Arthur. To interpret a work of
literature, to add one's own interpretation—'et de lor sen le sorplus
mettre'—was not in the twelfth century the prerogative solely of those
concerned with the exegesis of biblical texts.

Combined with this interest in interpretation was a change of
approach of certain of the Church Fathers. In their teaching, both
St. Bernard of Clairvaux and St. Anselm moved away from the
communal exercise to stress the importance for the individual to know
himself, and by knowing himself to rise to a knowledge of God.[4] A
source of great inspiration for St. Bernard was the Song of Songs,
and he felt that it should be expounded for other men. The men he
referred to were his fellow monks, and his exposition is solid food, and
of greater worth than the previous instruction they had received in

---

[1] quantum poma foliis, tantum allegoria historiis praecellit (F. Stegmüller, *Repertorium biblicum medii aevi*, iii, No. 3256), quoted by E. Vinaver, 'From Epic to Romance' in *Bulletin of the John Rylands Library*, vol. xl, No. 2, Mar. 1964, pp. 476–503, see p. 490.

[2] Quoted by E. Vinaver, art. cit., p. 490.

[3] Marie de France, *Les Lais*, ed. A. Ewert, v. 9–16.

[4] See R. W. Southern, *The Making of the Middle Ages*, 1953, Ch. V, 'From Epic to Romance'.

INTRODUCTIONxiii

Ecclesiastes and Proverbs.[1] The spirit in which the book is to be understood is described with precision:

> You must bring chaste ears to listen to this Discourse of love which we now have in hand; and, when you think about the lovers in it, you must not understand by them a man and a woman, but the Word and the Soul. And if I say 'Christ and the Church' instead of Word and Soul, the difference is only this: that by the Church is meant the unity—or rather unanimity—of many souls.[2]

St. Bernard's sermons were delivered to his fellow monks. He began to preach on this theme to his brethren at Clairvaux in or about 1135. He had preached eighty-six sermons on the Song when he died in 1153, and by this time he had covered only the two first chapters and a little of the third. The sermons are long, and their beauty and enthusiasm testify to the powerful force of inspiration which the Song had for him: his sermons did much to draw attention to this Book of the Old Testament, which enjoyed considerable attention in the twelfth century.

Guillaume de Saint-Thierry was inspired not merely by the writings of St. Bernard, but by the saint himself. He was invited to Clairvaux to join St. Bernard. Both of them spent a period of illness in the infirmary there, and the two men discussed the Song of Songs at length. Guillaume de Saint-Thierry was concerned above all with the different states of the spiritual life, and Bernard expounded to his friend those things which can be known only from personal experience and which are described in the Song of Songs. This sojourn at Clairvaux in the company of St. Bernard encouraged Guillaume to undertake his own *Expositio* of the work.[3]

Before he began this task, he was already familiar with other commentaries on the Song of Songs. Shortly after entering the new foundation of Signy in 1135, Guillaume prepared what can best be described as extensive notes on the work of St. Gregory on the Song of Songs,[4] and the Commentary on the Song of Songs as revealed in the work of St. Ambrose.[5] These preliminary researches and studies enabled

---

[1] St. Bernard, *On the Song of Songs*, translated by a Religious of the C.S.M.V., London, 1952, Preface, p. 21.     [2] St. Bernard, *In Cantica Canticorum Sermo*, lxi. 2.
[3] See Dom. J. Hourlier, 'Guillaume de Saint-Thierry et le Brevis Commentatio in Cantica' in *Analecta Sacri Ordinis Cisterciensis*, 12 (1956), pp. 105–14.
[4] *Excerpta ex libris Sancti Gregorii Papae super Cantica Canticorum*, Migne, *Patrologia Latina*, clxxx, pp. 441–74.
[5] *Commentarius in Cantico Canticorum e scriptis sancti Ambrosii*, Migne, *Patrologia Latina*, xv, pp. 1947–2060.

Guillaume to produce his own *Expositio* of the Song of Songs. Although the expressly allegorical interpretation of the book was usual, nay popular, in the twelfth century (St. Bernard himself describes it as 'a veritable forest of allegories'[1]), Guillaume's work is not just another allegorical interpretation. Familiar though he was with the commentaries of earlier fathers, Origen, St. Ambrose, Gregory, St. Augustine, Plotinus, not to mention his great contemporary Bernard, Guillaume de Saint-Thierry did not merely summarize and reproduce their ideas. His commentary is above all a moral one. He seeks to explore the meaning of the relationship of Bridegroom and Bride in terms of the relationship of Christ and the Soul. Though it clearly depends on that of his predecessors, his is an original work of remarkable insight and power.[2]

*        *        *

During the first half of the twelfth century, there was, therefore, in northern and central France a considerable interest in the interpretation and explanation of this particular Book of the Bible. The Song of Songs is concerned with Love, the Love of the Bride and Groom, the Love of Solomon and his Bride, which symbolized for different readers the love of Christ for the Church, or the bond which linked the Soul with the Divine Being. *Love, Amor,* or *Amour* is a word which can apply to a wide range of feelings, both profane and sacred. To see profane love and sacred love as two quite separate and even opposing ideals is to misunderstand the way in which the twelfth-century mind operated. Theories concerning human love of man for woman were a feature of secular literature towards the end of the twelfth century. Well known and influential was the work of Andreas Capellanus[3] *The Art of Courtly Love,* or the *De Amore Libri Tres,* adapted and rendered into French by Drouart de la Vache in his *Livre d'Amours.*[4] The growth of theories of courtesy and love, the flowering of romances of love and chivalry, as well as the rich harvest of love poetry, all testify to the great awareness of the problems of

[1] silva umbrosa latebrosaque allegoriarum (St. Bernard, *In Cantica* xvi, Migne, *Patrologia Latina,* clxxxiii, p. 849A). This phrase suggests what Baudelaire was to describe many centuries later as a *forêt de symboles.*
[2] The most useful edition of the work of Guillaume de Saint-Thierry is the edition and translation published by J. M. Décharet and M. Dumontier: Guillaume de Saint-Thierry: *Exposé sur le Cantique des Cantiques,* Paris, 1962 (*Sources Chrétiennes,* No. 82).
[3] Andreas Capellanus, *The Art of Courtly Love* translated by John J. Parry, New York, 1941, Sept. 1959.
[4] Drouart de la Vache, *Li Livre d Amours,* p.p. R. Bossuat, Paris, 1926.

love. The expression of this awareness was by no means restricted to tales of chivalric love. Within the very framework of the Arthurian romance of chivalry, one finds that authors, and presumably readers too, recognized that chivalric and secular love did not exclude the search of the Soul for God. It was during the third decade of the following century that earthly love and divine love came to be treated simultaneously in one work. The *Quest of the Holy Grail*[1] is not merely a romance about the Knights of King Arthur's Round Table; it is a work of religious inspiration, in which the author considers the revelation of the Divine Mysteries to Man.[2] It marks a culmination rather than a beginning, for almost a century earlier, as we have seen, St. Bernard, in his sermons on the Song of Songs, was considering questions of Divine Love and Grace. These sermons were preached at the very time when the Troubadours of Provence and the Trouvères of northern France were singing of earthly love.

At the beginning of the twelfth century, too, were produced the first French versions of the Bible. The Psalter was the first Biblical text to be rendered into the vernacular. The so-called Cambridge Psalter, based on the Latin translation of a Hebrew text, was made at Canterbury in about the year 1120.[3] Other translations followed, mostly in prose, but sometimes in verse.[4] The twelfth century did not, however, witness the translation of the Bible *in extenso*. Characteristic of this age is the production of translations of single books, especially the Psalms, the Historical Books, e.g. Kings and Maccabees, as well as the Apocalypse. At the very end of the century there was made a French summarized version of the Bible, of which one manuscript, now in the Bibliothèque de l'Arsenal in Paris (MS. 5211), survives. (It is an incomplete version, but it did point the way to the making of the full translation of the Bible into French which was undertaken in the early years of the thirteenth century, and of which a number of manuscript copies survive.)

---

[1] *La Queste del Saint Graal*, éd. A. Pauphilet, Paris (Champion), 1923 (*Les Classiques français du Moyen Âge*, No. 33).

[2] E. Gilson, 'La mystique de la grâce dans la *Queste del Saint Graal*' in *Romania*, vol. li (1925), pp. 321–47. On the Cistercian connections of the *Queste* see Pauphilet, *Études sur la Queste del Saint Graal*, Paris, 1925.

[3] For a full account of this, and other Old French versions of the Bible, see S. Berger, *La Bible française au Moyen Âge*, Paris, 1884.

[4] For an account of Old French versions of the Bible in the context of the history of the transmission of the Bible, see C. A. Robson, 'Vernacular Scriptures in France' in *The Cambridge History of the Bible*, vol. 2, *The West from the Fathers to the Reformation*, ed. G. W. H. Lampe, Cambridge, 1969, pp. 436–52. The verse translations are described

Translations into verse were also executed, and of these the most
complete is that of Herman de Valenciennes, who was a Canon of the
Cathedral of Valenciennes in the twelfth century. More than twenty
manuscript copies have come down to us. Partial verse adaptations
and verse renderings of individual books of the Bible were also popular.
In this climate of literary and theological writing, it is not surprising
that the Song of Songs should have appealed to poets in twelfth-
century France. From this period, two poems based on the Song of
Songs have survived. A third, which is also extant, was composed
at the end of the thirteenth or perhaps at the beginning of the fourteenth
century.

*       *       *

Of the two twelfth-century poems, the one which is the object of the
present edition is preserved in a single manuscript at Le Mans. The
other, a short work of some ninety-three verse lines, is not a trans-
lation so much as an imitation of the Song, and is preserved on the
reverse of the last folio of MS. B.N. lat. 2297.[1] It has been published
several times during the last hundred years or so.[2]

The translation of the first three chapters of the Song of Songs
preserved in MS. B.N. 14966 is of much later date. It is presented in
eight-line stanzas and begins with a more or less literal translation
of the Latin text followed by explanations and amplifications. The
author had no intention of translating more than the first three chap-
ters. The link between secular and religious literature is explicitly
made: after asking for the aid of Our Lady in the Prologue, the author
alludes to the *Roman de la Rose*, saying that his work is

> . . . plus honeste que n'est celle
> Dou romant c'on dist [de] la rose.
> (MS. B.N. fr. 14966, f° 1 v°)

Furthermore, he takes the opportunity to chastise monks:

> Par les renars au[s] grandes coues
> Entendés nonnains et canoinnes,
> (quoted by J. Bonnard, op. cit., p. 165)

by Jean Bonnard, *Les Traductions de la Bible en vers français au Moyen Âge*, Paris,
1884.
    [1] See ibid., Ch. XV, *Le Cantique des Cantiques*.
    [2] G. Paris, 'Petit Poème dévot' in *Jahrbuch für romanische und englische Literatur*,
vol. vi (1866), pp. 362–9; and W. Foerster and E. Koschwitz, *Altfranzösisches
Uebungsbuch* 1884 (seventh edition 1932).

and lashes them with a whip as suggested by the *Roman de Renart*. Though some translations are very happy ones,[1] the poem is marred by trivialities and outworn allegorical commentaries. It is none the less composed in a manner which shows technical competence, and it testifies to a continuing interest in the Song of Songs.

## III. *The Poem of Landri de Waben* (?)

Of the three surviving French adaptations and interpretations of the Song of Songs, the most extensive, and in many ways the most intriguing, is that preserved in MS. 173 of the Municipal Library of Le Mans, the only known copy of the work. It begins on f° 33 verso. There is an illuminated initial six lines high at the beginning of the text, whose first lines are:

> La matere de cest saint livre
> Vuelt tot le cuer avoir delivre . . .

but there is no title, rubric, or *incipit*. Four lines are left blank between the end of the previous work—a commentary on the book of Exodus—and the Song of Songs, but no rubricator or copyist has provided a heading as a guide to what follows. The ending of the poem too is devoid of *explicit* or any form of title. The author does not give his name anywhere in the manuscript. There is, however, an epilogue, separated from the main body of the text by two blank lines, which reads:

> Por l'oneur Deu premierement,
> Aprés por nostre enseignement
> E por celi cui jo present
> A Deu, quant jo le sai present,
> Ki me pramist k'ele por moi
> Deu prieroit, e fait, jo croi,
> Ai de rimer paine soferte.
> Or sui venuz a bogne certe.
> Ici vueil jo metre ma cire.
> Ne m'en orreiz ore plus dire,
> Mais tant requier que cist romanz
> Unkes ne viegne en main l'enfant
> (MS. Le Mans 173, f° 109 v°–110 r°, vv. 3495–3506)

---

[1] e.g. for *Lectulus noster floridus* (I, xv) we have

> Amis, floris est nostre lis
> Et bien parés de fleurs diverses,
> De violettes et de lis,
> De roses, de glais, de fleurs perses . . .

This important passage shows that the poem is not simply a pious 'labour of love' carried out for its own sake and for the edification of the writer; it was written for a patron, the lady to whom reference is made in the lines

> Ki me pramist k'ele por moi
> Deu prieroit, e fait, jo croi.
> (vv. 3499–3500)

This reference does suggest that the Old French poem on the Song of Songs, unlike St. Bernard's sermons on the Song of Songs which were presented to his brethren at Cîteaux, was an attempt to interpret the work for lay readers. Its form—octosyllabic couplets rhyming in pairs—was that which, from the middle of the twelfth century onwards, was employed for verse chronicles such as the *Roman de Brut* of Wace, a legendary history of Britain, the Arthurian romances of Chrétien de Troyes, some of which were composed for Marie de Champagne, the romances of Antiquity, for example the *Roman de Troie* of Benoît de Sainte-Maure, and the romances of Tristan and Ysolt composed towards the end of the twelfth century by Béroul and Thomas. By an amazing and fortunate coincidence, we have a reference to a work which would apparently resemble very closely the Old French version of the Song of Songs, in the History of the County of Guines written by Lambert d'Ardres. There it is stated that the Count Baudouin II of Guines commissioned the writing of a mystical interpretation of the Song of Songs in French, and that this was undertaken by a Landericus de Wabbanio. The French name of this otherwise unknown writer would be Landri de Waben. The full text of the reference is as follows:

Sed cum omnem omnium scientiam avidissime amplecteretur et omnem omnium scientiam corde tenus retinere nequivisset, virum eruditissimum magistrum Landericum de Wabbanio dum Ardensis honoris preesset comes dominio, Cantica canticorum non solum ad litteram, sed ad misticam spiritualis interpretationis intelligentiam de latino in romanum, ut eorum misticam virtutem saperet et intelligeret, transferre sibi et sepius ante se legere fecit. (*Lamberti Ardensis historia comitum Ghisnensium*, in *Monumenta Germaniae Historica*, ed. Pertz, vol. xxiv, p. 598)

The places mentioned here can all be identified without difficulty. Guines is in the Pas de Calais, some 10 kilometres due south of the town of Calais. Its population today is some three and a half thousand

INTRODUCTION xix

souls. Ardres, a still smaller township of some fourteen hundred inhabitants, is 17 kilometres SSW. of Calais, and about 8 kilometres from Guines. Waben now forms part of the canton and administrative district of Montreuil-sur-Mer.

The Count of Guines who invited Landri to carry out this enterprise was Baudouin II, who became Count of Guines in 1169. In 1176, on the death of his father-in-law Arnoul de Colvida, he acceded to the seignorie of Ardres, and in 1187 he was succeeded by his son Arnoul. This means that Landri de Waben must have worked on the *Cantica Canticorum* between 1176 and 1187. Nothing else is known of him, but when, over a century ago, Charles Richelet published some fragments of the work, he stated quite categorically: 'C'est l'ouvrage d'un poète du XIIIᵉ siècle, et vraisemblablement de Landry, trouvère normand, à qui André Duchesne, dans son *Histoire des maisons d'Ardre et de Couci,* attribue un pareil travail.'[1] André Duchesne no doubt had in mind the reference in the chronicle by Lambert d'Ardres, and somewhat uncritically Richelet accepted the poet Landri as the probable author, ignoring the fact that Landri de Waben would not, however, be a *trouvère normand* so much as a *trouvère picard*. The suggestion that he was the author of our poem was taken up again in the *Histoire Littéraire de la France*[2] and further confirmed by Gaston Paris, Herman Suchier, and Gustav Gröber. In his work on the versions of the Bible in Old French verse, Jean Bonnard devotes several pages to what he describes as 'Traduction du Cantique des Cantiques par Landri de Waben',[3] and, much more recently, F. Ohly in his *Hohelied-studien* speaks at some length of our 'Landri von Waben'.[4]

The case for Landri de Waben's authorship is based on two facts: on the one hand, the chronicle of Lambert d'Ardres mentions his work, and on the other, the poem in MS. 173 could be described in the terms used by the chronicle. Furthermore, as Jean Bonnard and others have pointed out, there is, at the end of the poem, a reference to St. Winwalois, a saint known in English as St. Winwaloe and in French as St. Guénolé:

> Sainz Gregories assez en conte,
> Sainz Winwalois raison aconte.
> (vv. 3491–2)

---

[1] Ch. Richelet, *Le Cantique des Cantiques*, Paris, 1843, p. 147.
[2] *Histoire Littéraire de la France*, vol. xv (1869), pp. 328–33, 479–83.
[3] Bonnard, op. cit., pp. 152–62.
[4] F. Ohly, *Hoheliedstudien*, pp. 280–302.

Why should this little-known Breton saint, a fifth-century abbot of Landevenech, be linked with a well-known saint such as Gregory? St. Guénolé is a popular saint in Brittany. A small fishing port bears his name in Penmarch Peninsula, some 30 kilometres south-west of Quimper in the west of southern Brittany, and his cult is now localized, but he has his place in the *Acta Sanctorum*. When, between A.D. 977 and 979, Norse invaders forced the monks of Landevenech to flee, the relics of the Breton saint were taken to Montreuil-sur-Mer and placed in a church quite close to Landri de Waben's place of origin, for Waben now forms part of the commune of Montreuil-sur-Mer. It is some 12 kilometres to the south-west on the Rue-Étaples road.

The case for Landri's authorship of the poem would seem to be proved 'beyond reasonable doubt', but certain difficulties have been overlooked or else too readily dismissed. The chronicle of Lambert d'Ardres makes it quite clear that the adaptation of the Song of Songs was made by Landri for one of the Counts. Now, in the epilogue, the poet of MS. 173 states clearly that he was writing for a lady:

> E por celi cui jo present
> A Deu, quant jo le sai present,
> Ki me pramist k'ele por moi
> Deu prieroit . . .
>
> (vv. 3497–3500)

Jean Bonnard gets over this difficulty by suggesting that 'Il ne faut sans doute voir là qu'une preuve de la galanterie de l'auteur, qui dédie à la comtesse l'œuvre qui lui avait été commandée par le comte'.[1] It would be possible to accept this suggestion if this were the only reference in MS. 173 to the circumstances of the composition. However, earlier in the poem we read:

> Ceste nostre exposicions
> Que nos de ces deus venz faisons
> Solonc le sens que Dex nos done,
> Plairoit a une altre persone.
> Mais cele por cui jo travail,
> Quar tot est suen, se jo rien vail,
> Certes molt s'esmerveilleroit
> S'ele altre chose n'en öoit,
> Quar jo li ai maintes foiz dit
> Qu'aster signe Saint Esperit,

[1] Bonnard, op. cit., p. 157.

Cist sens li plaist, cestui atent,
Cist li savroit plus dolcement,
E quant jo sai le sien plaisir,
Jo ne m'en puis mie taisir,
Quar faite vueil qu'ele por moi
Prist son ami, li Sovrain Roi.

(vv. 2363–78)

From this passage it would seem that the author had discussed on several occasions certain matters with the person for whom he was working. It is clear that the poet was directed by a lady:

Cele por cui jo travail (v. 2367)

To argue that *cele* could refer back to *persone* is to overlook the use of the third person feminine pronoun in the lines that follow. It is not clear why the interpretation of the significance of the South Wind should have been the subject of numerous conversations with a patron, but the passage does at least demonstrate that the patron's interest was more than a passing one. Is it possible to infer from this that the patron is the wife of the Count of Guines, the count who was particularly interested in the interpretation of religious literature? The evidence considered hitherto points to certain coincidences but the possibility that the poem mentioned in the chronicle of Lambert d'Ardres is the poem of MS. 173 must remain a hypothesis, an attractive hypothesis, until further evidence comes to light.

The last two lines of the work may seem enigmatic:

Mais tant requier que cist romanz
Unkes ne viegne en main d'enfant

(vv. 3505–6)

The author seems concerned that his work should not fall into the hands of children (*enfant*). The meaning of this request becomes clearer when we consider a passage earlier in the poem, in which the author expounds the comparison of the bride's brow with the pomegranate. This comparison is made in Song of Songs 4: 3:

Thy temples are like a piece of pomegranate within thy locks

The interpretation of this symbolism demands skill, which wrongly used can do great harm:

A grenate pomme entamnee
Dolce amie, puis comperer
Tes maiseles, et ten vis cler.

> Cho me plaist bien, mais molt vat plus,
> Li granz biens ki est dedenz repus.
> Voioms k'il a en la parole,
> Kar le letre defors afole,
> S'om ne s'i guarde sutcilment,
> Tost i a lait abuissement.
> Letre est colteaus en main d'enfent,
> Dont il a tost damage grant.
> Ki de coltel enfant apaie,
> Gart bien k'il ne s'en face plaie.
> Deus nos doinst ore issi parler,
> Ke nos vos en puissons garder.
>                         (vv. 1862–76)

In order to understand the word, God gives to man a power of interpretation which can, wrongfully used, be as wounding as a knife in the hands of a child. This explanation is not, however, simply a metaphor taken from everyday life. The term *enfant* is used elsewhere in a technical sense, and is defined with precision:

> Les jovenceles ont l'onor
> De toi amer, e le valor,
> Kar li enfant e li viellard
> Sont a tel chose nul reguard.
> Chaus doit hom enfanz apeler
> Ki commencié n'ont a amer.
> E cil sont dit viel par droiture
> Ki amerent, or n'en ont cure.
>                         (vv. 235–43)

A child is thus one who has not yet experienced love. In the context of this poem, love is a spiritual experience, as the prologue makes abundantly clear:

> Quar d'amor est li livres faiz
> ... ...           (v. 7)
> L'amor dont il ici parole
> N'est pas del siecle, n'est pas fole,
> Enz est amors e bon e sainte
> ... ...           (vv. 11–13)
> Ceste amors le saint cuer enivre.
>                         (v. 15)

St. Bernard of Clairvaux had used the phraseology of human love to portray the relationship between the soul and the Divine Being.

The poem on the Song of Songs is destined above all for those who are able to appreciate if not fully understand the mystery of God's love. Those who are able to comprehend such matters form the reading public which inspires the author:

> Mais jo parol plus haltement
> Quant jo sui entre sage gent
> (vv. 197–8)

But this is not to say that the treatment of the theme is unvaried. The author consciously adapts his technique to make his work accessible to a wider audience, and this is a duty which a writer should observe.

> Ne devez pas d'une mesure
> Doneir a toz le lor peuture.
> Varieté i doit avoir
> Se il i a point de savoir
> Se doneir puis, a chascon doigne
> Solonc son sens o sa besoigne.
> (vv. 2035–40)

Despite this assertion, the author in the last lines of the work feels strongly that the work could be dangerous if it were to fall into the hands of the unlearned.

It would be hazardous to argue that this conclusion proves that the work was designed for an exclusively non-lay audience; that, like the sermons of St. Bernard, it was composed only for the cloister. Time and time again the author stresses the range of his interpretations, and that to seek God through love, in the special sense which is intended here, is difficult:

> Voirs est ke roiste ert le montee
> (v. 1489)

or again:

> Roiste est le veie enekedent
> (v. 1563)

But this does not imply that few can take this road:

> Por cha a Deus cele montee
> A nos foibles amesuree,
> Ke nuls ne se puist escuser
> Par lo griece de la monter
> (vv. 1571–4)

Those who are prepared to become aware of love and of the Divine Being are not prevented from trying to become more fully aware. The child can grow older, the ignorant may learn:

> Or aiez bon antendement
> Quant vos orrez diversement
> Parler ceste seinte escriture
> (vv. 43–5)

The way to understand is carefully indicated:

> Icsi covient ententre metre
> La flor entendre de la letre
> (vv. 81–2)

After the milk of knowledge comes the more demanding food, the bread of wisdom:

> As petiz est laiz de science
> E as grans pain de sapience
> (vv. 185–6)

This allusion to bread and milk as spiritual foods re-echoes the sentiment of the Preface to St. Bernard's Sermons on the *Canticle*. Is the author not thinking of double audience? On the one hand for his brethren he provides a commentary which may be partly familiar, and on the other, for a layman, he provides 'food for thought' or satisfies to some extent the demand for a mystical explanation.

If this is the case, one is reminded of the passage quoted from Lambert d'Ardres:

> Cantica canticorum non solum ad litteram, sed ad misticam
> spiritualis interpretationis intelligentiam . . .

The poem of MS. 173 certainly fits this description. Furthermore, as we shall briefly indicate later, the language of the text is a northern, Picard dialect which is that of the region of Ardres and Waben. Is it possible then to declare, as others have done previously, that the work attributed by Lambert d'Ardres to Landri de Waben and the version of the Song of Songs which we are now editing are one and the same poem? Only one difficulty remains, the reference in the poem to a Lady for whom the author was working. With regret, one feels that, short of further evidence, this reference cannot be brushed aside as a mere gesture of gallantry. When Chrétien de Troyes speaks of Marie de Champagne as the lady who requested the *romance of Lancelot*, one does not proceed to argue that gallant feelings, which in the case of a romance of chivalric love would not be out of place, encouraged Chrétien to name Marie, rather than her husband, Henry the Lion, Count of Champagne. When Chrétien, later in his life, dedicated his *Perceval* to Philippe d'Alsace, Count of Flanders, this statement is accepted by critics. Moreover, critics of medieval literature do not lightly accept the observations made by authors in their prologues, as can be seen by the fact that the statements proffered by Geoffrey of Monmouth in the Prologue to his *History of the Kings of Britain* have been subjected to searching scrutiny.

To suggest that Landri de Waben must be the author of our poem is to believe that it is highly unlikely, if not impossible, for two writers in northern France to have conceived the idea of preparing a commentary in French verse on the Song of Songs. Given the lengthy commentaries in Latin by Guillaume de Saint-Thierry on the Song of Songs, as well as the many sermons of St. Bernard on the same theme, there is no reason why two writers should not have treated this theme in northern France. Furthermore, interest in the *Canticle* in this region was no doubt stimulated by writers like Guillaume de Saint-Thierry whose influence in this area must have been marked, for he was, after all, abbot of Signy. The attribution to Landri de Waben must therefore remain a possibility rather than a probability.

## IV. *The Present Poem*

The version of the Song of Songs which is preserved in MS. Le Mans 173 is in several ways unique: it is not just a poem about the meaning of the Song of Songs, even less is it a translation or a free adaptation of it into twelfth-century French; nor is it a vernacular version of the sermons and discourses written on the Song of Songs by twelfth-century fathers of the Church. But while it is true to say that it is none of these things, it is also, paradoxically, almost true to say that it is all of these things.

The poem follows the text of the Latin Bible very closely indeed. It extends from the beginning of the book down to verse 14 of Chapter 5 of the Vulgate Canticum Canticorum. And to facilitate the task of simultaneously following the poem and the Latin text, the latter is transcribed verse by verse, or phrase by phrase, in the margins by the side of the French text. Throughout, the very close relationship between the French and Latin texts is made manifest, and the poet follows the first five chapters of the Canticum Canticorum systematically verse by verse, phrase by phrase, omitting nothing, changing not at all the order of the ideas of the Vulgate text except, from time to time, to repeat certain verses and phrases.[1] For the greater part of the first quarter of the French text, the author, or scribe, copies the Latin text by citing a phrase of half a dozen or fewer words at a time. Towards the middle of the text, the verses are quoted in a less disjointed form, and on one occasion the margins of folio 88 recto and verso are almost completely filled with the continuous transcription of verses 2 to 7 inclusive of Chapter 3 of the Canticum Canticorum. Towards the end of the text, the pattern of shorter, much shorter, quotations is adopted once more. From these material indications at least, it would appear that the text is a translation into French of the Canticum Canticorum, and in one sense this is the case, for the greater part of the first five chapters is in fact translated.

The translation is, however, a framework for a much longer work. It is a series of pegs on which to hang many interpretations of the Song of Songs. The author provides detailed explications of each verse, almost of each word of the text he translates. These explanations are presented quite explicitly. One of the methods employed is called *allegorie*:

> Ceste sentence premeraine
> Allegorie nos amaine,
> Kar ço ke nos avomes dit,
> Tot est de Sainte Eglise escrit
> (vv. 113–16, f° 36 r°)

But Allegory is not the sole figure employed, for the author continues:

> Mais el sens de moralité
> La a dulceur e pitié
> (vv. 117–18)

Moreover, the author, or at least the copyist, is careful to remind the reader that the book is not to be read literally, but figuratively. When expounding the meaning of the little foxes (Cant. Cant. 2: 15), he gives one frequently suggested explanation, that they signify heretics, and before developing a second interpretation, namely that they are intrusive unworthy thoughts, he adds a marginal note: *altrement en moralité* (v. 1065).

---

[1] For example, Ch. IV, verse 4 is transcribed in the margin facing line 1915, and then subdivided into phrases which are transcribed separately and individually facing lines 1939, 1941, and 1953.

From the beginning of the poem the reader is not left in any doubt about the broad outlines of the allegorical interpretation which will be offered. There was nothing novel in the twelfth century in reading the Song of Songs, an Old Testament Book, as a prefiguration of the New Testament. The prologue shows explicitly that this book, attributed to Solomon, is a book about love:

> L'amor dont il ici parole
>
> ... ...
>
> . . . est amors e bone e sainte
>
> (vv. 11 and 13)

and it is the love

> A Jesu Crist e a sa mie
>
> (v. 23)

The bride, or rather 'amie', friend, of Christ:

> Ço est Sainte Eglise
> O l'arme sainte bien aprise
>
> (vv. 27–8)

The allegory then is a double one, that of the love of Christ for his Church and that of the union of the soul with God or Christ. Both of these interpretations have a venerable ancestry, as we have seen. That the Old Testament was a foreshadowing of the New was the dominant theme of twelfth-century Biblical exegesis. Did not Abbot Suger of Saint-Denis exemplify this by pointing out that the name of Eve (Eva), the first woman, who was tempted by the Devil, itself is a reflection of the opening words of the annunciation to Our Lady: *Ave* Maria? Similarly, in the domain of vernacular dramatic literature, the Anglo-Norman Adam play, often called the *Jeu* or *Mystère d'Adam*, emphasizes that 'as by man came death, by man came also the resurrection', for after the eating of the forbidden fruit Adam refers specifically to the redemption of man by the sacrifice made by Christ:

> Ne me ferat ja nul aïe
> For le filz que istra de Marie.
>
> (*Le Mystère d'Adam*, ed. P. Aebischer, vv. 381–2)

The poem of MS. 173 is characteristic of the twelfth century in this respect that systematically, verse by verse, an explanation, and multiple explanations on occasion, are given of the Song of Songs. Allegorical interpretations are numerous and rich in variety. Commentators could, and of course still can, see in almost any verse a meaning to suit their own particular argument: let one example suffice. The little foxes that spoil the vineyard (2: 15) are seen as heretics by J. Durham,[1] as well, quite independently of course, as by the author of the poem who likens them to 'eriteals' (v. 1047) or 'heritel' (v. 1061). The kiss of the Beloved is not only the means of joining two natures, the human and the Divine, it is the sign of the Son of God coming to seek his Bride the Church, on earth (v. 112). The kiss is a sign of peace. As the Bride is refreshed by the breasts of the Beloved (v. 172), so we learn of the double doctrine of the New Testament, and how St. Paul observed that the Old Law was austere and the New Law more suited to all men. The eulogy of the throat of the Beloved inspires the observation that through the throat food is received and speech issues forth (v. 449). The Song of Songs refers to the Lord as resembling a fine apple tree (2: 3). The fruits are the Holy Martyrs of the Church (v. 723). A reference to the river Jordan is immediately followed by the note that there Our Lord was baptized to wash away our sins (v. 855 et ss.). Even the Crown of Solomon has its special meaning: its twelve towers are the twelve apostles, the towers are made of gold which means wisdom, and of silver which means eloquence. The gems that adorn it represent virgin martyrs and confessors. The redness of the lips of the Beloved inspire reference to the Blood of the Passion (v. 1828 et ss.). The poet moves from the Bridegroom of the Song of Songs to Christ himself without always noting the transition: the cheeks of Christ are, for example, described as the first churches to be established (v. 3217) which echoes verse xiii of Chapter 5 of the Canticle: 'Genae illius sicut areolae aromatum consitae a pigmentariis'. Throughout his work the poet suggests that the Old Testament, a relatively obscure work, is difficult to understand, whereas the New Testament is relatively straightforward, and on one occasion he states this explicitly:

Mais del viez curt occultement
Del novel tot apertement
(vv. 3289–90)

The theme of the whole work is the redemption of mankind through Christ, a theme which is made to derive simply and naturally from the Song of Songs.

[1] The text of this commentary on the *Songs of Songs* is preserved in Bodleian MS. Opp. 625, and was edited by H. J. Matthews in *Festschrift zum 80en Geburtstag Moritz Steinschneider's*, 1896, pp. 164–85 and 238–40.

The author, although not by any means original in his interpreta-
tions, does not quote systematically his sources and authorities. He
makes reference in passing to the work of his predecessors. St. Paul
(v. 192) is mentioned in passing, the poet alludes to the eloquence
of Jerome, Augustine, and Gregory (v. 477), and the closing lines con-
tain the famous reference to Saints Gregory and Winwalois (v. 3484).
Nowhere is there a mention of St. Bernard or of Guillaume de Saint-
Thierry. The author makes no attempt to support each judgement or
interpretation by reference to an authority, as Richard de Fournival
was to do in the thirteenth century when writing on love.[1] This latter
author parades his learning by quoting St. Augustine, Cicero, St.
Jerome, etc., etc., at very frequent intervals, and can hardly write a
sentence which does not include a phrase such as: 'Li sages dist . . .' or
'Tulles dist'. The allegorical and other explanations of the Song of
Songs are then, for the most part, presented, if not as the author's
own, at any rate without overelaborate reference to authorities. The
explanations are not original by any means, and they are in many cases
framed according to an already established mode. This apparent lack
of originality has led critics, on occasion, to judge the work, if not
harshly, at least ungenerously. Thus Jean Bonnard comments: 'Le
commentaire ne présente aucune originalité; les explications allé-
goriques sont celles que l'on trouve partout . . .'.[2]

*       *       *

To judge the poem solely as a commentary on the Song of Songs
is to misjudge it completely. The author nowhere states that he intends
to produce a French equivalent of St. Bernard's *Sermons on the
Canticle* or Guillaume de Saint Thierry's series of studies upon it. His
work is at the same time less ambitious yet more far-reaching. If one
reflects upon the way secular writers on occasion approached their
sources, his purpose and the value of his work becomes clearer. A
well-known example of a secular writer who expressed a view on the
theory of literature is Marie de France, who, in the prologue to her
*Lais*, observes that the ancients used to express themselves obscurely
in their writings so that those who were to succeed them and study
their books might interpret the text and add to it from their own

---

[1] C. E. Pickford, 'The *Roman de la Rose* and a Treatise attributed to Richard de
Fournival' in *Bulletin of the John Rylands Library*, vol. xxxiv (1952), pp. 349–65.
[2] Bonnard, op. cit., p. 157.

minds.[1] But this means that her approach to literature, like that of many
of her contemporaries, was to expound its meaning and to add thereto a
personal interpretation (*et de lor sens le sorplus mettre*). In other words,
explication and personal interpretation are two essential ingredients
in literary composition. When one turns from a literary text, like
the *Lais* of Marie de France, to a Biblical text such as the Song of
Songs, it is natural to find in the latter an element, an important ele-
ment, of exegesis. The art of the writer of romance—and let us not
overlook the fact that the poet of MS. 173 describes his work as a
*roman*—was not by any means a free one, undisciplined and giving
licence to the imagination, but rather a carefully controlled and ordered
technique. The *Grammatica* taught in the medieval schools has been
accepted as playing a major part in the growth of medieval literary
techniques. This grammar is not merely an instruction in the correct
use of language—originally of Greek. The meaning of the term
became extended to the interpretation of poetry. As early as Quin-
tilian the dual nature of *Grammatica* was stressed—both the *scientia
recte loquendi* and the *poetarum enarratio*. With the twelfth-century
renaissance in France, literary training and literary art concentrated
not only on the art of story telling, but also on that of interpretation.
The budding writer learnt the importance of revealing the significance
of whatever he found in his model or source. As Eugène Vinaver so
tellingly puts it, 'In practice this meant either commenting on the
narrative or letting the characters themselves explain their feelings
and their behaviour.'[2]

In our version of the commentary on the Song of Songs, this is
precisely the technique which the author uses, or, more precisely, one
of the techniques. Not only does he from time to time intervene
directly to explain the text which he is presenting, as when he com-

[1]          Costume fu as anciens,
             Ce testimoine Precïens
             Es livres que jadis faisoient
             Assez oscurement disoient
             Por ceus qui a venir estoient
             Et qui aprendre les devoient
             Qu'il peüssent gloser la lettre
             Et de lor sen le sorplus mettre
             (Marie de France, *Les Lais*, ed. J. Rychner, *Prologue*, vv. 9–16)

[2] E. Vinaver, 'From Epic to Romance' in *Bulletin of the John Rylands Library*,
vol. xlvi (1964), p. 493 (the complete article, offering a superbly illuminating view of
literary theory in twelfth-century France, occupies pp. 476–503); see also E. Vinaver
*The Rise of Romance*, Oxford, 1971, Ch. II, 'The Discovery of Meaning'.

ments on Canticle 1: 1–12 (*meliora sunt ubera tua vino fragrancia unguentis*):

> Seignors, ci nos covient entendre
> Ke nos en puissoms raison rendre,
> Kar mameles, al dire voir,
> Suelent femmes nient homme avoir.
> Or sachiez donc ke par figure,
> Parole ici Sainte Escriture.
>
> (vv. 173–8)

or, again, when he states with some precision that after a digression he must return to the main theme and, at a given turning point in the work, begin the second book:

> Repairier veil a ma matere,
> E prier Deu le sovrain pere,
> Parler me doinst a son plaisir,
> Ose che non del tot taisir.
> Mielz veil semblanz estre al muel,
> Ke molt parler se lui n'est bel,
> Amors m'a mis a ceste escole,
> Kar d'amor est ceste parole.
> Molt puet amors, il me semont
> Entrer en cest livre secont.
>
> (vv. 1437–46)

But also, and more usually, it is the personages in the narrative who provide the commentary and the explanations. A characteristic example is the passage in which the King (*li Rois*) speaks to the Bride (*l'Esposee*), and having praised her hair, proceeds to praise her teeth, and to explain the significance of his praise, in this way providing a commentary on Canticle 4: 2: *Dente tui sicut grex tonsarum que ascenderunt de lavacro: omnes gemellis fœtibus et sterilis non est inter eas*. The meaning of the image can be far from clear indeed the King declares:

> Ceste parole semble dure,
> E a entendre molt oscure.
>
> (vv. 1797–8)

But the difficulty is not left unexplained, and the King continues:

> Mais or oiez ke g'i entent,
> Jo.l vos dirai assez briefment.
>
> (vv. 1799–1800)

This method of exposition is adopted throughout the poem, and the author has produced a work which, in some senses, is virtually unique. Although the writing of a romance in which the explanations offered by the characters of their own state of mind is by no means a rare phenomenon, the poet of MS. 173 goes beyond what so many of his contemporaries achieved. To elucidate a story was a technique of rhetoric which was widely used in post-Roman writing. Indeed the relationship between 'matiere' and 'san', subject matter and meaning, is one that has often been explored, but rarely better evaluated than by Eugène Vinaver, who uses the analogy from music and speaks of 'the two elements of the work as two series of layers, or strata, like two melodies superposed in contrapuntal arrangement'.[1] Our author presents his work in this manner, and also he uses the allegorical form in a particularly personal way.

It was not unusual for those who were paraphrasing sacred texts and presenting them in the vernacular to a secular public to use the figure of allegory. An allegorical explanation of the chosen theme is given, and this, in its turn, is followed by a homily. Thus, the temptation of the soul is described in terms of the capture of Jerusalem by the Lord of Babylon, that is to say by Satan. The allegory remains a pure illustration of the dogma which is being propounded.[2] But this is a slight extension of the technique adopted by Silvestre, who, in his Commentary in French on the *Pater Noster*, is satisfied with offering for each verse first a homiletic explanation and then an allegorical one.[3]

The poem on the Song of Songs is, however, presented in a rather different manner. Rather than give successively a series of interpretations, the author combines allegorical explanation and narrative. It is not unusual for the personages in the narrative to offer their comments in the form of allegorical explications. Thus when the Bride compares the Bridegroom to a young kid, she points out the meaning of the various leaps, or jumps, made by him:

Al cervecel rest il semblanz
Ki suelt faire les salz molt granz.
Cist cervecels tant debonaire
Savez kels salz il n'os faire.

[1] E. Vinaver, 'From Epic to Romance', p. 496.
[2] This example is taken from *De David li Prophecie*, edited by G. E. Fuhrken in *Zeitschrift für romanische Philologie*, vol. xix (1895), pp. 189–234.
[3] The *Pater Noster* of Silvestre is described in Bonnard, op. cit., pp. 145–6.

Le premier fist del sain son pere
Dusqu'en celi ki'l fist sa mere.
D'iluec saili dusqu'en le creche,
Ou il fu mis par grant destresce.
Par destrece de povreté,
Ou il vint par sa volonté,
Moltz fist del salz, mais nul en vain.
Le tierz salt fist dusk'en Jordain
Ou li Sires fu baptisiez
Por eslaver les noz pechiez.
D'iluec salli dusqu'en desert
Ou li deables, tot en apert,
De trois choses le tenta;
Mais en nule ne.l sormonta.
D'iluec sailli dusqu'en la Croiz,
Ou il sofri les granz destroiz,
Ou il sofrir volt passion
Por le nostre redempcion.
E de la Croiz ou mort reçut,
Fist salt el liu ou il mort jut
Quant il a Infer descendist
E as feels clarté rendist.
Aprés toz ces fist un grant salt,
De la terre la sus en halt;
E liement fu receuz,
El ciel dont il estoit venuz.

(vv. 861–90)

Here the author allows the characters themselves to present at some length a developed commentary. On other occasions it is the author himself who intervenes in the narrative to provide the commentary, as in lines 1605–10:

Salemons porte la figure
De Crist solonc Sainte Escriture.
Assez l'avez oï deseure.
Laissez kele parole keure.
Deus, ki tot set, bien nos ensent
Sire de son coronement . . .

where the comparison between Solomon and Christ is stated firmly on the authority of Scripture.

The interesting innovation which is made in this poem is that the biblical narrative and the commentary are carefully intermingled.

Indeed, to be precise, they are fused into a whole, and we are in the presence not of another more or less traditional commentary on the Song of Songs, but of a romance which is also at the same time an exegesis of the Song of Songs.

To call the work a romance is no exaggeration. At the beginning of the poem, the author describes it as

> cest saint livre
>
> (line 1)

a term which is re-echoed and emphasized a little later,

> Quar d'amor est li livres faiz
>
> (line 7)

and 'cist livres' in line 26.

This *livre* is in itself divided into two parts, each of which is also a *livre:*

> Entrer en cest livre secont
>
> (line 1446)

To use the one term to describe both the whole poem and the parts into which it is subdivided is not unusual. Long romances of chivalry, for example, were subdivided into *livres* or books.[1] In the closing lines of the work, the whole is described as a *roman*. In the final couplet, we read

> Mais tant requier que cist romanz
> Unkes ne viegne en main d'enfant.
>
> (vv. 3505–6)

This term *roman* is itself rich in meaning. It can apply to a work of literature which is primarily fictional, or it can refer more precisely to the language in which a given work is written. Chrétien de Troyes uses the term in this way when, in the opening lines of the romance of *Cligès*, he says of one of his own earlier writings

> et l'art d'amors en romans mist.
>
> (*Cligès*, ed. Micha, v. 3)

More familiar is the use of the word to denote a work of the imagination written in either verse or prose, and most frequently in the vernacular. This definition is absolutely appropriate in the case of the poem preserved in MS. 173, for it has so many of the characteristics

---

[1] C. E. Pickford, *L'Évolution du roman arthurien en prose*, Paris, 1960, Deuxième Partie, Ch. I, 'Le Livre'.

of a twelfth-century romance. From the starting-point of the literary explication which formed a part of the training in twelfth-century schools, the author moves on to create not simply a commentary on an already familiar text, but a completely new work of art. He has fused together the text and the allegorical exposition of it, which was an almost unique accomplishment in the rise of allegory during the century 1150–1250.[1] In a manner which at the time was unique, and which unfortunately was never subsequently adopted in this form, the author has combined in one work two currents of great strength, namely, on the one hand the tradition of religious, especially mystical, experience, and on the other that of the culture of courtly romance. It may be argued that one finds a combination of courtly chivalry and mysticism in the *Queste del Saint Graal*, but the *Queste* is a branch of the Vulgate Arthurian Cycle and is not an allegorical poem. Again, although in the *Mystère* or *Jeu d'Adam* the feudal relationship between *vassal* and *seigneur* is used to describe the relationship between man and God,[2] the play is primarily a dramatization of the first verses of the book of Genesis and could hardly be described as a fusion of the spiritual and feudal world.

The terms used to describe the bride are on the one hand the 'Espeuse' (v. 57) but more usually the secular term 'Damoisele', or a term with more courtly overtones 'amie' (v. 27). Similarly, the bridegroom is her 'ami' (v. 135) or 'li sire debonaire' (v. 30) whom she addresses as 'Bels sire' (v. 577). The courtly impression made by phraseology of this kind is reinforced by quasi-proverbial statements like that which opens the second part of the work:

> Amor ne puet prisons tenir
> Por rien ki ja puist avenir.
> (vv. 1447–8)

To begin a work with a proverb is a rhetorical technique recommended by the authors of the twelfth- and thirteenth-century poetic arts, e.g. Matthieu de Vendôme or Geoffroy de Vinsauf. It is found also in thirteenth-century romances such as the *Chastelaine de Vergi* or the *Roman de la Rose*. The greater part of the poem is presented

[1] H. R. Jauss, 'La transformation de la forme allégorique entre 1180 et 1240: d'Alain de Lille à Guillaume de Lorris' in *Humanisme Médiéval*, ed. A. Fourrier, Paris (Klincksieck), 1964, pp. 105–46, esp. 122–3. Jauss accepts the attribution to Landri de Waben without the slightest question.

[2] *Le Mystère d'Adam*, ed. P. Aebischer, vv. 1–80. See also vv. 2492 of the present text, and notes thereto.

in direct speech, in the form of conversation between two persons. This structure recalls the 'scènes à deux' of the *Chastelaine de Vergi* or more precisely the whole of the *Lai de l'Ombre* which is almost entirely one long conversation between a knight and a lady. Details of this kind are not mere isolated examples: the tone of the whole poem is both mystical and at the same time courtly, and so to dismiss the work as yet another run-of-the-mill unoriginal allegorical exposé of the Song of Songs is a judgement as unfair as it is inexact. The work happily preserved in MS. 173 is an example of the heights which could be reached by a clerkly writer who was commissioned by one of the small courts of northern France. The literary glories of Troyes at the time of Marie de Champagne cast such a light that it is easy to fall into the trap of believing that elsewhere was but shadow and darkness. The poem attributed to Landri de Waben serves as a reminder that well-known literary centres not only existed but were able to inspire poets who produced, if not always masterpieces, at least works which can still inspire and move the reader of the twentieth century.

## v. *The Manuscript*

Only one manuscript preserves the present poem. It is now to be found in the Municipal Library of Le Mans (Sarthe), France. It consists of 114 parchment leaves, numbered 1–114 in a modern hand, preceded by three fly-leaves lettered A, B, C. The leaves now measure some 195 × 147 mm. but they have been somewhat cut down by the binder's knife. Prickings and rulings are clearly visible, and most of the catchwords are still visible. It is divided into gatherings normally consisting of eight leaves. The text of the paraphrase of the Song of Songs occupies leaves 33 verso to 110 recto. The sole miniature of the manuscript, depicting against a plain gold background a man and woman who represent Christ and the Church embracing, is at the beginning of our text on folio 33 verso. The full contents of the manuscript are as follows:

Folio 1–33 verso: paraphrase of the book of Exodus;
folio 33 verso–110 recto: paraphrase of the Song of Songs;
folio 110 verso: short version of the *fabliau 'Le Vilain Asnier'*;
folio 110 verso–111 verso: Lamentation of Our Lady on the death of Our Lord;
folio 111 verso–end of manuscript: Prayer to God.

All the works are in French and all are in octosyllabic rhymed couplets.

A consideration of the language of the text would suggest that although the language of the original poem was northern or north-eastern French, the copyist was from the region of the Île de France. For example, in verse 1910 of our poem he 'corrects' the dialectal form *le roine* (where 'le' is the NE. dialect form of the unstressed feminine definite article) to *la roine*.

The same scribe has executed the whole of our text. It is difficult to determine whether he also copied the Latin text in the margins, a task which was carried out by a man who had an eye for the symmetrical arrangement of words in formal patterns. There is no indication in the text of the circumstances and the date of copying. It has usually been attributed to the early part of the thirteenth century. This dating may be a little early, for a careful comparison of the text with facsimiles[1] of dated manuscripts would suggest that it is in a hand which most closely resembles MS. 3139 of the Bibliothèque de l'Arsenal, a copy of the *Cycle de la Croisade* completed in 1286, though it is by no means unlike MS. Arsenal 3340, a copy of the *Roman de Troie* completed in June 1237.

To date the copy of MS. 173 as of the mid-thirteenth century is as precise as one can be in the light of our present knowledge.

There are no indications of ownership earlier than a note on folio 1 (Monasterii Vincentii Cenomanensis congregationis sancti Mauri catalogo inscriptus, 1719), and the stamp of the Abbey of St. Vincent du Mans at a much earlier date. Fragments of fifteenth-century accounts are on the fly-leaves, where can be read the names of the rue Dupineau, the street behind the Church of St. Remy, the rue du Bourg Rousset, the rue aux Juifs, and the abbey and convent of Belle-Branche. Thus the book was probably in the abbey of St. Vincent by the fifteenth century, it was certainly recorded there at the beginning of the eighteenth century, and it passed into its present keeping at the time of the French Revolution.

## VI. *Notes on the Present Edition*

Since the text of the adaptation of and commentary on the Song of Songs is presented in only one manuscript, the text of this copy is used as the sole basis of the present edition. It has been reproduced with as little change as possible. The editor has intervened only to

---

[1] Ch. Samaran et Robert Marichal, *Inventaire de Manuscrits portant des indications de copiste, de lieu et de date*, Paris (C.N.R.S.), Tome I, planche XIV and Tome II, planche XII.

the extent of adding modern punctuation, making the distinction between 'i' and 'j', and 'u' and 'v', using the acute accent to distinguish final stressed 'e' from final 'e' feminine, the cedilla to indicate a 'soft c'. Emendations are few in number, and are limited to those cases where the text can be shown to be defective, and departures from the manuscript are discussed in the notes. The footnotes contain those passages from the Vulgate which in MS. 173 reproduced the Latin text of the Song of Songs. Here we have deemed it useful to indicate modern division into chapter and verse. We have not thought it useful to transcribe the few variant readings from Richelet's century-old edition. The Commentary on the text includes discussion of those passages in which the text of the manuscript has been changed as well as attempting to throw light on the more obscure passages and to give some indications of the writer's treatment of the Song of Songs.

# THE SONG OF SONGS

La MATERE de cest saint livre
Vuelt tot le cuer avoir delivre,
Qu'il n'ait al siecle baerie
E toz soit vuiz de legerie.    4
Tel le requiert, quar altrement
N'avroit pas sein entendement;
Quar d'amor est li livres faiz,
E par grant sens en fu estraiz.    8
Li sages Salemons le fist,
Cui Deus a cest honor eslist.
L'amor dont il ici parole
N'est pas del siecle, n'est pas fole,    12

Enz est amors e bone e sainte,
Dunt il ne vient mals ne complainte.
Ceste amors le saint cuer enivre,
E d'altres cures le delivre,    16
Tot le cuer torne d'une part,
E d'un saint fu l'esprent e art,
Le cuer angoise e si destraint,
Mais nequident nuls ne s'en plaint.    20
Duce est de ceste amor le plaie,
Nuls ne le seit s'il ne l'ensaie.
A Jhesu Crist e a sa mie,
Qu'il sue fait par bone vie,    24
Apartient d'amors le parole,
Dunt cist livres partot parole.
L'amie, ço est Sainte Eglise,
O l'arme sainte bien aprise.    28
Por ceste amie a soi retraire,
Morut li Sire debonaire.
Morut, e son sanc precios,
Dona li puis, li merveillos.    32
Ne pooit par altre maniere
Mostrer conbien il l'avoit chiere.

v. 16: cuers, *expuncted* cures *written above.*

LA DAMOISELE come sage
Conoist bien ke par son ultrage          36
S'estoit de sen ami partie.
Por sen pechié l'avoit guerpie.
Ne li pooit biens avenir,
Mais or vuelt a lui revenir,             40
Quar tres bien seit ke nols n'a joie
Ki vueille aler par altre voie.

OR AIEZ bon antendement
Quant vos orrez diversement              44
Parler ceste seinte escriture.
Por cho ne vos soit pas oscure,
Ne soit de ço nuls esmariz.
Sovent parlera li mariz,                 48
Or l'espeuse, puis cist, puis ceste,
Si com raisons e droiz l'apreste,
Li compaignon le roi sovent,
E les puceles ensement                   52
Ki od la dame vont e vienent.
Itels persones i covienent,
E Synagoge a le fié,
Si come femme molt irié.                 56

L'ESPEUSE tot avant parole
Come sage e de bone escole:

'Por ke me laisse en plorement
Li miens amis tant longement?           60
Ja conoist il ma repentance,
Si le seit bien, n'est pas dotance.
S'il me guerpi, cho fu a droit,
N'en puis mentir a cest destroit.       64
Or m'en repent, e merci proi,
Ait mes amis merci de moi!
Ne puis mais altrement durer,
Ne puis sofrir ne endurer               68
Ke ja tant loinz soie de li,
Quar trop par en ai grant ennui.
Laira mi dunc tot tans doloir,

v. 71: Laira mil dunc.

Quant je n'en ai cuer ne voloir,    72
Desirrier ne altre pensee,
Fors a lui estre racordee?
Repairs a moi, viengne e me baist,    *
Por Deu sen maltalent abaist!    76
Port moi le baisier de sa boche,
C'est ço ki plus al cuer m'atoche!
Ja mais n'avrai ne bien ne aise,
Se ses baisiers ne me rapaise!    80

ICSI COVIENT ententre metre,

f° 35 v°    La flor entendre de la letre:
Quel mal ceste dame avoit fait
Dunt ele maine si gra[n]t plait    84
Ki ne peut estre pardonez
Se li beisiers ne fust donez?
Li maus dunt ele fu reprise,
Dunt ele fu en eisil mise,    88
Dura tres le mors de le pome,
En dusque Deu prist forme d'ome.
En la pome fu li meffaiz:
Por le pechié ke la fu faiz    92
Deus del home se departi,
E toz li siecles i parti.
Ainç n'en peut estre fait acorde
Dusque que par misericorde,    96
Li Fiz Deu sa umbra en terre,
Kar dunc vint il s'espeuse querre.
Dunc fu icil beisiers donez,
Ki primes fu tant desirrez.    100
Li cerz signes li plus entiers
De ferme pais c'est li baisiers.
Ainç l'espeuse ne fu seüre,
Dusque que homaine nature    104

f° 36 r°    E li filz Deu furent ensemble;
C'est li beisiers ki les assemble,
Si come veez par le beisier
Divers cuers ensemble apaisier,    108

v. 74: Fons *with 'n' expuncted and corrected to* 'r'.
*v. 75, *in left margin*: Osculetur me osculo oris sui. (*1: 1*)    v. 84: si grait plait.

E deus cors asembler e joindre.
Si s'asemblerent sens desjoindre
Deus natures: humanitez
L'une, l'autre fu divinitez.                                112

CESTE SENTENCE premeraine
Allegorie nos amaine,
Kar ço ke nos avomes dit,
Tot est de Sainte Eglise escrit.                            116
Mais el sens de moralité,
La a dulceur e pieté.
Al cuer toche plus dolcement
Cho ke chascons de soi entent.                              120

L'ARME CUI DEUS a espiree
E de s'amor l'a enivree,
En la chartre del cors enclose
Ne puet taisir, ne parler n'ose.                            124
Alkes le font si mal taisir,
Dont a Deu cuide desplaisir,
Mais amors vaint, se li fait dire
Cho ke vos vueil briement descrire.                         128

LAISE, fait ele, que dirai?
Tote de fail ja perirai;
Amors m'a mise en grant destroit.
Cil cui jo aim le seit e voit.                              132
A lui ferai de lui clamor,
Kar il me fait languir d'amor.
Mes Amis seit conbien jo l'aim,
E de quel cuer jo le reclaim.                               136
En cest siecle riens ne me plaist,
Ke plus i sui, plus me deplaist.
Quanque jo voi, tot m'est a fais,
Ne.l puet mes cuers porter en pais.                         140
Jo ne desir se lui sol non,
Ne sai se lui demant un don.
Jo li dirai, e tres bien sent,
Ke trop ferai grant hardement,                             144
Mais neportant ne lairai mie.
Destroit d'amor me fait hardie.

f° 36 v°

Viegne Li Dolz, e si me baist,                    *
D'un sol baiser mon cuer rapaist.              148

SA PRESENCE me doinst sentir,
Cho est li baisiers ko jo desir.

f° 37 r°    A soi me joigne par esperit,
Kar ço ai jo trové escrit:                         152
Ki par amor a Deu s'aert,
Ki tresbien l'aime, e bien le sert,
Uns esperiz est avec lui,
Ço vaint tot mal e tot ennui.               156
C'est li baisiers o jo aspir,
Por cui tant pleur e tant sospir.

APRÉS CESTE dolce complainte,
L'Espe[u]se par dolor atainte              160
Ne puet sofrir, n'ele ne volt,
K'ele sen ami n'aparolt.
Or dist: — Amis, n'est pas merveille,
Se t'amors le mien cuer esveille,          164
Kar toz ies dolz nis tes mameles
Sunt tant dulces, bones e beles,
Ke vin passent par leur dulceur,                  *
E longement tienent l'odeur.               168
La peuture ki d'eles ist,
Me refait tote e replenist,
E cele odeur ke jo i sent
Me fait grant bien, men cuer me rent.      172

SEIGNORS, ci nos covient entendre
f° 37 v°    Ke nos en puissoms raison rendre,
Kar mameles, al dire voir,
Suelent femmes nient homme avoir.          176
Or sachiez donc ke par figure
Parole ici Sainte Escriture.

LES DEUS mameles ke tant prise
L'espuse ki bien est aprise,               180

---

*v. 147, *in left margin*: Osculetur me osculo oris sui. (*1: 1*)
v. 160: Lespense par dolor.
*v. 167, *in right margin*: Meliora sunt ubera tua vino fragrancia unguentis optimis.
(*1: 1–2*)

Ço est espoir doble doctrine,
Ki toz les buens a soi acline,
Ke Deus par sen comandement
A mis el Novel Testament;                      184
As petiz est laiz de science,
E as granz pain de sapience.
Ces mameles a Nostre Sire,
E preste a cels ki sevent dire                 188
E preechier bien e droiture
A chascon solonc sa mesure.
Ces mameles eut aletties
Sainz Pols ki dist plosors fiées              192
A ces ki petit entendoient
E de granz choses soing n'avoient.
Jo ne vos ai rien preechié
Fors Crist et celui clofigié.                  196

f° 38 r°          Mais jo parol plus haltement
Quant jo sui entre sage gent.
L'austerité de la Viez Loi,
Ce est li vins, si com jo croi.               200
Cele estoit molt cruels e dure
A tote homaine creature.
La Loi de Grace est mielz vaillanz,
Ki toz norrist, petiz e granz.                204
Por tant est voire la parole
Ki vint de la devine escole,
Ke cil a cui tot est aclin
A mameles meillors de vin.                    208


LA DAMOISELE preuz e sage
Dist aprés par ardant corage
A son ami: — Certes, bels sire,
De toi puet om vraiment dire,                 212
Puis ke tu fus el mont venuz,
Est tes noms o eles espanduz.
Tes noms est Crist, ço est enoinz,            *
Ki grant bien fait e prés et loinz.           216
Tot men cuer oint e asoage,
E repos done a men corage.

*v. 215, *in right margin*: Oleum effusum nomen tuum. (*1: 2*)

Cist nons grant leece me fait.

Cant jo l'oï tote me refait. 220
Grant bien me fait, grant bien me done,
Cele parole o cist nons sone;
Wape me semble l'escriture
O jo ne truis ceste peuture. 224
Beals Sire chiers, tres duz Amis,
Li nons d'enoint c'est a droit mis,
Kar enoinz ies a grant planté
De ço dunt nos avons chierté. 228
C'est de grace dunt Tu faiz don,
La ou Te plaist, solonc raison.
Por çe T'aiment les jovenceles *
Forz en amor, sages e beles, 232
Kar bien sevent k'eles n'ont rien
Se par Toi non, et tot del Tien.
Les jovenceles ont l'onor
De Toi amer, e le valor, 236
Kar li enfant e li viellard
Font a tel chose nul reguard.
Chaus doit hom enfanz apeler
Ki comencié n'ont a amer. 240
E cil sunt dit viel par droiture
Ki amerent, or n'en ont cure;
Cil ne n'ont mie d'amer valor,
Cist le perdent a deshonor. 244

—SIRE, trai ma pensee a Toi, *
Ma pensee, mais tote moi,
Trai me aprés Toi, ke ne remaigne
El mont ke jo truis tant estraigne, 248
Done me efforz d'aler avant,
Ço est li traires ke jo demant.

LES PUCELES ki sunt meins sages,
Kar sage rent li longs usages, 252

*v. 231, *in right margin*: ideo adolescentule dilexerunt te nimis. (*1: 2*)
v. 239: ce haus doit hom.
*v. 245, *in right margin*: trahe me post te. (*1: 3*)
v. 247: Traii (*second 'i' expuncted*).

Vienent avant e nient ne prient,
Ainz s'afichent forment e dient:
—Nos iroms totes le grant cors                    *
O que nos maint la Tue odors.                    256
Odor unt grant li ungement
Dunt Tu ies uinz, chascon le sent.

L'ESPOSE ki fu debonaire,
Enhorte celes de.l bien faire,                    260
Par sen example les envie
De querre gloriose vie:
Vie de contemplacion,
Dont Deus li avoit fait grant don.                264

—LI ROIS, fait ele, m'a menee                     *
f° 39 v°        En son celier, e enivree
D'un cler, vermeil, savereus vin.
Jo croi del boire seraphin.                       268
Ceste ivresce est de Deu amer,
De lui servir e reclamer,
De lui loer e graces rendre,
Del mont despire, e al ciel tendre.               272
So vos volez cest bien atraire,
Servez Celui ki ço puet faire.

APRÉS A DIT al soverain Roi;
—De moi, Sire, e de ces Te proi.                  276
Nos n'avomes de nos nul bien,
Tot sunt de Toi, e tot sunt Tien.
Por ço raisons, ki tot adresce,                   *
Qu'en Toi soit nostre leece,                      280
De Tes mameles nos sovient,
Dunt grant biens e grant joie vient.
Meillors de vin sunt Tes mameles,                 *
Ço sevent bien cez noz puceles,                   284
Quar la duresce de le Loi,
Lor est atempree par Toi.

*v. 255, *in right margin*: curremus in odorem unguentorum. (*1: 3*)
*v. 265, *in right margin*: Introduxit me rex in celaria sua (*1: 3*)
*v. 279, *in left margin*: Exultabimus et letabimur in te. (*1: 3*)
*v. 283, *in right margin*: Memorem uberum tuorum super vinum. (*1: 3*)

Lᴉ ᴅʀᴏɪᴛ T'aiment, e unt bon droit,     *
Kar par Toi sunt e bon e droit:     288
f° 40 r°     E il ne sunt bon, ne n'unt droiture,
Ki vers Toi n'unt d'amer grant cure.

Aᴘʀᴇ́s ᴄᴇᴢ diz, s'est retornee
As jovenceles l'Esposee.     292
Bien seit ke jovence s'esmaie
D'asez petit, si les rapaie:
— 'Por Deu, fait ele, ne vos desplace,
Se vos veez ma brune face,     296
Se jo sui noire par defors,     *
Dedenz sui clere come ors.
Mes amis m'a descoloree,
Por cui jo sofre mainte colee.     300
Sovent m'en dist om grant laidures,
E fait choses ki molt sunt dures.
Faverkié unt li pecheur,
Desor men dos a grant sejur.     304
Mais sofri por moi ennui,
E jo le vueil sofrir por lui.
Dedenz le cuer la o Deus voit
Est ma beltez, com estre doit.     308
Kar a lui sol vueil jo plaisir,
E de tot faire a sen plaisir.'
Ço dist l'Espouse a ses puceles
f° 40 v°     K'ele vuelt faire dedenz beles.     312
Filles Jerusalem les nome,     *
N'i ramentoit femme ne homme.
De charneus generacion,
Ne seit rien contemplacion.     316

—Oɪᴇᴢ, fait ele, e entendez,
Dunt vos ensivre me devez.
Tels hom vuelt faire altrui damache,
Ki malgré suen s'onor porchace.     320
Savez ou la parole tent,
Por moi le di, de moi l'entent,

*v. 287, *in left margin*: Recti diligunt te. (*1: 3*)
*v. 297, *in left margin*: niger sed sed (*sic*) formosa. (*1: 4*)
*v. 313, *in left margin*: filie ierusalem. (*1: 4*)

Kar simple e povre e petite ere
Entre les fils k'avoit ma mere. 324
Il combatirent contre moi, *
E mal me disent a desroi,
E jo sofroie tot en pais
Kanque disoient li malvais. 328
Por ço se bien sai esguarder,
M'a om mise as vignes guarder: *
Icil sunt faulz arbre sens fruit,
Ki de bien faire ne sunt duit. 332
Mais ki bien fait e Deu reclaime
Cil est la vigne ke Deus aime.

f° 41 r° Vigne estuet foir e femer,
Colper, lier, eskarchoner. 336
Confessions la vigne fuet,
Sens ço bon fruit porter ne puet.
E la memorie des pechiez
I met le fiens novel e viez. 340
Raisons colpe les malvais rains,
E les biens laise entiers e sains.
La lois Deu i done liens
Dunt a le vigne vient granz biens. 344
Li bon home en sunt eskarat
Ou n'a triche ne barat,
Cil sostienent par oreisons
La vigne dusqu'en mosteisons, 348
Dusqu'a cel tens que li reisin
Puissent par mort rend[re] lor vin.
En moi ne puis tel paine rendre *
E as altres m'estuet entendre, 352
Mais li loiers que jo.n espoir
Iert granz se jo.n faz mon pooir.

MOLT m'estroit bien, se jo savoie
O jo bons homes troveroie. 356
Ne sai del grain geter la paille:
f° 41 v° C'est une riens qui me travaille.

*v. 325, *in left margin*: filii matris mee pugnaverunt contra me. (*1: 5*)
*v. 330, *in right margin*: posuerunt me custodem vineis. (*1: 5*)
v. 350: mort rendent lor vin.
*v. 351, *in right margin*: Vineam meam non custodivi. (*1: 5*)

Le mont a nule ypocresie,
Cui vaine glorie a molt saisie                    360
S'oi loe molt les altres chosé,
E vent la fuite por alosé.
Kar me mostre chans, soverains paistre,            *
Qui Tu meïsmes deignes paistre                    364
Des viandes celestiels
Qui sunt plus doces que nuls miels,
Qui sunt cil ou Tu Te reposes
Entre les liles e les roses.                       368
Kar cil sol bel hostel Te sont,
Ki neteé e amor unt,
Quant li solaus lor est plus halt,
Cho est quant sunt d'amor plus chaut.              372
Donc i feus Ta reposee,
Tot belement a recelee.
Bien sai que tels meridienne,
E pais e joie nos ameine,                          376
Mostre les moi, que jo les sache,
Bien ensivre par droite trache,
Que Tu aie par aventure
Damache o grant entrepresure;                      380
Quar compaignon privé se font
A Toi pluisor ki pas ne.l sunt,
Qui chievres paiscent, nient aigneals,
Lor acoster ne m'est pas beals.                    384
Cist mal e ces temtacions
Sunt a mon cuer granz passions.
Molt ai travail, mais desor tot
Criem les herites e redot,                         388
Quar cil se font Tien compaignon,
E se n'i a se semblant non.
Ne voldroie aprés els vaier,
Iço me doit bien esmaier.                          392

Li sires asez cortoisement
Respont a cest complaignement:

f° 42 r°

*v. 363, *in left margin*: Judicamur quem diligit amam mea. ubi pascas ubi cubas in meridie. (*1: 6*)
v. 387, MS.: desor toz *with 'z' expuncted and 't' substituted.*

— Jo ki fis tote creature
Conois bien humaine nature.                          396
Li mal font l'ome a soi conoistre,
Por ço les lais venir e croistre.
Cil qui ne sent griece ne mal,
Est tost montez en nair cheval.                      400
Li mals fait bien, n'est pas dotance,
Ki done a homme coneisance,
K'il puet de soi e par soi faire
Quant Jo li vueil ma main retrere.                   404
Jo t'ai faite e bele e sage:                           *
Guarde ne te tort a damage,
Se tu por ço t'enorgueillis,
Puis ne t'aim Jo, ne ne te pris                       408
S'orguels i vien, tant com un pois,
Tu meïsmes ne te conois;
Puis va fors de ma compaignie,                         *
Kar Jo n'ai soig de tele amie.                       412
Donc pais tes kievres, con cil font
Qui tu blasmas; ore a pur front
Done fius tes bues, tes bues pormaine,
Que li orguels molt tost amaine.                     416
Ço sunt li malvais desirrier
Dont il vienent maint encombrier.

SE TU ne n'as totes ces aises,
Cuides por ço ke me desplaises?                      420
A m'anciene chevalcie                                  *
Ki vient de Egypte tote lie
Quant la maisnie Pharaon
E tote si corre e si baron                           424
Perirent en la Roge Mer,
Posa t'ai faite resembler.
En ces larmes de grant destresce,
Ke cil a ki vers Deu se dresce                       428

f° 42 v° (margin next to line 404)
f° 43 r° (margin next to line 427)

---

*v. 405, *in left margin*: Si ignoras te O pulcherrima inter mulieres. (*1: 7*)

*v. 411, *in left margin*: Egrede et abi per vestigia gregum et pasce eclos tuos inter tabernaculam pastoris. (*1: 7*)

*v. 421, *in right margin*: Equitatui meo in curribus Pharaonis assimilavi te amica mea. (*1: 8*)

Ne pueent vivre li pechié,
Tost i sunt mort e trebuchié.
Mais e li juste desirrier
E li pensé vers moi entier,                    432
Li afeet e les voluntez
Dont en toi est la grant plentez,
Cist pueples a seur trespas,
Il n'i perist ne halt ne bas.                  436

BELE, tu m'aimes, e jo toi,
Kar tu me portes droite foi.
Tu as joes de torterele,                       *
Kar tu ies caste e douce e bele.               440
Joes mom, nient altre menbre,
Kar tu seiz bien, se il t'en membre,
Ke as joes e al reguart
Apert femme de bone part.                      444
Tortre n'a soin d'altre assemblee,
Quant de son per est devisee;
E tu ne vuels nul altre amer,
Ne t'en porroit nuls entamer.                  448

BELE, ten col toz li monz prise               *
Por la noske que g'i ai mise;
E tu meisme resplendies
Por l'or et por les margeries.                 452
Cist tant bels dons clot bien ton sain,
Ke nuls n'i ost metre la mein.
Par le col passe la sustance
Ki norrist l'ome e avance.                     456
E par le col ist la parole
Ki del cuer sort et fors envole.
Tes cols, Amie, cost tes sens,
Dont jo grant bien e saie e pens,              460
Par cui trespasse li mangiers
Ki de sor toz est buens et chiers:
Cho est la sainte norreture
Que hom trueve en l'Escriture,                 464

f⁰ 43 v⁰

*v. 439, *in right margin*: Pulchra est gene tue sicut tortoris. (*1:9*)
*v. 449, *in right margin*: Collum tuum sicut monilia. (*1:9*)

Qui tels morsels reçoit sovent,
Fel est si as altres n'en rent.
Par le noske de charité
T'ai le sens a cho atempré;        468
Tels est li cols, tels est le noske,
Fols est qui rien charnel i soske.


ENCOR feroms un apareil;        *
Unques femme n'out sen pareil        472
f° 44 r°        Jo e cist altre bon ovrier
Que tu avras merveilles chier.
G'i metrai le comencement,
Tot de fin or, molt richement:        476
Jeromes, Augustins, Gregories,
Lamproietes i frunt ories,
E cist e altre bon ovrier,
Se penerunt del fabricher,        480
Avec men or i mellerunt
Argent, et de cel overrunt.
Jo fis la noske e tot l'ovrage,
N'i eut altrui ne fol ne sage.        484
Mais ore a faire les enors
L'uevre en iert lor, e miens li ors.
Jo i met l'or de sapience,
Il ovrent d'argent d'eloquence.        488
Par ces deus choses assemblees
Sunt les oreilles aornees.
Les lamproietes varielees,
Qui sunt bien en l'argent formees,        492
Sunt des paroles li tresor
Dunt escolier font maint estor.


QUANT l'espeuse est si aornee,
f° 44 v°        Vers ses conpaignes est tornee.        496
—Veez, fait ele, que Amis
Del sien en moi, li miens amis,
Molt m'a doné, mais bien sui certe
Ke ço n'est pas par ma deserte.        500

*v. 471, *in left margin*: Murenulas aureas faciemus tibi verbiculata et argento. (*1: 10*)

Li rois selonc moi s'acota,
Ainç por mes mals rien n'i dota,                    *
De nard avoie un ramissel,
Dont voloie faire un chapel.                    504
Mes Amis en senti l'odor,
Par tant m'a mise a cest honor.
Cil arbres suelt grant odor rendre,
E sa racine est crasse e tendre.                    508
Charitez est ceste racine,
Ki vers toz mals a medecine.
De grace encraisse e atenroie
Le cuer qui vers Deu se ravoie.                    512
De racine de charité
S'eslieve ovre de pieté;
C'est li arbres, cist a molt rains,
E toz les a De buen fruit plains.                    516
Mais jo.n tenoie un molt petit,
Si com vos ai conté e dit,
f° 45 r°          Par cui tendoie a le corone,
Ke Deus en ciel as petiz done.                    520
Por tant petit m'a grant bien fait,
Tot a men cuer a lui atrait.

MES AMIS est faisels de myrre,                    *
A cest mien cuer, qui le desirre,                    524
Ke est mirre c'est amertume,
Ce est li martels, mes cuers l'englume.
E neporquant ele me plaist,
E Deu en pri k'ele n'abaist,                    528
Quant mi sovient que por moi fist
Le persone de Jhesu Crist,
Comment por moi fu circomcis
E laidengiez sovent, e pris,                    532
Liez, batuz e demenez
Tant laidement e tant penez,
Comment il soffri passion
Por la moie redempcion,                    536

*v. 502, *in left margin*: Cum esset rex in acubitu suo nardu mea dedit odorem suum.
(*1: 11*)
*v. 523, *in right margin*: fasciculus myrre dilectus meus. (*1: 12*)
v. 525: *An initial 'c' has been expuncted by the copyist. It is the initial of the following line.*

Jo ne m'en puis assez doloir,
Ne jo al main ne al soir;
Un faiscelet fait de cest rains
Mes cuers quant Deus i met les mains.                540
Cil en men cuer demoera,                               *

f° 45 v°          Ja se Deu plaist ne s'en movra.

CESTE dolors me tolt men sens,
Mais nekedent kant me porpens                        544
De la sue surrection
E de la sainte ascension,
Roisin de cypre est mes amis,                          *
Tost m'a grant joie en men cuer mis.                 548
Roisins me set sor toz roisins,
Sor les lointains, sor les voisins,
Tote m'enivre et rent odor
Plus que balsmes en sa valor,                        552
La o meillor rendre le suelt,
Ço est es vignes o om le cuelt.

LI ROIS entent que cele dist,                          *
Coment lui loe, e soi despist,                        556
Coment se tient povre e despite,
Femme tant bele e tant eslite,
Donc l'aparole asez briefment:
—Bien pert a ton dementement                         560
Ke molt ies bele, dolce Amie,                          *
Que quo li cors de ce me die,
Bele ies dedenz, bele ies defors,
Bele ies en arme, bele ies en cors;                  564

f° 46 r°          Dedenz de vertuz aornee,
Defors de bien faire atornee.
Bele ies de celestiels dons.                           *
Li tien ueil sunt ueil de colons;                     568
Li oeil dedenz del esperit,                            *
Cil sunt molt cler, simple e eslit,

*v. 541, *in right margin*: Inter ubera mea cominorabitur. (*1: 12*)
*v. 547, *in left margin*: botrus cypri dilectus meus michi. (*1: 13*)
*v. 555, *in left margin*: in vinieis engadi. (*1: 13*)
*v. 561, *in left margin*: Ecce tu pulcra es amica mea. (*1: 14*)
*v. 567, *in right margin*: Ecce tu pulcra. (*1: 14*)
*v. 569, *in right margin*: Oculi tui columbarum. (*1: 14*)

Tost ont veü li mal oisel,
Quant il vers toi fait son cembel.          572
Bien eslisent le meillor grain,
De quanque jo.n tiegn en ma main.
En als n'a puint de covoitise,
Malice en est ariere mise.                  576

CELE respont et dist: — Bels sire,
Tu conois tot, mais bien puis dire
Que Tu feroies molt grant feste
De buenes meurs, de vie honeste,            580
Kant Tu loes ceste frarine,
Cui jo ne pris une fordine.
Mais Tu ies beals oltre mesure,               *
N'est pas merveille, enz est droiture,      584
Quar donerre ies de toz biens,
Cho set mes cuers kant Tu i viens,
Bele est la devine nature,
Bele est humaine, e nete e pure,            588
En Tei Abel, e Deu, e ome,
Sor toz ies bels, c'en est la somme.

QUELS ke je soie, il m'est granz fais
Taisir les biens que tu me faiz,            592
Nient en moi seule, mais en totes
En cui tu fiez, gis o acotes.
En nos par Toi est faiz uns liz              *
Soef, flairanz, bels e floriz.              596
A cel lit faire est pietez,
Pais e justice e veritez,
Ainç nuls om n'ot tels camberieres
Kant jo les sent, molt les ai chieres.      600
De liles et de fresces roses
Est faiz li liz ou Tu reposes.
Kar chasteez e veraie amors
Est Tes repos e Tes sojors.                 604
Cest apareil sont les vertuz,
Quant Tu viens o les venuz.

fo 46 vo

*v. 583, *in right margin*: Ecce tu pulcher es et dechorus. (*1: 15*)
*v. 595, *in left margin*: lectulus noster floridus. (*1: 15*)
v. 605: cest [aparail *crossed out by scribe*] apareil.

BELS est li liz e le maisons
Ke nos en nos cuers Te faisons.                    608
Nos le faisons, mes Tu, bels sire,
Ki toz les biens puez faire et dire

fº 47 rº           De cedre sunt tot li cevron,                    *
E li cypres sunt environ,                          612
Qui font tote le lacheure.
Tot cho m'est bel por le figure
Quar cho faiz Tu tot vraiement
Por nos doner entendement;                         616
Kar par samblant des corporels
Seit om les biens esperitels.
Li cedre sunt arbre mult halt
E odor rendent ki molt valt,                       620
Kar il n'i puet avoir duree
Serpents ne beste envenimee.
Li cedre durent sens mesure,
Ne criement ver ne pureture.                       624
Tot cho par droit nos senefie
Charité doble e pure vie.
Ces eslievent maison el cuer,
Venim n'i sofrent a nol fuer.                       628
Li venims est orguels, envie,
Glorie, luxure, felenie.
Cist cedre a toz jorz durerunt,
Mais altre bien trespasserunt.                     632
Cist doivent bien solonc raison
fº 47 vº           Doner grant force a la maison.
E li cypres croiscent en halt,
Peuz as cedres petit en falt.                      636
Cist noz figurent les vertuz
Dont li cuers est laienz vestuz,
E la font une lacheure
Dont tote l'uevre est plus seure,                  640
E belté donent al palais
O venir suels, or n'i viens mais.
Mais ore i vien, ore i repaire,
Ki tant ies francs e debonaire.                    644

*v. 611, *in right margin*: tigna domorum nostrorum cedrina et laquearia nostra cupres-
sina. (*1: 16*)

Li ROIS entent k'ele velt,
Dont se complaint, e dont se delt,
Bien seit la chose ou ele tent,
Ke quiert, ke vuelt, o ses cuers tent, 648
Ke tot son cuer velt en Deu metre,
Nient del siecle plus entremetre.
—Bele, fait il, Tu quiers repos,
E qu'avec toi sovent repos. 652
Mais par victorie a om corone,
Par travail l'a cui Deus le done.
Par cho covient el champ venir
E la l'estor bien maintenir. 656

f° 48 r°   Ke li espirs delivrement
Puist e par soi e par sa gent
Les mals, les vices sormonter,
E les malvais deliz donter, 660
E en sa char e en l'acrui,
Dont il revienent maint annui,
Griesce, jamais esperance,
Doit fors buter tote dotance. 664
Viengne i amors ki tot eshaite,
E fois avec l'espee traite,
Aprés la lere chevalerie,
Si ert la bataille tost ferie. 668
Je sui la flors ke cil avra
Ki loialment se combatra.
Flors sui del champ, por ceste glorie    *
Doit om bien rendre a la victorie. 672
Mais qui de cho s'eslevera,
Tote se paine i perdera,
Kar jo sui liles des valees,    *
O les eaues sunt avalees, 676
Des umles cuers e des ploranz,
Fiere loiers vient des granz.

A CEZ paroles voit doter

f° 48 v°   Li rois s'amie, e redoter 680

*v. 671, *in right margin*: ego flos campi. (2: 1)
*v. 675, *in right margin*: et lilium convallium. (2: 1)

Les granz cures e la grant paine,
Ke tels mestiers od sai amaine,
Ke ele ne seit ne rien n'en sent,
Kant toz ses cuers a Deu entent.                    684
E dist: — La flors que plus est pure,
Plus tost sent d'une pointure,
M'amie a filles ki le quaiscent                     *
Les pensees ki de li naissent.                      688
Celes li sunt males voisines,
Com al lilie sunt les espines.
Molt le grievent ices pointures,
E plus resoigne les plus dures.                     692
En ces tribuls metre ne s'ose,
Kar ele est simple e tendre chose.
Mielz volroit ore un petit prendre
Ke plus assez al long atendre.                      696
Mais por Deu doit paine sofrir
Cil ki ses biens volra sentir.

CELE respont — Si com jo pens
As paroles nient al sens,                           700
Al sens ke la devine amaine,
Ne se prent pas parole humaine.
fº 49 rº         Ele velt, tant puet om entendre,
Loenge por loenge rendre,                           704
E dist: — Si com li dolz pomiers                    *
Est sor arbres salvages chiers,
E les fruiz bels e d'odor plains,
Dont se s'entent sovent les mains,                  708
Si ies Tu, sire, precios,
Desor tes filz, e glorios.
Li tien fruit sunt trestot si bien,
Tu les fesis e il sunt tien.                        712
Cil sunt ti fil en l'Escriture,
Du cui Tu prenz e guarde e cure,
Ki Toi honeurent come pere
E Sainte Eglise come mere.                          716

*v. 687, *in left margin*: sicut lilium inter spinas sic amica mea inter filias. (*2: 2*)
  *v. 705, *in right margin*: sicut malus inter ligna silvarum, sic dilectus meus inter filios.
(*2: 3*)

Itel filz sunt li Saint Martyr,
Cui morz ne peut de Toi partir,
E li altre Saint ensement
Ki firent ton comandement.                    720
Cil sont arbre de paradis
Bon fruit e bel avront totdis.
Leur fruit, cho sunt li bon ovrage
K'il el mont firent come sage.                724
Cil fruit rendent al mont odor
f° 49 v°    E as bons ont bone savor,
Mais li tiens fruiz sor tote rien,
Est bons e dolz e plains de bien.             728
Dolz est al cuer, dolz a la boche,
Se la dolchor al cuer atoche.

MOLTZ jors desirai aveir                      *
Cest arbre e desuz lui seir.                  732
Tant ke g'i sis, e si trovai                  *
Molt plus ke jo ne desirrai.
Kar le kaleur me toli l'ombre
Ki grant mal fait e molz encombre,            736
E m'amena tant soef ore
Ke dolcement le sent encore.

PUIS cho m'a li rois amenee                   *
En son celier e abevree.                      740
M'enivra de tel ivresce,
Ki done al cuer molt grant destresce,
E de bien fair, e de bien dire,
Issi fet cil jurer mes Sire.                  744

ADONC m'aprist molt dolcement                 *
De charité lor ilevement
Ke Deus sor toz doit estre amez,
Sor toz serviz et honorez.                    748
f° 50 r°    E aprés Deu, soi amer doit
Li hom ki velt amer droit.

*v. 731, *in left margin*: sub umbra illiusque desideram sedi. (2: 3)
*v. 733, *in right margin*: et fructus eius dulcis gutturi meo. (2: 3)
*v. 739, *in left margin*: Introduxit me rex in cellam vinariam. (2: 4)
*v. 745, *in right margin*: ordinavit me karitatem. (2: 4)

Kar cil vers soi amor ne n'a
Son proisme coment amera                    752
Cu'il amer doit come soi,
Solonc le comant de le loi?
Nostre proisme le tierz lui tient
En l'amor ki par ordre vient,               756
E cist tierz lius a molt degrez,
Kar molt i a diversitez
Tant com chascons est Deu amis
Doit estre amez, c'en ai apris.             760

OR SAI cui je doi plus amer,
E je plus l'aim, tot m'est amer
Kanques je sent, kanques je voi,
Se je Toi n'ai, dolz filz a roi,            764
Deus dit: 'Va!' et je n'en voi mie,
Je croi n'en porterai ja vie.
Deus, ke ferai, le cuers me falt?
Se jo ne l'ai riens ne me valt.             768
Se secors n'ai prochainement,
N'en puis vivre el, es bien le sent.
f° 50 v°          — Damoiseles, ne vos ennuit,
De flors m'apoiez e de fruit,               *772
Flores e pomes cha m'aportez.
. . . . . . . . . . . .

Tenez men cuer par bone odor,
Kar jo languis tote d'amor.                 776
Flors est de bien comencemenz,
E fruiz en est complissemenz.
Vos, compaignes, ki Deu cremez,
Ces dous choses en moi semez,               780
Ke jo me puisse a bien atraire
E fruit de bones ovres faire.
Ce sunt les flors, ce sunt les pomes,
Ki font a Deu plaisir les omes.             784

CONTEZ por Deu des ancesors,
De trois ou quatre les meillors

---

*v. 772, *in left margin*: Falcite me floribus, stipate me malis quia amore langueo. (*2: 5*)
v. 774: *There is clearly a line missing, as can be seen from both the sense and the rhyme. The copyist has not left a blank. The lapsus is the result of an oversight.*

Dont comença lor bone vie,
E en quels biens fu acomplie.                    788
De cho me volroie apoier
E men ami de moi proier.
S'il ma vie voit amendee,
Il m'avra tost reconfortee.                       792
Sa senestre mon chief tendra                      *
E sa destre m'embracera.

f° 51 r°      Li chies dedenz, c'est la pensee
Ki de ses biens iert sos levee                    796
De sacramenz de Saint Eglise,
E d'altre biens de mainte guise
K'il tient trestoz en sa senestre.
Cil de la sus sunt a sa destre.                   800
De ces granz biens tant en avrai
Ke rien plus ne demonderai.


Li ROIS estoit ariere alez
Por ce qu'il fust plus demandez.                  804
Or i revient e [mot] ne sone
Mais tant li fait, et tant li done,
Ke de dolçor s'est endormie.
Kant li rois voit dormir sa mie,                  808
Donc a parlé as jovenceles:                        *
— Je vos conjur, chieres puceles
Ki vers Jerusalem tendez
E ses filles vos ramembrez,                       812
Par les chevrels e par les cers
Ki vont corant par les desers,
Ke vos m'amie n'esveillez,
Ne li por rien ne traveilliez;                   *816
Tant com li plaist, tant se repost,

f° 51 v°      E nols ne soit ki trobler l'ost.
En contemplacion l'ai mise.
Ce est li repos k'ele plus prise.                 820

---

*v. 793, *in left margin*: leva eius sub capite meo et dextera illius amplexabitur me. (2: 6)
v. 805, MS.: e molt ne sone.
*v. 809, *in right margin*: Adiuro vos filie Jerusalem per capreas cervosque camporum.
(2: 7)
*v. 816, *in left margin*: ne suscitetis necque evigilare faciatis dilectam quo adusque
ipsam velit. (2: 7)

Vos ki porsivre le solez
Tant dolz repos ne li tolez.
Il revenra li tans d'ovrer,
Ne porroit donc pas recovrer.                    824
Filles de Jerusalem vos nom,
Dont fu getez li premiers hom,
Por ce, ki volez revenir
E la droite voie tenir.                           828
Or ne vos soit donkes oscur,
Ke par ces bestes vos conjor.
Chevrels ignels les lius boeus
Tressalt e toz les espineus.                      832
Li cerf unt a serpenz haine,
Si com Nature les escline.
Tot ço figure les vertuz
Par cui li cuers est maintenuz                    836
Contre vices e vaines cures
E mals serpenz od lor pointures.
Se vos volez tel compaignie,
N'esveilliez pas ma dolce amie.                   840

f° 52 r°        CELE S'ESVEILLE sodement,
Ne dormoit mie fermement,
E dist: — Ha, Deus qu'ai jo oï?
Ce est la voiz de mon ami,                        *844
E Deus aide, je le voi,
E Deus kar venist il a moi.
Il salt es monz ki sunt plus halt,               *
E les tertres del tot tressalt,                   848
Es halz parvient en petit d'eure,
Mais es meneurs rien ne demeure.
Por ço me criem ke jo n'i faille,
E k'il del tot ne me tressaille                   852
Kar il set bien quele je sui.
Ne valt escusemenz vers lui.
E il resemble le chevrel                          *
Ki toz jors quiert le liu plus bel.              856

*v. 844, *in left margin*: Vox dilecti mei. (2: 8)
*v. 847, *in right margin*: ecce iste venit saliens in montibus et transiens collens. (2: 8)
*v. 855, *in right margin*: similis est dilectus meus capree hinnuloque cervorum. (2: 9)

Les laiz tressalt dont il n'a cure;
Issi l'aporte sa nature.
Por ma laidor qui molt m'ennuie,
Criem jo tot jors qu'il ne me fuie. 860
Al cervecel rest il semblanz
Ki suelt faire les salz molt granz.
Cist cervecels tant debonaire
Savez kels salz Il n'os faire. 864
Le premier fist del sain son pere
Dusqu'en celi k'Il fist sa mere.
D'iluec saili dusqu'en le creche,
Ou Il fu mis par grant destresce, 868
Par destrece de povreté
Ou Il vint par sa volonté.
Moltz fist del salz, mais nul en vain.
Le tierz salt fist dusk'en Jordain 872
Ou li Sires fu baptisiez
Por eslaver les noz pechiez.
D'iluec salli dusqu'el desert
Ou li deables, tot en apert, 876
De trois choses Le tenta;
Mais en nule ne.l sormonta.
D'iluec [sailli] dusqu'an la Croiz,
Ou Il sofri les granz destroiz, 880
Ou Il sofrir volt passion
Por le nostre redempcion.
E de la Croiz ou mort reçut,
Fist salt el liu ou il mort jut 884
Quant Il a Infer descendist
E as feels clarté rendist.
Aprés toz ces fist un grant salt,
De la terre la sus en halt; 888
E liement fu receuz
El ciel dont Il estoit venuz.

APRES CES moz, le voit venir,
E dist kar ne s'en puet tenir: 892
Or vient, or vient li dessirez
Dont ja mes cuers n'avra asez.

v. 879, MS.: salili.

fº 52 vº

fº 53 rº

Jo le voi la ester tot droit,                               *
Aprochiez est de no paroit.                                896
Se il en luec ne s'entendist
Jo croi ke tost avant venist,
Mais par treilles et par fenestres
Esguarde cha quels est [mes estres].                       900
Quant il en moi sa grace espant,
Jo di ke donc vient il avant.
Mais la paroiz ki nos devise,
Cho est ma char le mal aprise,                             904
Cele est toz li encombremenz
De nos chastes enbrachemenz.
Cho le detient, mais bien le voi,
Ke volentiers reguarde a moi.                              908
Mon cuer haucent et font destroit
f° 53 v°         Les manieres dont il me voit.
Quant il m'esguarde par la treille,
Adonc mes cuers alkes s'esveille                           912
A porpenser de mes pechiez
Dont ne puet estre esleechiez.
Mais ce meisme, bien le sent,
Me vien de son reguardement.                               916
Quant par fenestre a moi reguarde,
Donc m'est avis ke mes cuers arde.
Donc s'eslieve par une joie
Ke je dire ne vos porroie.                                 920
Par tant sai jo ke sa veue
Est largement sor moi venue.
Kant me sovient de son reguart,
Molt haz le cors ki m'en depart.                           924
Il ne vuelt pas chaienz venir
Issi come je le desir.
Mais molt me fait riche semblant
Com amant doit faire a amant.                              928
De la defors parole a moi                                   *
De bon semblant, kar bien le voi.

*v. 895, *in right margin*: en ipse stat post parietem nostrum despiciens, per fenestras, prospiciens per cancellos. (*2: 9*)

v. 900, MS.: quels est mest est.

*v. 929, *in left margin*: En dilectus meus loquitur mi: surge, propera amica mea, columba mea, formosa mea. (*2: 10*)

— Vien ent, fait il, ma dolce amie,
[Mieus] covient un poi ta vie. 932
f° 54 r° Ma columbele, lieve toi, vien,
Ne demorer de faire bien,
Vien en cha fors, e si te haste,
Ne redoter travail ne laste. 936
N'est pas saison de someillier;
Ouvrer doit hom et traveillier.
Kar li ivers est trespassez, *
Ki fist al mont del mal asez. 940
E la grant pluie e la gelee
Avec l'iver en est alee.
Granz ivers est, e grant froidure,
Kant prés tote humaine nature 944
Ert engelee a tel desroi
K'il n'i avoit kaleur de foi.
Grant ert la pluie de laidures
Des paroles aspres et dures 948
Ke cil de totes parz sentoient
Ki de bien faire se penoient.
C'est trespassé de grant partie,
S'il en remaint, ce ne nuist mie. 952
El plain esté voit om grant pluie
Ki grant bien fait, et si annuie.
Tels paroles annuient l'ome
f° 54 v° Ki biens li faut, c'en est la somme. 956
N'est se bons non al cuer cist plaist
Cui li ramenbre ses mesfaiz.

FLORS aperent en nostre terre, *
Ce est el cuer cui Deus defferre 960
E delivre de la gelee
Dont cele terre ert enserree.
Flors sunt comencement de bien.
Cueil en, ma dolce, e si les tien. 964

v. 932, MS.: muex [sic] covient.
v. 935, MS.: *the copyist has corrected* fors si te haste *into* fors e si te haste.
*v. 939, *in right margin*: iam enim hyems abiit et recessit. (2: 11)
v. 947, MS.: *the copyist has corrected* ert de pluie *into* ert la pluie.
*v. 959, *in right margin*: flores apparuerunt. (2: 12)

Se tu as tel comancement,
Li fruiz venra plenierement.

OR EST li tans de laborer                    *
En ces vignes, e de colper,                 968
D'oster de les tot le malvais,
E tot le bon laissier em pais.

LA TORTORELE nos envie,                      *
Cui voiz ne suelt pas estre oie,            972
La lois maldit cels ki vivront,
E sor terre fruit ne feront.
De casteé n'estoit parole,
De toz fust tenue por fole.                  976
Or le reçovient li plus sage,
Sains maldiçon e sans damage.
f° 55 r°     Fruit doit hom faire, nient d'enfanz,
Mais des ovres a Deu plaisanz.              980
Nostre est a droit icele terre,
Ki la voiz out de la tortorele,             *
Kar cil cuers est de nostre guarde,
Ki chasteé maintient e guarde.              984

A CEST comencement d'esté                    *
A ja sunt fruit tenpriu geté
Nos figiers: c'est Sainte Glise
Ki molt est ore halt asise.                 988
Mais cist figiers premierement,
Fu molt grevez de tote gent.
Escus en fu li fruiz temprius,
Ki donc estoit povres et vils.              992
Ce est li apostoile e li martyr
Ki ne volrent de moi partir,
Mais par martyre trespasserent
A la gloire dont il digne erent.            996

*v. 967, *in right margin*: tempus putacionis advenit. (2: 12)
*v. 971, *in left margin*: vox turturis audita est. (2: 12)
v. 979, MS.: doitn (*copyist has expuncted 'n'*).
     v. 981: *Is the correct reading* terre icele, *which would restore the rhyme, or have two lines been omitted by the scribe?*
*v. 982, *in right margin*: in terra nostra. (2: 12)
*v. 985, *in right margin*: figus protulit grossos suos. (2: 13)

Les Vignes donent bone odor                    *
Kar grant plenté i a de flor:
Bone ovre n'iert ja bien celee,
Loinz en espant la renomee.                     1000

Vien enz, dolce, de gracie plaine,              *
f° 55 v°    Se tu dotes travail ne paine,
Fui t'ent as pertuis de la piere,
E al cavain de la mesiere                        1004
La met ton cuer, donc entendras
Ke tu por grant petit rendras.
Voies mes mains, voies mes piez
Tant dolerosement perciez.                       1008
Se cho ton cuer n'esmuet asez,
Voies la plaie de mon lez,
Dont il eissi del sanc grant onde,
Kar ele fu grande e parfonde.                    1012
Cho firent li felon a tort,
Ki me volront vaincre par mort.
Men cuer perchierent a la lance
Sans nule dote de venjance.                      1016

Haste toi, bele, e siu me trace,
E mostre moi la tue face.                        *
En mes oreilles sunt te voiz,
E me die toz tes destroiz.                       1020
La face juce la pensee,
Ne puet estre longes celee.
Tost s'i demostre le leece
S'ele est el cuer, o le tristece.                1024
f° 56 r°    Por tant est ci [f]ace apellee
La volentez dedenz celee.
Kar e le cuer e ses pensez
Juge le sole volentez.                           1028
Par voiz doit om le cuer ovrir
Cui malvais sens faisoit taisir.

---

*v. 997, *in right margin*: vinee florentes odorem suum dederunt. (2: 13)

*v. 1001, *in right margin*: surge amica mea, sponsa mea, columba mea, et veni in fora-
minibus petre et in cavernis macerie. (2: 13–14)

*v. 1018, *in left margin*: ostendi michi faciem tuam. Sonet vox tua in auribus meis.
(2: 14)

v. 1025, MS.: pace.

Ce est la some de la raison.
Jo vel ke par confession                                    1032
Soit mostree ta volentez,
Dont te venra de bien plentez.
Dolce chose m'est a oïr                                        *
Te voiz, et te face a veir,                                 1036
Buen m'est e bel. Ke tot ten estre
Sache sovent por moi li prestre.
Kant tu li diz, tu le dis moi,
Jo sui presenz, e trestot oï.                              1040

AS COMPAIGNONS vient la parole,
Kar lor Sire les aparole:
— Pernez, fait il, ces volpiseles                             *
Ki les vignes, de flor tant beles,                         1044
Vont par le siecle devastant
Damache i puet avoir molt grant.
Damnez, fait il, ces eriteals
f° 56 v°         Ki vont muchant par ces bordeals          1048
E suddinent la simple gent
Ki petit ont d'entendement,
E damnent noces e batesme
E totes uncions de cresme,                                 1052
Nis le sacrement del alter
Osent cil paltonier blasmer.
Ces vulpilles tolront les iglises
S'eles ne sunt alkes tost prises.                          1056
Totes les iglises par le mont
Une sole vigne me font,
Une sole par unité,
E de foi e de charité.                                     1060
Celes vastent li heritel:
Cho ne m'est pas ne bon ne bel.
Por tant ai jo rové veillier
Ma dolce Amie, e traveillier.                              1064
Tot cho pöons altrement dire.                                 *
Prendre, comande Nostre Sire,

*v. 1035, *in right margin*: vox enim tua dulcis et facies tua decora. (*2: 14*)
*v. 1043, *in right margin*: capite nobis vulpes parvulas que demoliuntur vineas. (*2: 15*)
*v. 1065, *in left margin*: altrement en moralité.

Sens demorer les vuolpiseles,
Cho est les pensees noveles                    1068
Ke diables en cuer envoie,
Ki de tot bien, s'il puet, desvoie
f° 57 r°          Por estaindre devocion
E por destorber oreison.                    1072
Ces vuolpiseles doit om prendre,
Son cuer seignier e bien defendre,
Quar altrement del tot perist
La vigne qui laienz florist,                    1076
Ki fait bon fruit s'ele est guardee
E a son droit est coltivee.
De cho comande a ses Amis,
As angeles de tot bien apris,                    1080
K'a cest ovre me tent les mains,
Kar ne puet tuit travals homains.

LA DOMOISELE ot son ami,
Ke dolcement parole a li,                    1084
Ke soefment le reconforte,
E tant de bien faire l'enorte,
E ke tels ai d'ors lor baille,
Ke nule chose n'i defaille.                    1088
Donc a parlé a ses mescines
Ki prés estoient ses voisines:
— Bien aperçois, fait ele, e voi
Ke mes amis i est a moi.                    1092
E jo certes iere a lui,                         *
f° 57 v°          Ja ne.l lairai por nul annui.
Bien doi savoir ke ço lui plaist,
Ki de purs liles se repaist                    *1096
Pur ce de cuer ce li delite,
C'est sa viande plus eslite.
Cho le repaist ore, e fera,
Tant com cist siecles durera.                    1100
Quant a declin ira cest umbre                  *

---

v. 1079: *The copyist has written* cho me comande *and has then expuncted* me.
*v. 1093, *in right margin*: dilectus meus michi et ego illi. (*2: 16*)
*v. 1096, *in left margin*: qui pascitur inter lilia. (*2: 16*)
*v. 1101, *in left margin*: donec aspiret dies et inclinentur umbre. (*2: 17*)

Ki toz nos tient, e toz encombre,
E li vrais jors esclarcirra,
Ki ja puis fin ne sentira.          1104
Il iert en toz, e toz en lui,
La avra noces sans annui.

LA VOLROIT ele ja venir
E ja le desirré tenir.          1108
Mais faire estuet premierement
Cho dont ele a comandement.
Bien seit ke faire li estuet,
Mais par soi aemplir ne.l puet.          1112
Por cho requiert al aideur,
Meime son comandeur,
E dist: — Bels sire, a moi repaire,
Kar jo ne puis par moi rien faire.          *1116

f° 58 r°

Plusors choses m'as comandees
Ki ja sans Toi n'ierent finees.
E jo, coment me combatrai
Sains Toi? Certes, ja ne.l ferai.          1120
E des vignes jo n'en sai rien
Sains Toi, n'i puis faire nul bien.
Vuolpiseles, jo ne.s sai prendre
Se Tu ne vels avec entendre.          1124
Kar certes Sire, poissanz rois,
Jo meïsme ne me conois.
E coment iert devant Toi bele
Ma vois, ki sui une muele?          1128
Tu ies fontaine de toz biens,
Tot iert bien fait, se Tu i viens.
Jo Te volroie avoir toz jors,
Mais ne Te plaist si lons sejors.          1132
Se jo Te voi alkes sovent,
Ço m'iert a grant confortement.
Al cevrolet Te fai semblant,
Ki sor ces tertres va saillant.          1136
Fai toi semblant al cervecel
Ki cort de sor les monz Betel.

*v. 1116, *in left margin*: revertere. (2: 17)
v. 1137: *The scribe adds this line in the right margin.*

Kant ces bissetes sunt caciés,      *

E des brachez sunt eslongiés,     1140

f° 58 v°     E perdu unt des chiens la noise,

Donc se restunt, e lor empoise.

Si s'en revienent a l'oie

Des chiens ki ne targent mie.     1144

Kant il sunt prés, donc se refuient

Puis revienent, si se deduient

Ai[n]si revien a la fiee,

Dolcz Sire, e de Toi me fai lié.     1148

De tant Te proi, kar a venir

Ne puis a Toi toz jors tenir.

Fai noz cuers monz, hauz par vertuz,

Ke Tu ne.s truises de bien nuz.     1152

Kar tres bien sai ke Tu n'as cure

De mont o n'a bone pasture.

Fai nos Betel, c'est Deu maison,

Ke tu i viegnes par raison.     1156

En maison Deu doit Deus venir,

Deus doit sa maison maintenir.


SIRE EN Toi tot guart tes comanz

De ces biscetes les semblanz.     1160

Tu ies li cies, e nos li membre.

De tes membres sire, Te membre.

Fai nos semblant a ces bissetes

f° 59 r°     De cler veir, de guarder netes,     1164

Ke de loinz poissons esguarder

Ki nuire puet, e nos guarder

E nos buens primes ensement

Ki maisons Deu sunt veraiment.     1168


NE SE DOIT pas targier ne faindre

Ki ço k'il chace vult ataindre.

Damoiseles, jo vos vueil dire

De cel Seignor o mes cuers tire,     1172

En kel maniere jo le quis,

E al querre kel paine mis.

*v. 1139, *In right margin*: similis esto, dilecte mi, capree, hinuloque cervorum super montes Betel. (*2: 17*)

v. 1147, MS.: Aisi.

Molt i porrez de bien aprendre,
Se vos a moi volez entendre.                        1176
Bien m'en sovient ke jo gisoie                         *
Ja en men lit e reposoie.
La quis jo sovent mon ami,
Mais ne trovai, ce pesa mi,                          1180
Kar nuiz estoit, nuiz d'ignorance
Mist ariere cele esperance.
Bien a la teste de sens vuide                          *
Ki Deu trover en deliz cuide.                         1184
Jo me levai de cel mien lit,
E mis ariere tot delit.

f° 59 v°   Quis mon ami par la cité,
Demondoie [e]nt la verité                            1188
Par les rues et par les places
Quis longuement les sues traces.
Par les rues de vie estroite
Le quis, kar cele est la plus droite.                   1192
Par les places de lasque vie
Le quis, mais la n'estoit Il mie.
As guardes ving de la cité,                            *
Cil le m'eurent tost endité.                          1196
A Deu conoistre tost amainent
Li buen maistre, quant il s'en painent,
Ki del parfont de l'Escriture
Sevent traire buene peuture.                         1200
Kant ses guardes oï trespassé,                         *
Donc trovai jo lo desirré.
Pluisor nos dient molt de bien,
E il meisme n'en font rien.                          1204
En cho covient c'on les trespast
Ainz ke om Deu tiengne e embrast,
Kar par dire e nient ovrer

*v. 1177, *in right margin*: in lectulo meo quesivi per noctes quem diligit anima mea.
Quesivi illum et non inveni. (*3: 1*)

*v. 1183, *in right margin*: Surgam et circuibo civitatem per vicos et plateas querens
quem diligit anima mea. Quesivi illum et non inveni. (*3: 2*)

v. 1188, MS.: Demondoient la verite.

*v. 1195, *in left margin*: Invenerunt me vigiles qui custodiebant civitatem. Num quem
diligit anima vidistis? (*3: 3*)

*v. 1201, *in left margin*: Paululum cum pertransissem eos inveni quem diligit anima
mea. (*3: 4*)

Ne le puet om mie trover. 1208
Devocions de cuer le trueve,
f°60 r° Kant il Deu plaist ke il les mueve.
Mais a ce failent bien sovent
Li gros ventre e li vis rovent. 1212
En terre de delicies plaine
Ki la Le quiert, il pert sa paine.
Mais nekedent pieté en eut
De moi se.l trovai kant Lui pleut. 1216
Se.l tieng bien ferme, e le tenrai *
Tant ke ma merre le menrai.
Sainte Iglise, cho est ma merre
De cui jo sui sans charnel perre. 1220
Ceste grant joie li dirai
E parchoniere l'en ferai.
Toz jors li ferai mais entendre
A lui avoir, e paine rendre, 1224
S'ele bien vuelt, n'i faldra mie,
Posé a k'il apele sa mie.
Tant ferai jo k'ele l'avra,
E en son cuer le guardera. 1228
La li ferai un molt bel lit, *
Molt precios e molt eslit.
Ja ne.l laira, s'ele men croit,
Ainz le tenra molt bien estroit. 1232

f° 60 v° LI ROIS entent la damoisele,
E ses compaignes en apele
E dist: Ma dolce amie dort,
Or cuide estre venue a port. 1236
Sachiez ke s'ele ne dormist,
Ja ne pensast ce k'ele dist.
Mais il n'a sens, il n'a raison
Ki dort par contemplacion. 1240
Ore est molt riche, or est a aise,
Nule rien n'est ki li desplaise.

---

*v. 1217, *in right margin*: tenui illum nec dimittam donec introducam illum in domum matris mee. (*3: 4*)
v. 1226, MS.: kil la pele sa mie.
*v, 1229, *in right margin*: et in cubiculum genitricis mee. (*3: 4*)

S'om cho li tolt, granz iert li dels,
Or vos ajur, par les cevrels                    1244
E par les cers, ne l'esveilliez,                   *
K'a agriece ne li soiez.
Or vos covient entente metre,
A bien entendre ceste letre.                    1248
Kant Deus parole a creature,                      *
Ne.l fait mie a nostre mesure.
Cho ke lui plaist al cuer aspire:
Ne li estuet altrement dire.                    1252
Par ses menistres ensement
Parole Il asez sovent.
Kant il cuer e buke eskelt,

f° 61 r°    A annuncier ce ke il vuelt            1256
De ces bisses, dont il a ajure
Les puceles, dist l'Escriture
Ke cevrels quiert la place bele
E li cers vils se renovele,                      1260
Kar les serpenz quiert e manjue,
Par cui se pels tote li mue
E de ses cornes se descharge,
Kar li venins point ne se targe,                 1264
Ainz les bolist, e aive vive
Li fait querre, ki le delivre.
Kant but en a, toz est novels,
Tot se mue, cornes e pels.                       1268
A sage ome n'est pas dotance
Ke ci n'ait grant senefiance;
Kar li chevrels cels senefie
Ki tot jors mainent nete vie,                    1272
E li cers est de Deus figure
O il ot grant entrepresure.
Mais par baptesme sunt lavé
E dedenz tot renovelé,                           1276
E des larmes de penitence
Dist cho meime la sentence.

f° 61 v°    De totes genz a Deus plus chieres,

---

*v. 1245, *in left margin*: adjuro vos, filiee Jerusalem, per capreas cervosque camporum, ne suscetetis. (3: 5)
  *v. 1249, *in left margin*: neque evigilare faciatis dilectam donec ipsa velit. (3: 5)

E li angele ces deus manieres,                    1280
Mais desor toz prent le meillor
Ki garde entierement s'onor.
A honor est e a grant aise
Ki ne fait rien ke Deu desplaise.                 1284
A ces dous manieres de genz
Apartient cist ajuremenz.

OR REVENONS a la parole.
Li rois as puceles parole,                        1288
Ne velt qu'il i ait tant hardie,
Ki pas esvelt la sue amie.
Cele se dort, mais ses cuers veille,
Kar uns fus l'art, ki bien l'esveille.            1292
Ele al siecle ne voit ne n'ot,
Ne rien ne sent, ne n'i dist mot.
Mais ses cuers art e toz remet,
Si come encens kant om le met                     1296
Sor les charbons por odor rendre.
Tant en pooms dire e entendre.
Mais nuls ne puet sentir ne dire
Coment i ovre Nostre Sire.                         1300
Li cors remaint, une virgele
f° 62 r°                         S'en eslieve grellete e bele:
Une vergele de fumiere
De bon odor e a Deu chiere,                        1304
Ki des angles la compaignie
Esmuet par une sainte vie.
— Ki est, font il, cele pucele,                   *
Ki la monte pers a vergele                         1308
De fumiere ki d'encens ist,
E cui tote odor replenist?
Com est succils, e bele, e pure,
Sains malvaistié, sains vaine cure.                1312
Ele s'en vient par le desert
Tot plain de mals, e rien n'i pert.
En li pert bien ke ne se sent,
D'altrui pechié, ki n'i consent.                  1316

*v. 1307, *in right margin*: que est ista que ascendit per desertum sicut virgula fumi ex
aromatibus mirre et thuris et universi pulveris pigmentarii? (*3: 6*)

Uns desers est cils monz l'aval,
Peu i a bien, e molt de mal.
Mais ki fait cho ke raison dite
Entre les mals a grant merite,                              1320
Kar estre el fu e nient ardoir
Fera molt grant corone avoir.

LA DAMOISELE ert endormie
Tolue al mont, en Deu ravie.                                1324

f° 62 v°    Or s'esveille tot de son gré,
E dist cho ke li est mostré.
— Jo vi, fait ele, un bel palais,
Unkes soleus n'ert plus clers rais.                         1328
D'or, de pierres ert la faiture,
Meillors c'onkes ne fist Nature,
Chascune solonc sa maniere
Rendoit a la meison lumere.                                 1332
Toz ert de saphir li celez
E al semblant del ciel formez.
Estoiles d'or le destincloient,
Soleus e lune n'i failoient.                                1336
En cel palais veoie un lit.                                   *
Ne vos avrai ja descrit
Ne sa belté ne sa valor,
Par tot sembloit uevre d'amor.                              1340
De liles, de roses noveles
E d'altres flors freches e beles
Eirt faiz cil liz; e si veoie
Uns dras de cui jo ne pooie                                 1344
Por rien conoistre la maniere,
Mais tant sai jo k'ele ert molt chiere.
Unkes artifiere humains
f° 63 r°    As dras faire ne mist les mains.                1348
Li rois Salemons i gisoit
E en tel lit se delitoit.
Al lit guarder estoient mis
Sexante fort, tot de grant pris.                            1352

*v. 1337, *in right margin*: en lectulum Salomonis sexaginta fortes ambiunt ex fortissimis
Israel omnes tenentes gladios. (*3: 7–8*)

Chascons avoit ceinte s'espee
K'ele li fust bien aprestee                    *
Ke par nuit ne s'i embatissent
Telz genz ki damache i fesisent.                    1356
Volez ore ke je vos die
Kel preu cho fait a nostre vie?
Ne cuides pas ke nuision
Aviegne riens se por nos non,                    1360
Par travail d'ome e par miracle
Fait Dex el cuer un tabernacle,
Un bel palais esperitel,
Ainç mortel ueil ne virent tel.                    1364
La descent li vrais Salemons.
A Jhesu Crist covient cist nons,
Kar Il est cil ki les pais fait
Si com li nons le nos portrait.                    1368
Cil i descent, cil s'i repose,
S'a son talent trueve la chose.

f° 63 v°    Cho est se om del cuer li oste
Kanques deplaist a si grant oste                    1372
E apareille de vertuz
Ançois k'il i soit descenduz.
Ors charité nos senefie,
Ki le forche est de bone vie;                    1376
E les pierres en l'or plantées,
Ovres en charité fondees.
Safir semblant al tres pur ciel
Mostre vie celestiel;                    1380
E les estoiles senefient
Vertuz ki la vie enluminent.
El lit liles par sa blanchor
Mostre de chasteé la flor.                    1384
Li grain dedenz semblant a or
Signent l'esperitel tresor
Ou nostre chasteez doit rendre,
N'en doit altre loier atendre.                    1388
N'a en son lilie nul grain orie
Ki chastes est por vaine glorie.

*v. 1354, *in right margin*: et ad bella [fortes *expuncted by the scribe*] doctissimi
unius cuiusque super femur filum [*sic*] propter timores nocturnos. (*3: 8*)

Rose senefie martire:
Ceste flor aime Nostre Sire.                          1392
Granz martyres est penitence
Kant li espirz a la char tence,
E fait aler par tels sentiers
K'ele sivrot plus volentiers.                         1396
Ces flors et altres font le lit
Ou Deus repose par delit.
De cest sien lit sunt guardeur
Li bon, li saint preecheur                            1400
Ki nos enseignent bien a faire
E de toz mals le cuer retraire.
Cist sunt li fort, cist li sexante
Dont la chançon d'amor no chante.                     1404
Forz les covient estre en bon uevre,
Kar bien enseigne ki bien uevre.
E sexante les covient estre,
Leur nombres est solonc lor estre:                    1408
Cest nombre ont cil ki governer
Lor cinc sens sevent e torner
As meurs de char cui Deus eslit
E cui il doze apostles fist.                          1412
Cinc e doze monteploier
En foi nos pet bien avoier,
Cinc foiz doze sexante sunt,
Doze foiz cinc altretant funt.                        1416
Ki les cinc sens a cho remaine,
K'il ensivent ceste dozaine,
Lui doit om faire guardeor
De la maison Nostre Seignor.                          1420
Tel chevalier guardent le lit,
Donc nos avomes devant dit
Par example, par oreison,
Par sainte predication.                               1424
Espees unt, le Deu parole,
Dont cil bien fiert ki bien parole.
Les mals destraint, blasme e argue,
E puis le vin en olie mue.                            1428
A ces armes par tel maniere
Puet om diable metre ariere.

Sor lor quises unt lor espees,
La sunt eles a droit posees.                    1432
Kar cil qui velt altrui reprendre
Tot avant doit il a soi entendre,
E de sa char le mal trenchier
Dont il altrui velt blastengier.                    1436

REPAIRIER VEIL a ma matere,
E prier Deu le sovrain pere,
Parler me doinst a son plaisir,
Ose che non del tot taisir.                    1440
Mielz veil semblanz estre al muel,
Ke molt parler se lui n'est bel,
Amors m'a mis a ceste escole,
Kar d'amor est ceste parole.                    1444
Molt puet amors, il me semont
Entrer en cest livre secont.

f° 65 r°

## II

AMOR NE PUET prisons tenir
Por rien ki ja puist avenir.                    1448
S'il a tant fait ke li cuers arde,
N'i a mestier serre ne guarde.
Tost se mostre, tost se descuevre,
O par paroles, o par oevre.                    1452
Cho voit om bien tot a delivre
Par les paroles de cest livre.
L'Espeuse ne s'i puet taisir,
E ne.l fait pas por mielz plaisir;                    1456
Mais grant amor ki son cuer art
Le torne tote de se part,
E fait loer celui k'ele aime,
Cui son seignor son ami claime.                    1460
Lui loe, e ço k'a lui apartient:
Maison, lit, son siege ensement:
— Li rois, fait ele, Salemons,
Riches e bons en toz ses dons,                    *1464
A fait un siege a lui porter
E delitier e reposer.

f° 65 v°

*v. 1464, *in left margin*: ferculum fecit sibi Salomon. (*3: 9*)

Ainç mais oevre ne fu tant chiere,
Ne d'ovrage ne de matere.                    1468
Faite est l'uevre a bien prés tote
De fustz ki de porrir n'ont dote:
C'est des buens fustz del mont Liban,        *
De cho fu faite par maint an,               1472
Kar ne fu pas tost consumee
Uevre de tant grant renomee.
Columbeles i ot d'argent,                     *
E d'or un appareillement                    1476
Ki le chief le roi retenoit
Kant el cel siege reposoit,
Cel precios reclinatorie
Apele nostre livres orie;                   1480
Mais les pierres e li esmail
Mis en l'uevre par grant travail,
E rent plus chier ke tot li ors
Voire ke uns riches tresors.                1484
Porprins degrez fist al monter;              *
Nuls ne porroit bien raconter
Le grant belté de lor faiture.
Uvre fu sains entrepresure.                 1488
Voirs est ke roiste ert le montee
Mais charitez l'a atempree.
Por les foibles, por les puceles             *
Ki d'amer estoient noveles                  1492
Fist li rois entre les degrez
Une voie legiere asez.
A ces paroles a ovrir
Covient les iuls del cuer ovrir.            1496
Paine e travail i covient rendre,
Ki bien le volra faire entendre.
En fort escrin gist li tresors,
Petit i prent om par defors.                1500
Jo vos dirai cho ke j'en sent,
Cil ki tot seit, Deus mi ensent.

f° 66 r°

*v. 1471, *in left margin*: de lignis Libani. (*3: 9*)
*v. 1475, *in left margin*: columpnas fecit argenteas reclinatorium aureum. (*3: 10*)
*v. 1485, *in left margin:* ascensum porpureum. (*3: 10*)
*v. 1491, *in right margin*: media caritate constravit propter filias Jherusalem. (*3: 10*)

Li sieges ke la Dame prise
E loe tant, cho.st Sainte Glise. 1504
Li rois ki son siege l'a faite
Est Jhesu Crist, ki toz eshaite,
Cui nons est oiles espanduz
As cuers ou il est descenduz. 1508

f° 66 v° Cist rois est li verais Salemons,
Kar faisanz pais sone cist nons.
Cist le fist grant kant il en soi
Joinst dous paroiz par droite foi. 1512
Cho.st les juius e les paiens
K'il traist a soi e fist toz siens.
De cez fu Sainte Eglise faite,
E de le gent de cez estraite. 1516
Cist sont sieges Nostre Seignor,
Ne mie tot, mais li meillor,
Cui li espiritels Libans
A fait dedenz de vertuz blans. 1520
Ces covient il doler avant
Qu'a l'uevre fusent covenant.
Par veilles, junes, aspretés,
Discepines, enfermetez, 1524
Ces coinnies doivent doleir
Le tort, nient le droit afoler.
Le charpantier ki n'a mesure,
Maine nient sens mais aventure. 1528
Chaus ki Deus torne d'one part
Dole il bien, il en seit l'art,
E en son siege les alive

f° 67 r° Par sa puissance juste e pive. 1532
Chascons i a plus ke son droit,
Mais ne sunt pas tot d'un endroit.
Li un sunt eschamel as piez,
E ki tant a molt en est liez. 1536
Es altres siet li rois laienz
E ordene ses jucemenz.
Kar tot cho fait o dist li sire
Ke illor fait, o faire, o dire, 1540

v. 1514, MS.: ka [*expuncted*] ki l traist.
v. 1533, MS.: Chasicons *corrected to* chascons *by expuncting the* '*i*'.

En chaus cui vie est bone e pure,
Ki del siecle n'ont soin ne cure,
Cline son chief li sovrains rois,
E repose tot a son cois.                                    1544
Il n'est point las, mais par figure
Parole issi Sainte Escriture,
Kar toz li cuers en Deu repose,
Ki sent en soi tant digne chose.                           1548
Les columbes de fin argent
Ki font le siege fort e gent
Sunt li maistre de Sainte Eglise,
Par cui ele est de bien aprise.                            1552
Kar comune est ceste sentence,
Kar genz senefie eloquence.

f⁰ 67 v⁰     Hauz est li sieges e vaillanz,
Mais li travalz i est molt granz                           1556
A tant monter ke li om soit
De cest siege, com estre doit.
Grief montera, cui Nostre Sire
Met en son siege par martyre.                              1560
A cho reguardent li degré
Ki de vermeil sunt coloré.
Roiste est le voie enekedent;
Amors i va legierement,                                     1564
Ki bien desire sans dotance,
Riens ne li nuist fors demorance.
Certes Amors e Desirriers
Font les tormenz asez legiers.                             1568
Mais ne sont mie tot espris
D'une maniere, ne apris
Por cha a Deus cele montee
A nos foibles amesuree                                      1572
Ke nuls ne se puist escuser
Par le griece de la monter;
Jounes ne viels, foibles ne forz,
C'est as petiz molt granz confortz.                        1576
Li petit sunt les jovinceles,
f⁰ 68 r⁰     Filles Jerusalem noveles;
Kar de novel ont repentence
Des mals, et de bien coneissance.                          1580

Monter i pooms sens martyre
Par bien ovrer e par bien dire,
Par almosnes, par oreisons,
Se nos nete vie menons,                                    1584
Kar altrement en orz vaisseaus
N'estroit a Deu nuls presenz bels.

OR REVOLRA parler l'espeuse.
Oiez parole merveilluse                                    1588
E dolce com est mielz en ree
Kant le raisons iert assignee: —
Issiez, fait ele, damoiseles,                              *
Filles Sÿon, vaillanz puceles,                             1592
Issiez de chambre e de maison,
E voiez le roi Salemon.
A tot le mont leëce done,
Cho ke li rois porte corone                                1596
Ke sa mere li a donee
Al jor k'ele fu esposee
Kant a son cuer eut grant leëce
E d'amor fine grant destresce.                             1600
Par tels paroles les envie
Totes l'espeuse, sains envie.
Ne velt pas seule avoir se joie,
Mais les altres en met en voie.                            1604

SALEMONS porte la figure
De Crist solonc Sainte Escriture.
Assez l'avez oï deseure
Laissez kele parole keure.                                 1608
Deus, ki tot set, bien nos ensent
Sire de son coronement.

LA CORONE est d'or e de pierres
Molt precioses et molt chieres.                            1612
Toretes doze i a levees
D'or e d'argent bien destinclees.
Li apostle cui Deus eslist
E prechier son nom lor fist                                1616

f⁰ 68 v⁰

---

*v. 1591, *in right margin*: Egredimini et videte filie Syon regem Salomonem in diademate quo coronavit eum mater sua in die desponsationis illius et in dieletitie cordis eius. (*3: 11*)

Sunt doze tors en la corone
Dont le merre son fil corone.
D'or sont por lor grant sapience,
Argent i a por l'eloquence.                                    1620
Solonc les tors sont bien asis
Cil ki por Deu furent ocis.
Cist sunt rubin, e cil sardines,
f° 69 r°        Cist grenat, cil alemandines.                   1624
Vermeil sunt tot, mais se deserte
Done a chascon se color certe.
Cui Deus done de juner grace,
Abstinence le fait topace                                      1628
Par le paleur e le froidure,
Cho.st de topace la nature.
Les saintes virges, Deu espeuses,
Sunt esmeraugdes precieuses.                                   1632
Li confessor selonc lor cries
I sunt o perle o margeries.
Ceste corone fist de soi
La genz hebriue al soverain roi,                               1636
Kant il deigna de li char prendre
Ke longement eut fait atendre,
Kant jointes furent dous natures
En un selonc les Escritures.                                   1640
Ainç a bastir cest mariage
N'i prist om guarde de parage
Nature humaine plus haut prendre
Ne peut, ne l'autre plus descendre.                            1644
Molt vint as omes grant leece
Aprés cele longe destresce
f° 69 v°        De desirier et d'esperance
Cui molt fait grief grant demorance.                           1648

UNS LIVRES altrement nos dist
De la corone Jhesu Crist:
Des quatre vertuz principals
E des affectes naturals                                        1652
Nos fait un bel ordenement  ·
E entremelle avenantment.
Des vertuz est la premeraine

Prudence ki toz biens amaine,                    1656
E atemprance est la seconde
Cil ki l'a de toz biens abunde.
Force est la tierce; e la quarte
Est justice ki les droiz guarde.                 1660
Li quatre affecte sunt leece,
Esperance, crieme e tristece.
Ces uit covient entremeller
A la diademe former.                             1664
Entre prudence e atemprance
Sortist leece, se balance:
N'est pas a droit issi nomee
S'ele n'est sage e atempree.                     1668
Entre atemprance e force siet
f° 70 r°    Tristece, k'ele trop ne griet.
Mais mesure i mete atemprance
E force i doinst bone soffrance.                 1672
Aprés entre force e justise
Est esperance a droit mise.
Ki puet a son cuer faire force,
E de par droit vivre s'efforce,                  1676
Cil doit avoir bone esperance
Del bien qu'il quiert, e sens dotance.
Entre justice est e prudence
Crieme solonc ceste sentence.                    1680
Kar es justes ki Deu ont prés
Est bone crieme tot adés.
Es sages est crieme essement
Ja sage n'ierent altrement.                      1684

.    .    .    .    .    .    .

f° 70 v°    Kar les vertuz chou n'est le pure    1693
Sunt de grace, nient de nature.
E les vertuz e altres biens
Done Jhesus a toz les siens.                     1696
Il meimes en a coronc,
Kar tot est sien kanqu'il lor done,

---

v. 1684 and 1707: *The lower half of folio 70 has been cut away. As a result vv. 1685–92 and 1708–14 have been lost. Traces of a large capital letter at the beginning of v. 1685 remain.*

v. 1693, MS.: K Kar les. *The first letter of* Kar *is partially erased.*

E sue en est la seignorie
Ke la corone senefie.                                    1700
Il a l'onor, mais le porfit
Trestot en ont li sien eslit.
La virgne de cui deigna naistre
Li Sovrains Rois, li Sovrains Maistre                    1704
Le corona, kant Il nature
Humaine prist de sa char pure,
Kar quanque nos avons conté

    .     .     .     .     .     .     .

f° 71 r°

Li ROIS entent la grant leece                           1715
De la roine e sa destresce.                             1716
Bien set ke par destroit d'amor
Fait tel parole de s'onor.
Oï a tot, mais or l'apele
E dist: — Amie, molt ies bele                            *1720
Molt ies bele, jo ki tot voi,
Lo mult ce ke jo sai en toi.
E ovre e predications
Te fait bele, e l'intencions                            1724
L'uevre bone; kar bien me sers
Kant ne te puet tenir de sers,
Ke n'en viegnes come fumerete
Ki d'encens ist subtils e nete,                         1728
E molt est buens li tiens sermons
Par cui tes compaignes semons
E en eles tote la gent
Venir a mon coronement.                                 1732
Simples iulz as come colons,                              *
Cho te fait digne de mes dons;
Mais dedenz a ki molt plus valt,
Ki ton esprit fera molt haut.                           1736


Li TIEN chevel unt le semblant                            *
f° 71 v°            A ces chievres ki vont montant

---

*v. 1720, *in right margin*: quam pulcra es amica mea quam pulcra es. (*4: 1*)

*v. 1733, *in left margin*: Oculi tui columbarum asbque [*sic*] eo quod intrinsecus latet. (*4: 1*)

*v. 1737, *in right margin*: capilli tui sicut grex caprarum que ascenderunt de monte Galaad. (*4: 1*)

De Galaad, e ades vont
Duke soient en som le mont.                1740
De multitude des chevels
Par cui li chies desor est bels:
Cho sunt les cogitations
Dont nos le cuer glorefions,                1744
Ki vont el mont Galaad paistre,
La les conduist li Soverains Paistre.
Galaad, cho dient li sage,
Sone monceals de tesmoignage.                1748
Monceals ne di pas petiz mon,
D'amassement li vient cist nons.
Amassees sunt en la foi
Ke nos avons del Soverain Roi,                1752
Moltes choses dont tesmoign furent
Cil ki por foi guarder morurent.
Avant i est Trinitez mise,
Ki l'Unité pas ne devise,                1756
E ke Jhesus por nostre vie
Prist char de la Virgne Marie;
Nostre fois, a k'il fu temptez,
Batuz e laidement menez,                1760

Tot cho volt il sofrir e faire
Por nos a son service atraire.
Aprés sofri gref passion,
Dont nos avons redempcion.                1764
E al tiers jor resucita,
E voianz moltz en ciel monta:
E vos grant moncel assemblé
Ki tesmoigns a de verité.                1768
Tesmoign en sunt nient uns ne doi,
Mais cent millier, o plus, jo croi,
Ki por ceste foi confermer
Furent ocis en terre en mer.                1772
De cest moncel ke nos disons
Montent les cogitations
A cler veir e bien entendre
Tant com Raisons se puet estendre.                1776
Li cler veirs od le monter
Les fait a chievres comperer,

Ki toz jors al plus halt savoient
E cler plus d'altres bestes voient.                    1780
Encor i a raison greinor:
Chievre figure pecheor,
Por le pueur k'ele rent

f° 72 v°          A cho senefier se prent.                    1784
E pensees ki vers Deu tendent,
Que plus de purté i entendent,
Plus se dampnent e plus s'aeguent:
Cho lor semble k'eles puent.                    1788
Alons avant! Sivons le livre,
Kar de cest pas sumes delivre!

Ço DIST li Rois a l'Esposee,
Cui de ses crins a tant loee:                    1792
— Ti dent semblent berbiz tondues
Ki del lavoir sunt eischues.                    *
Berbiz ki portent dous aigneals,
E norissent e cras e beals.                    1796
Ceste parole semble dure
E a entendre molt oscure.
Mais or oiez ke g'i entent,
Jo.l vos dirai assez briefment.                    1800
Sainte Escriture apele denz
Les motz, les bons castiemenz
Dont la sainte arme par parole
Mort ceals cui vie ele seit fole.                    1804
Ne poet sofrir lor laiz oltrages,
Dont vient as armes granz damaches.

f° 73 r°          Ire lor mostre par semblant,
Dont el cuer n'a ne tant ne quant.                    1808
El cors les trait de Sainte Eglise
Kant sa semence i est reprise,
Si com li dent traient el cors
Cho ke il truevent par defors.                    1812
Bien puet parler teste levee
Cil cui vie est en bien privee,

---

*v. 1794, *in left margin:* Dente tui sicut grex tonsarum que ascenderunt de lavaco: omnes gemellis fetibus et sterilis non est inter eas. (*4: 2*)

v. 1799: *The copyist has written* atentent *which he has corrected to* entent *by expuncting the first two letters,* 'at'.

Ki par ses faiz e par ses diz
A le semblant des Deu esliz                    1816
Ki sunt berbiz par innocence
Part tot sofrir en pacience,
Lavees par confession
Despoillies de lor toison,                     1820
Kar guerpiz unt les charneus biens
Ke nuls sages ne tient a siens:
Dous founs unt, c'est doble amor,
As proismes grant, a Deu g[r]eignor.           1824

Li ROIS reparole a s'amie
E dist: — Bele, molt prois ta vie,
Se jo t'aim bien, n'est pas merveille,
Tes levres semblent bende vermeille.           *1828
Bende les crins al chief ramaine,
E ceste en bien disant se paine,
Ke n'esloignent del Soverain Roi
Cil ki prés sunt par droite foi.               1832
Le color a del sacrament
K'ele preeche purement.
E del Saint Sanc k'ele reçoit
Devotement com faire doit,                     1836
Ceste meisme bende estraint
Les crins al chief kant ele vaint
Le baerie, e les pensees
Ramaine al cuer dont furent nees               1840
Ke ele mielz ne porroit faire
Ke par parole avant retraire
La gloriose Passion
Dont li monz a redempcion.                     1844
A cestui sens par droit encline
E ammaine la bende sanguine.
— A moi, fait il, plaist e amolz
Li tiens parlers ki tant est dolz.             1848
Dolz, voire as buens, kar as malvais
Est li bien dires a molt grant fais.

fº 73 vº

v. 1824, MS.: a deu geignor.
*v. 1828, *in right margin*: sicut coccinea vita labia tua et eloquium tuum dulce.
(*4: 3*)

Sofrir ne puent bone odeur
Cil ki norri sunt en pueur.

1852

LI ROIS, ki tot seit e tot voit,
Loe s'amie come il doit,
Il parole si come il.
Mais la dame, ki tient por vil
Kank'ele valt e ele puet,
Ne tant ne kant ne s'en esmet
Se de tant non k'en se maissele
Monte colors, s'en est plus bele.
Donc dist li Rois a l'Esposee:
— A grenate pomme entamee,
Dolce amie, puis comperer
Tes maiseles, e ten vis cler.
Cho me plaist bien, mais molt vat plus
Li granz biens ki est dedenz repus.
Voioms k'il a en la parole,
Kar le letre defors afole,
S'om ne s'i guarde sutcilment
Tost i a lait abuissement.
Letre est colteaus en main d'enfent,
Dont il a tost damage grant.
Ki de coltel enfant apaie
Gart bien k'il ne s'en face plaie.
Deus nos doinst ore issi parler,
Ke nos vos en puissons garder.
Pomme granate est defors pale:
Cho defors est com une male,
E dedenz est si bels tresors
Molt dessemblantz a cho defors,
Cho sunt li grain de tel color
K'onkes nuls hom ne vit meillor:
Ne blanc ne roge simplement,
Des deus prennent atemprement.
Rogeurs ki regne d'une part,
Se mecle al blanc, kant jo l'esguart.
Ne sai del blanc comencement,
Ne del roge definement.

1856

1860
*

1864

1868

1872

1876

1880

1884

1888

*v. 1861, *in right margin*: sicut fragmen. (*4: 3*)

Issi sunt les colors meslees
L'une del altre e atemprees.
L'escorche est figure del cors
Ki molt est vils kant l'arme est fors.                    1892
E plus pales est verais amanz,
Kar d'amor vient le paleur granz.
Li grain dedenz sunt les vertuz
Dont li espirs est bels vestuz.                           1896
A ces se melle le blanchors
Del inocence, e maint toz jors.
f° 75 r°   Tot enluminent esclarcist
Li fus d'amor ki del cuer ist.                            1900
Par ces vertuz conoist sa mie
Li Rois ki tot a en baillie.
Por cho les apele maisseles
K'il loe tant e tient por beles,                          1904
Kar maisseles sont conessance
Dunt li membre altre n'ont puissance.
La chose que li Rois tant prise,
Ki dedenz est el cuer asise,                              1908
Ce est la dolçors des sovrains biens
Cui la Roine tient a siens.
Kar ja les sent ja.n a l'odor,
Ki ja li done grant dolçor.                               1912

ENCOR PAROLE de s'amie
Cil ki tot set, e rien n'oblie: —
— La tor David semble tis cous                            *
O nuls ne salt se il n'est fous,                          1916
Kar escu mil environ pendent
Ki seure vers toz le rendent.
Ne crient assalt ne aventure,
Kar il n'i falt nule armeure                              1920
Que forz om puist ne doie avoir                           *
f° 75 v°   Ne que om puist nullui savoir.
Ceste parole est molt oscure,
Al sens covient metre grant curc.                         1924

v. 1910, MS.: le roine *corrected by copyist to* la roine.
*v. 1915, *in right margin*: sicut turris david collum tuum. Que edificata est cum pro-
pugnaculis, mille clipei pendent ex ea. (*4: 4*)
*v. 1921, *in right margin*: omnis armatura fortium. (*4: 4*)

Par le col vient norrisemenz
A toz les menbres fors e enz.
Li cous de predication
Est menistres, e d'orison.                              1928
Li cous ajoint li chief al cors.
Tot cho voit om as uels defors.
Por cho li cous est par droiture
De sainte parole figure;                               1932
Quar de li vient sa noreture
A l'esperit e sa peuture,
E li joint Deu a Sainte Eglise.                         *
Par cho l'a il a soi conquise.                         1936
Quant amors la parole amaine
De conscience pure e saine,
Donc est tors ki ne crient assalt,                     *
Ainz le redoutent bas e halt.                          1940
Donc i verriez mil escuz pendre,                       *
Ce est mil raisons a bien defendre.
Li escu la defension
Mil note la perfection.                                1944
f° 76 r°         Darz e lonces, espees nues,           *
Ja cho sunt raisons agues
A destruire malvaise vie.
Par mi l'escu d'yprocresie.                            1948
Ici notez ke l'Escriture
Ki de tot prent e guarde e cure,
Ne dist mie tor simplement
A faire ceste enseignement.                            1952
La tor David nomeement,                                *
I met a cest comperement.
Li rois David est Nostre Sire
Cui la tors est, bien le puis dire,                    1956
Kar qui ke die la parole
De sainteé, c'est de s'escole.
Ensorquetot, David, cist nons,
Si come nos apris avons,                               1960

*v. 1935, *in left margin*: le chief al cors.
*v. 1939, *in left margin*: sicut turris. (*4: 4*)
*v. 1941, *in left margin*: mille clipei. (*4: 4*)
*v. 1945, *in left margin*: omnis armatura fortium. (*4: 4*)
*v. 1953, *in left margin*: sicut turris David. (*4: 4*)

O fors par main sone por voir
O desirrable a veoir.
Cist dobles sens te peut aprendre
O tis cuers doit chascun jor tendre.          1964
Issi combat e nuit e jor
Isse defent toi e t'onor,
Qu'a le parfin por le victorie

f° 76 v°        Voiés le Desirré en glorie.                 1968


LI ROIS ne se taist pas atant
De sa mie, ainz passe avant: —
Bele, fait il, tes dous mameles               *
Ke jo te guart, plaines e beles,              1972
Unt le semblant de dous chevrels
Ki vairelees unt les pels,
Ki par ces lilies vont paischant
Par le grant chaut dusqu'al roisant,          1976
Quant soefs ore suelt lever
E umbres a declin aler.
Cho nos doinst Deus si bien entendre
Qu'alques de fruit i puischons prendre.       1980
As deus mameles repairons,                    *
Dont nos briefment parlé avons.
Toz li laiz vient d'une fontaine,
Qe Deus par ces conduiz amaine               1984
A norreture des enfanz
Cui li besoins en est molt granz.
Maiz cez choses e altre teus
Sunt signe des espiriteus.                    1988
La sainte arme, c'est la pulcele
Cui Nostre Sire espose apele.

f° 77 r°        En celi sort une fontaine
Ke de tot bien est toz jors plaine:          1992
Fontaine de misericorde
Cui ne troble nule discorde.
De ceste fontaine ist li laiz
Dont chascon jor est granz biens faiz.       1996

*v. 1971, *in left margin*: duo ubera tua sicut duo hinuli capree gemelli qui pascuntur
in liliis. Donec aspiret dies et inclenentur umbre. (*4: 4–5*)
    *v. 1981, *in left margin*: due ubera tua. (*4: 4*)

Cho est almosne esperiteus
E essement le corporeus.
Les mameles dont cho descent
Sunt les vertuz o cho apent.                    2000
Cho est amors e pietez,
En ces dous a del bien asez.
Cez unt as cheverlaz semblant                    *
En moltes choses; tot avant                    2004
En cler veir, quar voirement
Covient veir bien e sovent
Cui om puist paistre par droiture
Del lait de la Sainte Escriture.                    2008
A tel puet om cest mes offrir
Ki pais ne le porroit sofrir.
E tel ja ki plus demande
N'a soign de legiere viande,                    2012
De la viande corporel
Poums par voir dire altre tel.
Buen doner fait al bosoigneus
S'en doit ki done estre soigneus                    2016
Bien doit gardeir, ki le sien done
Le liu, le tens e le persone.
Oindre la coe a cras porcel
N'est a se oine buen ne bel.                    2020
'Mais puet s'estre, vos me direz,
A lait coment iert comperez
Corporez biens, solonc raison?'
'Semblance fait comperison,                    2024
Jo respont, que si nos aprist
Li apostles, la ou il dist
Ke li paistre ki guarde fait
Del folc en doit avoir del lait.'                    2028
Quar, c'est a dire par figure,
Que cil ke del puple a la cure,
Doit estre parchoners des biens
A chaus cui il repaist des siens.                    2032
Notez es vairelees pels
Un sens ki molt est buens e bels.
Ne devez pas d'une mesure

*v. 2003, *in right margin*: sicut duo hinuli. (*4: 5*)

**f° 77 v°** (margin)

Doneir a toz le lor peuture. 2036

Varieté i doit avoir
Se il i a point de savoir.
Se doneir puis, a chascon doigne
Solonc son sens o sa besoigne. 2040
Li ceverlaus es liles paiscent *
Quar les vertuz forment encraiscent:
Des flors de la Sainte Escriture
En chaus ki quierent teil pasture. 2044
E cho avient quant li solausz *
De justice est esevers plus hauz:
Quant il lor rent greignor chalor
E plus lor done de s'amor. 2048
Mais quant li jors tant atenduz,
Tant desirreiz estra venuz
E les umbres ierent passees *
Ki kuevrent ore nos pensees, 2052
Dunc ne paistrunt li ceverlat,
Ne cha ne la, tot ierent mat,
Quar fors ierent mis les cures
De porcerkier les Escritures. 2056
Donc iert toz cist travals quaiseiz
Quar tot savront de Deu asez.

ICI MOSTRE bien l'Escriture
Dont Nostre Sire a greignor cure. 2060
Il a loees les maisceles,
Les dens, les crins e les mameles,
Les altres membres essement
Solonc lor droit, mais nequedent 2064
Ne pramist pas k'il i alast
Ne qu'il por cho le visitast.
Or a trové ki miez li plaist,
Mais del loer des tot se taist, 2068
Quar nuls loenges n'i sofist,
Si come es altres choses fist.

*v. 2041, *in right margin*: qui pascuntur in liliis. (*4: 5*)
*v. 2045, *in left margin*: donec aspiret dies. (*4: 6*) (*also 2: 17*)
*v. 2051, *in right margin*: et inclinentur umbre. (*4: 6*) (*also 2: 17*)
v. 2068: *the copyist has written* raist *which he corrects to* taist *by expuncting the initial* 'r'
*and placing a* 't' *above the line.*

Tant dist: — Al mont de mirre irai
E en lui mansion ferai.                                    *2072
Al tertre vueil aler d'encens
E demoreir tant com jo pens.
Mirre senefie amertume
Quar amere est, c'est sa costume.                          2076
Molt a de myrre en son corage
L'espose Crist, ki tant est sage.
Kant se porpense k'il sofri
Sains son meffait e tot por li                             2080
Les comps tant durs, e les liens
Que il sofri, tien ele a siens

f° 79 r°          Li clous k'il eut par mi les piez,
Est en son cuer fort enfichiez                             2084
Les clos des mains; tote la croiz
Met en son cuer li granz destroiz.
Cele corone del Saint Chief
Li fait al cuer dolors molt grief.                         2088
Trestot par compassion sent
Qua[n]qu'il sofri corporeilment.
E lest uns espirz avec lui,
Se sont com un tot li anui.                                2092
Molt a de mirre en cesti part
Al cuer celi ki d'amor art.
Mais d'altre part e d'altre guise
E d'altre mirre est molt soprise.                          2096
Quar soi blasme, contre soi tence
Por ses mals, por sa negligence;
Son cuer blasme, ses uels, ses mains,
E toz ses menbres tient a vains                            2100
Quant cho ne font k'il doivent faire
Por le Seignor tant debonaire.
En le buene uevre qu'ele fait
Crient ele qu'alcon puint n'i ait,                         2104
Ki tote l'uevre mete al nient:

f° 79 v°          Cho redote forment e crient.
Doble materie a ci de plaindre,
E se ne sai les quels est graindre:                        2108

*v. 2072, *in left margin*: vado ad montem myrre et ad collem thuris. (*4: 6*)
v. 2090, MS.: quaquil.                    v. 2091, MS.: E lest uns uns espirz.

Cez amertumes dessemblanz
Meteiz en un, s'iert uns molt granz.
Cestui apele mont de mirre
Cil ki tot bien aime e desirre. 2112
Or revueil dire del encens
E del tertre cho que jo.n pens.
Encens senefie oreison
Ki molt valt, faite par raison. 2116
Al ciel en va subtils et nete
Come d'encens le fumerete,
Ki se flechist e uns tors fait,
Puis se radrece e sus s'en vait. 2120
Quar l'oreison ja tant n'iert pure
Puet retardier homaine cure.
Mais quant cest mal sent la pensee
Tost est l'oreisons rafermee. 2124
Tertre unt a non li mont meneur
Ke des granz monz n'ont pas l'oneur:
A cez est la comperisons
Que Jhesus fait des oreisons. 2128

f° 80 r°

Que s'amie cest mot entende
E plus s'esforst e a plus rende
Del mont e del tertre essement.
Nos avons dit assez briefment 2132
Por nos estruire; nos volt dire
Par ces figures Nostre Sire
Que molt li plaist fine oreisons;
Mais plus li plest contricions, 2136
Quar celi a tertre apelee
E ceste al mont est comparee.

Li rois revient a son loenge:
—En Toi, fait il, n'a nul chalenge, 2140
Tote es bele ma dolce amie, *
En Toi n'a maile ne putie,
E Deus ki puet cho bien entendre
Est nule o il n'ait a reprendre. 2144
Sainz Johans dist: —Se nos disons
Que nos mal ne pechié n'avons

*v. 2141, *in right margin*: tota pulcra est amica et macula non est in te. (*4: 7*)
D 398 D

Plainement sumes menteeur
De nos armes deceveeur.                              2148
Mais Nostre Sire, ki tot seit,
Ki toz biens aime e toz mals het,
Ne met en taille ne en conte
f° 80 v°          Cho ki tost fine, e nient ne monte.         2152
Cho tient a nient ki finer doit
Tot altresi com ja n'estoit.
Comment qu'or soit la creature,
Remanra bele e nete e pure,                         2156
Cui Deus eslist a parmanoir,
E al regne del ciel avoir.


OR DIST: — Vien de Liban, amie,                      *
Vien de Liban, ne targier mie,                      2160
Vien enz, tu ieres coronee
Des greignors monz de ta contree
Des lius ou gisent li lion,
E li liupart avras le don.                           2164
Ceste pramesse est molt estrange,
Sen altre sens ne le nos change.
Or nos ensent come faire suelt
Cil ki tot puet quanque il vuelt.                   2168
Libans senefie blanchor
De vertuz nient d'altre color;
Bien est grant monz la halte vie
Ki de vertuz est bien florie.                        2172
En cest mont est la damoisele
Cui li rois claime tote bele.
f° 81 r°          Deu aime e quiert, a Deu entent,
Grant bien e grant dolçor i sent.                   2176
Mais tot cest bien qe jo vos cont
Tient ele a soi, tot le repont.
Se l'a son desirrier e tient,
D'altrui besoign ne li sovient.                     2180
Por che la voiz Nostre Seignor
Li mostre voie asez meillor.

*v. 2159, *in left margin*: Veni de Libano soror mea sponsa veni de Libano veni coron-
aberis de vertite [*sic*] amana de vertice Sanir et Hermon de cubilibus leonum de montibus
pardorum. (*4: 8*)

De molt grant bien a mielz l'apele,
E pramesse li fait novele.                                    2184
Il vuelt del bien qe Il li fait
Soient pluisor a bien atrait,
E li prince meesment
Cui le torbe fuit de la gent,                                2188
Kar legiers est pules a traire
A cho qu'il voit les plus halz faire.
Por cho par droit vuelt qe s'espeuse
Soit des plus halz plus curieuse,                            2192
E par aspres repernemenz,
E par dolz reconfortemenz,
E par assiduel priere
Mete les mals espirz ariere,                                 2196
Ki de lor cuers unt faiz leur liz

fº 81 vº    E en als font toz leur deliz.
Cist sunt lion par leur fierté,
E liupart par lor cruelté.                                   2200
Li halt home, cho sunt li mont
U cez bestes lor gistes font.
De ces monz li pramet corone
Li Rois ki toz biens gueredone.                             2204
Par ces avra le grant loier
A cui tot doivent traveillier.
Granz honors iert quant ses amis
Dira: — Cist sunt par Toi aquis,                           2208
Cui Sathanas a son servige
Avoit tornez, or sunt mien lige.

CHO DIST li Rois: — Espose, suer,                           *
Molt as parfont navré mon cuer                             2212
D'un de tes crins et d'un tien ueil
Cui jo resguart, si con jo sueil,
Molt m'atalentent tes mameles
Ki tant sunt nobles e tant beles.                          2216
Enointes semblent ambesdeus                                 *
D'uns ungemenz molt precieus.

*v. 2211, *in left margin*: vulnerasti cor meum soror mea, sponsa, vulnerasti cor meum in uno occlorum [*sic*] tuorum et in uno crine. (*4: 9*)

*v. 2217, *in left margin*: colli tui. Quam pulcre sunt mamme tue soror mea, sponsa, pulcriora ubera tua vina [*sic*] et odor unguentorum tuorum super omnia aromata. (*4:9–10*)

Des mameles avons nos dit
Novelement en cest escrit,    2220
Mais por le los des ungemenz
Est faiz cist recomencemenz.
Del uil, del crin nos covient dire
Qe tant par aime Nostre Sire,    2224
Dunt cil a dit ki nient ne ment,
Qe la plaie d'amor d'amor ensent.
De deus uels est enluminee
L'arme feaus ki Deu agree.    2228
Li uns porvoit a vie active,
Li altre a la contemplative.
Li premiers mostre c'om doit faire
Qu'om doit les mals a bien retraire,    2232
Doner as povres sustenance,
Tenir par tot droite balance,
D'altrui besoing avoir grant cure
E soi guarder d'entrepresure.    2236
Li altre uels tent a le haltesce
Nostre Seignor e sa grandesce,
Mais comprendre ne le puet mie
Parfaitement en ceste vie.    2240
Cist esguarde cum cist est pius,
Cui comprendre ne puet nuls lius,
E vint el ventre virginal
Prendre armes a destruire mal.    2244
Il esguarde la pieté
Par cui Deus prist humanité,
E que por nient, u por petit,
Done as siens le sovrain delit.    2248
Cist est li uels ki Jesu Crist
A si plaie, com Il nos dist.
De celui crin ki l'a navré
Vos redirai la verité.    2252
La sainte arme dont nos parloms
A crinz, ses meditacions,
Ki li naiscent de la pensee
Ki chiés del anme est apelee,    2256
Ausi come li crins del cors
Naiscent del chicf cha de defors.

Un en i a cui Deus tant aime
Qe saiete d'amor le claime. 2260
Quar il dist qu'il en est navrez
Si come vos oï avez.
Cil crins, c'est li porpensemenz
De son nientage, e fors e enz, 2264
De sa vilté, de sa poverte,
De sa nuesce tant aperte
Qu'ele ne puet ses mals ataindre,
Ne de nul selonc sen droit plaindre, 2268
Qu'ele ne puet a cho monter
Qe ses pechiez puist raconter
Si qu'aprés la confession
N'i truist toz jors un mal crin 2272
Que trop est pereceuse et nive
Que ne puet estre false e brive
Si come cil ki monte e monte
E se.l n'oïe, quar n'en prent conte. 2276
Cist crins plaist molt Nostre Seignor,
Tant qe la plaie en sent d'amor.
Mais cho n'est mie morteus plaie,
Amors en fera bien la paie. 2280

O R REPAROLE a son plaisir
Li Rois ki tot a a baillir:
— Bele, cui pers n'est suz le ciel, *
Tes levres sunt ree de miel, 2284
Si com li miels ist de le ree,
Sort en toi, suer, dolçors mielee,
Veraie dolceurs que Deus amaine,
Ki vaint tote dolceur humaine. 2288
Desus ta langue est miels e laiz *
Dont tu les desirreus repais.
Quant Deus avevre cel armarie
De ses granz biens, mais cel sacrarie, 2292
La parole ki fors en ist,
Paist les oanz e replenist:

fo 83 ro

fo 83 vo

*v. 2283, *in right margin*: favus distillans labia tua sponsa. (*4: 11*)
*v. 2289, *in left margin*: mel et lac sub lingua tua. (*4: 11*)

64 THE SONG OF SONGS

Parole dolce e ordenee
Est miels e laiz e plaine ree. 2296

L'ODOR, SUER, de tes vestemenz *
Vaint ensens e toz ungemenz.
Li vestement sunt les vertuz
Dont li renons est granz eissuz. 2300
Cho est l'odeurs, la renomee
Ki par le mont en est semee.

DOLCE, TU IES jardins enclos *
Ou ge sovent gis en repos. 2304
Tu ies fontaine soz gelee,
Ki deseur totes bien m'agree.
Li soiels guarde les secrez
Qe nuls n'en soit avant mostrez 2308
S'a celui non cui om velt faire
Consachable de son afaire.
f° 84 r° Tels est tis cuers, quar bien conoiz
A cui tu descovrir le doiz. 2312

DE TON JARDIN petit lous dis,
Odeurs en ist de Paradis,
Quar il n'est mie de bien vuiz *
Ainz est toz plains de noble fruiz. 2316
Plus est tis cuers de vertuz plains
Que n'est grenate de ses grains.
Cipres e nardes e canele,
Croc, aloains, fistle novele, 2320
Tot li bons fust del mont Liban
Sont en ton cuer novel tot l'an.
Quar les vertuz pas ne s'oblient
Que ces especies senefient. 2324
Chascune fait que faire doit,
Ni vuelt laiser point de son droit.

*v. 2297, *in left margin*: et odor vestimentorum tuorum sicut odor thuris. (*4: 11*)
*v. 2303, *in left margin*: Ortus conclusus soror mea sponsa, ortus conclusus, fons signatus. (*4: 12*)
*v. 2315, *in right margin*: emissiones tue paradisus malorum punicorum cum pomorum fructibus Cypri cum nardo. Nardus et crocus fistula et cynamomum cum universis lignis Libani mirra et aloe cum universis primis unguentis. (*4: 13–14*)

Ki des especies conistra
Les qualitez, bien entendra 2328
Quele especie que senefie
E que tot valt a bone vie.

Tu ies fontaine des cortilz *
Ou tels especes e tant gentiz 2332
Croiscent par ton arosement.
f° 84 v° Durs est li cuers ki ne s'en sent
Quant de ta nete conscience
S'espant l'aique de sapience. 2336

Tu ies li puz d'aique vivant *
Ki de Liban vient acorant.
Sapience est en toi parfunde,
Ki toz jors sort, croist e abunde. 2340
Quar de la vient a grant esploit
Dont si faite aique venir doit
Del verai Liban de Jhesu Crist,
Le mont des monz, ki le mond fist. 2344

A tel gardin si bien planté,
Si bien enclos, si arosé,
Ne puet nuisir li venz de bise *
Ki les arbres granz e forz brise, 2348
Ne li mols venz ki tot corrunt
Auster n'i fait mal ki nient mont.
Lieve ce bise, auster or sufle,
N'i ferunt mal tot vostre sufle. 2352
Faire porrunt mon gardin plain
D'encens, mirre e d'aloein.
Quar quant il a tres bien venté,
Dunc vienent gommes a plenté. 2356
f° 85 r° Bise figure adversité,
Auster li mols prosperité:

*v. 2331, *in right margin*: fons ortorum. (*4: 15*)
*v. 2337, *in left margin*: puteus aquarum viventium que fluunt impetu de Libano.
(*4: 15*)
*v. 2347, *in left margin*: surge aquilo et veni aster, perfla ortum meum et fluent aromata
illius. (*4: 16*)

Mais cist n'abat, ne cist n'eslieve
Cuer ki Deu crient, rien ne li grieve.　　2360
Enz en est plus encens en oreison,
En myrre larmes, en aloe devocion.
Ceste nostre exposicions
Que nos de ces deus venz faisons　　2364
Solonc le sens que Dex nos done,
Plairoit a une altre persone.
Mais cele por cui jo travail,
Quar tot est suen, se jo rien vail,　　2368
Certes molt s'esmerveilleroit
S'ele altre chose n'en öoit,
Quar jo li ai maintes foiz dit
Qu'aster signe Saint Esperit.　　2372
Cist sens li plaist, cestui atent,
Cist li savroit plus dolcement.
E quant jo sai le sien plaisir,
Jo ne m'en puis mie taisir,　　2376
Quar faite vueil qu'ele por moi
Prist son ami, li Sovrain Roi.


LI ROIS S'AMIE a molt loee,
fº 85 vº Jarding enclos l'a apelee,　　2380
Quar il seit bien qu'il i planta
Dont ele unques ne se vanta.
Ainz tient clos en sa conscience
Le grant arbre de sapience　　2384
E l'ysope d'umilité
De suz l'arbre de charité,
E mulz altres toz de bien plains,
Quar toz planta devine mains.　　2388
Mais nequedent une froidure
I suelt venir, quant ele i dure
Bien fait les arbres decrier
A florir e fructefier.　　2392

v. 2361: *the copyist has crossed out* encens, *and has added* en *above the line before* oreison.
*He has then restored* encens *by a marginal note.*

v. 2362: *the copyist has crossed out* mirre *and indicated the spelling* myrre *by a marginal note. Then by means of double dashes and triple dots, as well as marginal notes, he indicates the correct order of words.*

Ceste froidure amaine bise
Ki tenre chose a tost soprise.
Quant bise cesse e auster vente
E la dolce ore se presente,                           2396
Donc a jardins buene saison,
Donc i a fruit ultre raison.
Cho fait par ses comandemenz
Li Rois des Rois, Deus de ces venz.              *2400
— Fui, fait Il, bise. Auster, tu vien!
Sofle en jardin, fai com el mien!

f° 86 r°       Donc aparra la grant plenteiz
Des biens ke jo ai planteiz.                          2404
Nostre Enemis, ki par faiture
Eirt beals sor tote creature,
Quant sa folie ot entreprise,
Volt son siege drecier vers bise.                    2408
La volt regner, c'est l'acoisons
Por que li est donez cist nons.
Auster li pius, a cui gelee
Ne puet longes avoir duree,                          2412
Saint Esperit nos senefie,
Ki des buens est lumiere e vie,
Ki fait en son avenement
Larmes venir abundantment,                           2416
Done vertuz, ovrer enseigne,
Les mals oste, les biens engreigne.
Por cho fait Deus bise fuir,
E cestui fait avant venir.                            2420


L'ESPOSE, cho qu'ele ot loer
Son ami li vult presenter:
— Viegne, fait ele, mes amis                            *
Manjust del fruit qe il a mis                         2424
En mon jarding, jo ne li voi,
f° 86 v°       Mais il le chist cui jo bien croi,

---

v. 2393, MS.: ceste [flo *expuncted*] froidure.

*v. 2400, *in left margin*: surge aquilo et veni auster perfla ortum meum et fluent aromata illius. (*4: 16*)

*v. 2423, *in right margin*: veniat dilectus meus in ortum meu, ut comedat fructum pomorum suorum. (*5: 1*)

Jarding e fruit il a tot fait,
E tot est sien, ci n'a nul plait.                    2428
Or se delit en sa faiture,
E ait de moi, se lui plaist, cure.


LI ROIS entent la damoisele
Ki molt li plaist, e si l'apele:                     2432
— En mon jarding vien, suer amie,                      *
Jo ai ma myrre ja cueillie,
Mes especies de bone odor
Ai cueillies en lor valor.                           2436
De mon miel ai mon mangier fait,
E bois mon vin avec mon lait.
Mangiez, bevez tot avec moi.
Li mien ami, jo.l vos otroi                          2440
A cest convi, a cest grant bien,
T'apel jo dolce, vien, i vien,
Vien i par contemplacion,
Aprés i sera mansion.                                2444
Cist jardins est esperitals,
Nuls n'i entre ki ne soit sals.
La sunt ja mis cil ki sofrirent
Amertumes quant il vesquirent,                      *2448
f° 87 r°         Ou por la loi Deu maintenir,
Ou por lor mals espeneir.
La sunt ja mis tot essement
Li saint, por cui enseignement                      *2452
E par cui bone renomee
Sainte Eglise est si honoree.
Cil i sunt ki par dolceur                              *
Avisent l'amor Nostre Seignor                       *2456
E cil ki de bien eninvererent                          *
Les fervenz cuers cui maistre il erent,

---

*v. 2433, *in left margin*: veni in ortum meum, soror mea, sponsa messui mirram meam
cum aromatibus meis. Comedi favum cum melle meo: bibi vinum meum cum lacte
meo, comedite amici et inebriamini, karissimi. (*5: 1*)
  *v. 2448, *in left margin*: mirra. (*5: 1*)
  *v. 2452, *in right margin*: aromata. (*5: 1*)
  *v. 2455, *in right margin*: favus. (*5: 1*)
  *v. 2456, *in right margin*: mel. (*5: 1*)
  *v. 2457, *in right margin*: vinum. (*5: 1*)

E ki de pure estorie peurent     *
La simple gent, quar plus ne seurent,    2460
E des greignors e des petiz
A Nostre Sire les deliz.     *
A cez, fait il, buen esguarder
Por prendre example e por guarder   2464
E les evres e les vertuz
Dont si granz biens lor est venuz.

L'ESPOSE entent que li rois dist,
E bien volroit qu'il le mesist    2468
En son jardin. Mais ele dote,
Quar tels n'a soing d'entrer ki bote,
E tels pramet la chose a faire

fo 87 vo     Cui on i puet a paine atraire.    2472
Abysme sunt li Deu juise,
Ne volroit pas estre soprise.
En son cuer dist par un grant plait,
Se il li vuelt, por que ne.l fait.    2476
Ja ne puet om avoir la joie
D'aleir a lui, s'il ne.l envoie,
Nis a cho dignement roveir
Ne puis sans lui voie trover.    2480
Il m'apele mais s'il voloit,
Je demorance n'i avroit.
Il puet trestot, jo ne puis rien,
Or face tot, quar tot est sien.    2484
Quant ele fu bien porpensee,
A ses compaignes s'est tornee
E lor reconte une aventure
D'une anciene entrepresure:    2488
—Jo dorm, fait ele, e mes cuers veille,  *
Sovent avient ceste merveille;
Ne faz complainte ne clamor,
Quar jo le tieng en fief d'amor.    2492
Quant tels somels jadist me tint
Par une foiz mes Amis vint.

---

*v. 2459, *in right margin*: lac. (*5: 1*)     *v. 2462, *in right margin*: comedi. (*5: 1*)
v. 2472, MS.: cui on [n *expuncted by the scribe*] ipuet.
*v. 2489, *in left margin*: ego dormio et cor meum vigilat. (*5: 2*)

f° 88 r°

—Evre, dist il, Amie bele,         *
Ma dolce suer, soies ignele,       2496
Tu n'as ore cho ki t'agree,
Mais mes chiés est plains de rosee.
E de mon chief le chevel tot
Sunt plain des gotes de la nuit.       2500
Jo m'esveillai, quar bien oi
La dolce voiz de mon ami.
E dis: — 'Jo ai mes piez lavez,
Coment les ferai mailentez?       2504
Coment iere revestue
De ma cote dunt jo sui nue?'
Mes amis mist par la fenestre
Ki pres estoit, sa main, la destre.     2508
Sor moi le mist adonc sans dote,
E j'oï peur e tremblai tote.
Adonc ne peu jo mais soffrir:
Se me levai por l'uis ovrir.      2512
Mais tot avant maniai ma mirre,
Unques meillor ne peu eslirre.
Tot en degoterent mi doit,
Quar cho vient faire par droit.      2516
Plus tost que peu men uis ovri,

f° 88 v°

Mais n'i trovai pas mon ami.
Donc me clamai: Chaitive, fole,
Dont me menbra de sa parole,      2520
— Ki m'amie fait tote decorre,
Quant mes Amis me vuelt socorre,
Si come l'aique clere e nete
Al fu s'en va par fumerete,      2524

v. 2495, MS.: Veire [*expuncted by the scribe*] eure, dist il.

*v. 2495, *in right margin as far as v. 2517 thence in left margin to v. 2525*: vox dilecti mei: aperi mihi, soror mea, amica mea, columba mea, immaculata mea, quia capud meum plenum est rore, et cicinni mei guttis noctium. Expoliavi me tunica mea quomodo induar ea? Lavi pedes meos quomodo inquinabo eos? Dilectus meus misit manum suam per foramen et venter meus intremuit ad tactum eius. Surrexi ut aperirem dilecto meo. Manus mee distillaverunt mirram et digiti mei pleni sunt myrra probatissima. Pessulum ostii mei, aperui dilecto meo, at ille declinaverat at atque [*sic*] transierat. Anima mea lique/[*f° 88 verso in left margin*]/-facta est, qua dilectus locatus est. Quesivi et non inveni illum. Vocavi et non respondit mihi. Invenerunt me vigiles qui circuerunt civitatem. Percusserunt me et vulneraverunt me. Tulerunt pallium meum custodes murorum. (5: 2–7)

Si dekeurt m'aneme dolcement
Quant ele sa parole entent.
— Donc me fait tant li miels, dolz sire,
Que jo ne.l puis ne ne sai dire. 2528
Assez le quis, nel poi trover.
N'est pas legiers a recovrer,
Quant l'en le pert par sa deserte
Si come jo fis bien, en sui certe, 2532
Altre chose est, s'il se tient chier,
Por embraser le desirrier.
Jo le perdi par me peresce,
Si.n eut mis cuers mult grant destresce. 2536
Tote esmarie me troverent
Cil ki gardes de la vile erent.
Vienent a moi, tornent, si fierent,
Bien me batirent e plaierent 2540
E me tolirent mon mantel,
Povres estoit, de drap sens pel,
N'i avoit nule forreure
Ki defendist de la froidure. 2544
Molt a de miel en ceste ree
Que nos avoms ici trovee.
Or covenroit fors le miel traire:
Deus le nos doinst dignement faire. 2548
Nostre sire bote a la porte
Quant il le feel homme enorte
Dedenz en contemplacion,
Defors par predication, 2552
E iscir del lit de sun repos
Por grant fais prendre sor son dos.
Laiscier atans son bien, sa joie,
Por les erranz remetre a voie. 2556
Quar les portes sunt les oreilles
U il amaine granz merveilles
Des sainz peirres ki par leur mortz
Firent en foi leur proismes forz, 2560
E del oneur que cil avront,
Ki ferunt bien, et bien dirunt.
La vient li rois qui la sus maint,
Somont sa mie, e se complaint 2564

f° 89 r°

f° 89 v°

Que sa chaveleure est plaine
Des gutes que la nuiz amaine.
Cheveus apele chaveleure
Cui i ont al chiés lor vie pure.                    2568
Il est li chiés, mais a grevance
Sunt plain de gotes d'ignorance.
Cil ont mestier d'ignele aiue
Sor cui tels nuiz est espandue.                     2572
Por cho i est cele apelee
Ki de tel nuit s'est mielz guardee.
Mais ele dote, quar ja mais
Volroit sa vie avoir em pais;                        2576
Ne seit des choses la mesure,
Se crient par tot entrepresure.
Ses piez, cho est ses volentez,
Adeviciez del mont l'avez,                           2580
Se ne volroit pas rembeer,
Por cho se dote a relever.
Le cote des mundaines cures
Rodote, trop li erent dures.                         2584
Qant ore est si que jus l'a mise
Ja n'iert sien vuel par li reprise.

f° 90 r°

Mais ses amis i met la main,
Quant de gracie fait le cuer plain.                  2588
Donc se leva sans grevemence
E prist mirre de penitence
Tant ke si doit en deguterent
Sor chaus ki porpensé n'en erent.                   2592
Li doit notent discrecion
Quar il i a division.
Ki plus a fait, plus doit sofrir
Por ses pechiez espeneir.                            2596
Donc ovri l'uis, quar a son prestre
Dist e ses uevres e son estre.
Le pesle osta de la dotance
Ki faisoit cele demorance.                           2600
Ainz vuelt bon example doner
Que nullui vueille aroisoner.
Premiers vuelt faire, e aprés dire,
Quar si l'enseigne Nostre Sire.                      2604

Son uis ovri, mais n'i trova
Celui ki faire li rova.
Donc fu dolente e esmarie,
E molt se tint a malbaillie.                    2608
Donc li sovint de la grant joie

f° 90 v°  Que ele avoit quant ele eirt coie,
Quant ne rendoit nullui raison,
Ne ne parloit se a Deu non,                     2612
Quant s'arme as piez Jhesu ploroit,
E en lui tote dekoroit.
Jamais n'i cuide recovrer
Quant son ami ne puet trover.                    2616
Guardes ki del puple unt la cure,
Ki sage sunt del escriture,
Le troverent tote eswaree
Mais dolcement l'ont apelé.                      2620
Ferirent le des darz d'amor
E firent plaies sans dolor.
Le mantel dont ele eirt coverte
Li tolirent e firent certe                       2624
Des choses qu'ele ne savoit
E dont sovent doté avoit.
Quant s'en para, molt li fu bel
Qe ele eut perdu cel viez mantel.               2628
Jamais fuz fui, ne fust a aise,
Tant le faisoit froide e malvaise.
Tot cho conte la Deu Amie                        *
As puceles, puis se lor prie                     2632

f° 91 r°  Que, s'eles voient son ami,
Ne.l oblient, mais dient li
Tot belement e sens annui
Coment ele languist por lui.                     2636
Cho qu'ele filles les apele
Jerusalem n'est pas nuvele.
Chascon apele on sovent
Filg de la chose o il plus tent.                 2640
— Jo vos conjur, fait ele, bien
Que vos ne m'obliez por rien.

*v. 2631, *in left margin*: adiuro vos filie Jerusalem si inveneritis dilectum meum
annuncietis ei quia amore langueo. (*5: 8*)

Hardiement li poez dire
Quar volentiers l'orra li Sire.                                    2644

CEUS KI connoissent le Seignor
No respondent fors a boneur.
Les altres ki sunt d'altre gent,
C'est des Juius, quar bien l'entent,                              2648
Li demandent: — Ki.st cil amis                                      *
Dunt tis cuers est issi sopris,
Por cui nos as tant conjurez
E tantes foiz amonestez?                                          2652

CELE RESPONT: — Jo vos dirai
De lui ce que dire en porrai.
Blancs est e roges mes amis,                                        *
f° 91 v°        Cho m'a mon cuer d'amor espris.                   2656
Il a la blanchor de vertuz
Dont il est toz a plain vestuz.
Li altre en unt mais de sa main
Mais il les a sans don forain.                                    2660
Li altre en unt, mais a mesure,
Nuls a suen ues ne les mesure.
Li fols en a la grant plenté,
Li altre en unt par sa bonté.                                     2664
Il est toz blancs, e es blancs lius
Vuelt demorer li dolz, li pius.
Li dolz aigneals prent sa pasture
Entre les lilles de vie pure.                                     2668
Il meisme a teil rogeur
Que nuls ne penseroit meilleur.
Une coleurs le fait vermeil
Dont jo merveilles m'esmerveil.                                   2672
Li saint rogirent par martyre,
Molt firent bien, ne.l puis desdire:
Mais chascons d'aus por soi ovra,
Chascons ço qu'il queroit trova.                                  2676

*v. 2649, *in right margin*: Qualis est dilectus tuus ex dilecto quia sic adjurati nos?
(*5:9*)
*v. 2655, *in right margin*: dilectus meus candidus et rubicundus electus ex milibus.
(*5:10*)

Mais cist de cui doleur me plaing
Ne fu pas mort por son guaaing.

Il sels se volt a mort livrer,
Por toz les altres delivrer. 2680
Ceste rogeurs de mil eslite
Est en mon cuer a droit escrite.

BLANCS EST e roges mes amis
Cho m'a mon cuer d'amor espris. 2684
Quant li dolz rois, li poestis,
Fu pris par les felons Juius chaitis,
Pilate por la renomee
Que il estoit de Galilee 2688
Ki terre estoit le roi Herode,
Si com escrit est el Saint Code,
Por cho que le roi volt atraire
A pais, qu'ançois ne pooit faire, 2692
Li envoia par ses messages
Le Roi des Rois, come mal sages.
Herodes ne.l prisa noient,
Vestir li fist blanc vestement, 2696
Par son gabois, nient por oneur,
Si renvoia mon dolz Seigneur.
Or me semble que jo le voie
Raleir ariere par la voie. 2700
Pilate vient, si la parole,

Mais il n'en puet traire parole.
A derains itant respont:
— N'est pas mes regnes de cest mont. 2704
Quant cil oï parler de regne
Pa[r] ses gas dist: — Veez cum or regne!
Mantel de porpre avons tot prest,
Veste li ont, quant il rois est! 2708
Cho fu tot fait, ceste rugeur
Porta por moi cil dunt jo pleur.
Por moi sofri molt grant ennui,
E jo, que puis faire por lui? 2712
Blancs est e roges mes amis,
Cho m'a mon cuer d'amor espris.

v. 2706, MS.: pas ses gas.

Blanchors porte asuagement,
E rogeurs espeventement.                                         2716
Soes as buens, e a felons
Est mes amis plus que lions.
Blancs e roges est mes amis,
Cho a mon cuer d'amor espris.                                    2720
Ces deus coleurs que jo vos di
Portent li menbre mon ami.
Les uns fait blancs lor innocence,
E lor justise od sapience.                                       2724

f° 93 r°      Les altres qui puis lor pechié
Sunt a bien faire radrecié,
Fait roges lor confessions,
Leur honte, leur confusions.                                     2728
N'est pas merveille s'on a honte
Quant hom ses griés pechiez raconte.
Mais cele honte est profitable,
Ki maine a vie parmanable.                                       2732
Li Hauz Deus ki lo pople fist
Ces deus parties en eslist.
Ce est justes, e peneanz
La tierce parz, ki molt est granz.                               2736
Sains ignocence, e sains justise,
Sains penitence, qu'aient prise,
Traira la coe del dragon
Ki fu mostrez en vision.                                         2740


BELS EST mes sire Jesu Críz
E de cent mil milliers esliz.
Cil est beals, e tot si menbre,
Dont jo.n dirai cho que m'en menbre.                             2744
Ses chiés est ors toz esmerez,                                      *
Ja nuls a lui n'iert comperez.
Cho est devine sapience
f° 93 v°      Ki desor toz a excellence.                          2748
L'umaine sapience est bone,
Buen tresor a cui Deus le done.
Cele des angles est plus pure
Quar plus sotils est leur nature.                                2752

*v. 2745, *in right margin*: capud ei aurum optimum. (*5: 11*)

Mais la devine est ors tres fins
A cui li monz est toz aclins.
Ceste est li chiés, mais li chevel
Sunt plus vaillant qu'il ne sunt bel,　2756
Quar as palmiers ki plus sunt halt
Unt senblance ki molt i valt.
Mais d'altre part a noirs oiseals
Unt un senblant ki pas n'est bels.　2760
Solonc le chief covient parleir
Des crins, se droit volons aleir.
Li crin al chief sunt coverture　*
Quar li crin sunt doble nature:　2764
Que la Deu sapience prist
En terre, quant ome se fist,
Cors e aneme eut come verais om,
E quanques est d'ome est par roison.　2768
De cez nos est li chiés coverz
Ki est as angles descoverz.

f° 94 r°　Palmiers est signe de victorie,
Dont li venquerre a molt de glorie.　2772
Nature humaine est cist palmiers:
En Jhesu Crist cho sent li fiers
Ki par cez armes est destruiz
E les enfers des bons est wuiz.　2776
Cist crin sunt noir come corbels
Ki plus est noirs qu'altre oisels.
Noir sunt par tribulacion,
Annui, doleur, irrision,　2780
Quar selonc larme eut il annui,
Si com il est escrit de lui.
Come vrais om mort redota
Tant que de lui sancs degota　2784
Solonc le cors, fu molt grevez,
Pris e liez, a cort menez,
Feruz, gabbez, jugiez a tort,
Fors la cité menez a mort.　2788
Horriblement furent percié
Ses lez, ses mains, e si bel pié.

*v. 2763, *in left margin*: Come illius sicut elate palmarum nigre quasi corvus.
(5: 11)

De cez griecez chascune amaine
Noirtume a la char humaine                    2792
Dont coverte est la deiteiz
En Jhesu Crist, bien le saveiz.
D'or fin a chief li miens amis
Dont jo conteir vos ai pramis.                 2796
Cele digne concepcions
Dont vint nostre redempcions
Est chiés, cho est comencemenz
De Crist ome, e des sacremenz,                 2800
Par cui vie nos est rendue
Ki par pechié nos eirt tolue.
Mais le chief cuevrent un cavel
Noir come pennes de corbel                     2804
Ki ne laischent le chief veoir
En la belté k'il a por voir.
Ainz eslongent de la creance
Fols cuers, e metent en dotance.               2808
Ces comes sunt les esposailes
De la Virgne, e ses relevailles
Li luius ou li enfes fu nez
E la creche ou il fu trovez.                    2812
Aprés la circomcisions
U comença la passions,
Tot cho aumbre la purté
Del saint chief, e la verité.                   2816

D'OR FIN a chief li miens Amis
Dont jo conter vos ai pramis.
Li chiés est Criz, li Filz Marie,
Mis doz Amis, mis cuers, ma vie.               2820
Cist est toz orz, e ors tres buens,
Quar toz les sens passe li suens.
Les comes ki de tel chief pendent,
Cho sunt li juste ki l'atendent,               2824
Ki l'ont a peirre e a seignor,
E sunt a lui joint par amor.
Cist sunt palmiers, venqueeur sunt
E de lor char e de cest mont,                  2828

v. 2800: *Three letters have been erased after crist* (en *and* ?).

Palmier treshaut, quar del diable
Sunt venqueeur fort e durable.
Si com palmiers ki puis cent anz
Portant fruit dure par long tanz,　　2832
Mais il sunt noier, selonc le cors,
Come corbels, c'est par defors,
Quar li corbels n'a plus noirtume
Plus qu'altre oisels, fors en la plume,　　2836
E par defors sunt noir li saint,
Quar il sofrent des travals maint,
De faims, des sois, de vesteures
f° 95 v°　　Que il portent aspres e dures.　　2840
Des malades, des bosoignos,
Plus ke de soi sunt corros,
Totes les tribulacions
Fait leur de granz compassions.　　2844
Deliz de chair heent e fuient,
Totes laidures leur annuient,
Si come char ki par victorie
Tendent a parmanable glorie.　　2848

COLUNS RESANBLENT li sien ueil,
Por cho l'aim tant, e amer vueil.
Colons resamblent sur rusceals　　*
D'aiques coranz viez e noveals　　2852
Ki lavees de tres dolz lait,
Sor aiques granz unt siege fait.
Cho nos doinst Deus si bien entendre
Que nos gracies l'en puischons rendre.　　2856
Dolceurs, simplesce est acoisons
De compereir uels a colons.
Li ueil Crist sunt a cele cure
E cele entente simple e pure,　　2860
Que il sor nos chascun jor met
Ki sumes d'aiques ruscelet
f° 96 r°　　Quar n'avommes establité,
Tot sumes en muableté.　　2864

*v. 2851, *in left margin*: Oculi eius sunt columbe super rivulos aquarum que lacte sunt lote & resident juxta fluenta plenissima. (*5: 12*)

E ruiscelet sumes nient riu,
Quar molt avomes petit liu.
Petit a le comperison
Di de cez uels, e par raison, 2868
Quar leur ve[u]e est par tot tote,
Mescreanz est ki de ce dote.
Dui sunt cist ueil, quar pietez
Les a d'un lait novel lavez. 2872
Cist laiz dunt Deus grant bien nos fist
Est cho que Il del nostre prist
Quant il prist char en la pulcele
Ki de totes est damoisele. 2876
Par cui nos Deu trovons plus prest,
Quar or seit il coment nos est,
Seit voire par experiment,
Se reguarde plus dolcement 2880
A nos, e a nostre povreté,
Que il prist par sa volenté.
Mais nequedent de la sentence
De la devine sapience 2884
Ne s'eslongent en nul afaire

f° 96 v° Li ueil ki tant sunt debonaire.
Cist saint colon, ki par tot voient,
Ne s'esmuevent, ne ne s'esfroient. 2888
Toz jors seent a la plenté
Des aiques sains muableté,
Que sainz espirs sovent amaine,
E toz jors sunt en lor fontaine. 2892

TOT CHO POUMS altrement dire:
Saichier nos vuelt Deus Nostre Sire.
Li ueil Jhesu sunt li bon maistre
Ki governeir doivent e paistre 2896
Les oelles de Sainte Eglise,
Sains fiel, sains mal de covoitise,
Quar comperei sunt as coluns
Teus com descrire nos voluns. 2900
Colons n'a fiel ne felenie,
Il n'a point d'ire ne d'envie.

v. 2869, MS.: vene.

Coluns ne tolt ne ne ravist,
Ne de proie ne se warist.                    2904
En halte tor ou en halt mur
Pose son ni, grain conkelt pur
Dont il norrist ses columbels,
Quar il les a sovent novels.                  2908

f°97 r°  Volentiers vole a compaignie,
Tels sunt ses meurs, tels est sa vie.
A tels oiseals sunt comperé
Cil ki Deu ueil sunt apelé.                   2912
Ne doit prelaz avoir costume
De retenir fiel d'amertume.
Ne doit nullui porteir envie
Ne agrever par felonie.                       2916
Se il tolte, tient a guaaigne,
Ne ne prent cure ki s'en plaigne.
Se de tolir quiert acoisons,
Escoulés est, n'est pas coluns.               2920
S'il se poroint e apareille
Le chaperon mel a l'oreille,
Esterkist soi sor le cheval,
Les povres fait ester l'aval,                 2924
N'est pas colons ki tant est fiers,
Ainz est ostoirs ou esperviers.
Li prelaz doit del Escriture
Les grains cueillir, c'est la peuture         2928
Qu'il doit doneir as desirreus
Ki de tel pain sunt familleus.
Li bons prelaz en halte tor

f° 97 v°  A mansion, e fait sejor.               2932
Se il par cuer s'est eslevez
En sus des terienetez,
E ja par contemplacion
A en ciel conversacion,                       2936
Li apostles le dist de soi,
E bien est voirs, tres bien le croi,
Nos n'avons pas fait wageure
D'aleir a Deu cest aleure.                    2940
Sor ruisels d'aiques doivent estre            *

*v. 2941, *in left margin*: super rivulos aquarum. (5: 12)

Li buen prelat e li saint prestre.
Les aiques puples senefient,
Si come les Escritures dient,                           2944
Ki toz jors curent en la mort.
C'est mers ki n'a rive ne port,
A cez doivent estre ententiu
Chascons as siens, e en son liu,                       2948
E sor als metre paine e cure
Qu'il n'i remaigne entrepresure.
Laveir les doivent en dulz lait,                          *
Si come li altre a aus ont fait.                       2952
Laveir en lait est belement
Chastier l'ome e dolcement.

f° 98 r°          Cho va selonc natureil loi,
Mais ce ne doit nuls faire a soi.                      2956
Judas lava son vestement
En vin. Faisomes ensement,
Quar cho covient a repentant
E ses pechiez regehisant.                             *2960
Vins senefie austerité:
Selonc justice e verité,
Doit ses pechiez chascons jugier,
Nient escuser ne alegier.                              2964
Mais raisons est qu'il face altrui
De bien ce qu'altre a fait a lui:
Cho est ovre de charité.
Par mi tot cho l'auctorité                             2968
De l'Escriture doivent tenir
A lor puple, bien meintenir.
Ne sunt pas tot d'une maniere,
Li un s'amendent par priere.                          2972
Les uns covient espeventer
E par parole acravanter.
Li altre par blandissement
Prennent de bien comencement.                        2976
Chascons mals a sa mecine,
f° 98 v°          E toz jors vienent, che ne fine.

*v. 2951, *in left margin:* que lacte sunt lote. (*5: 12*)
    *v. 2960, *in left margin:* Judas non traditor sed filius Jacob. (*Cf. Genesis, 49: 11:* Lavabit
in vino stolam suam.)

Mais l'apoteke d'Escriture
Trueve a toz mals lor propre cure.                    2980
Por cho doivent seir al livre
Tant come il ont de tans delivre,
E des buens diz des sainz aprendre,
Dont il puiscent lor deité rendre.                    2984
S'il cho ne font, n'ont pas l'oneur
Qu'il soient ueil Nostre Seigneur.
Tot cho voloms altrement dire.
Or nos aiut Deus, Nostre Sire.                    2988
Ysaias cho m'est avierre:
Trova set uels en une pierre:
Set gracies de Saint Esperit
Sunt li set ueil, pluiseur l'ont dit.                    2992
La pierre est Crist: por voirz le sai,
Quar l'apostle tesmoing en ai.
Deus quant lui plaist ces uels a uevre,
E a son buen de chascon uevre,                    2996
En l'esperit de crieme tramble,                    *
Quanqu'il reguarde tot ensemble.
En l'esperit de piété                    *
Reguarda Deus la foibleté.                    3000

f° 99 r°    Pierron ki renoié l'avoit
Trois foiz, al mielz que il savoit,
Par seul reguart le fist plorer,
Quar lui n'oï cil mot soner.                    3004
Abel en esperit de science                    *
Reguarda Deus quant la presence
Sains fu les dons Abel esprist
E toz les dons Caÿm despist.                    3008
Quar il seit bien que est en ome
Les cuers conoist, c'en est la some,
E bien puet corre en ceste ligne,
Che que il dist d'une provigne                    3012
Que plus avoit el temple offert

*v. 2997, *in left margin*: .i. spiritus timoris.
    *v. 2999, *in left margin*: .ij. spiritus [etatis *crossed out and expuncted by the copyist*] pietatis.
    *v. 3005, *in right margin*: .iij. spiritus scientie.
    v. 3006, MS.: dex [la foiblete *expuncted by the copyist who has confused this line with line 3000*] quant sa presence.

Que li riche ome, e s'est apert
Qui offrirent mars e esterlins
E cele n'eut mais deus ferdins.                      3016
Deus le corage del donant
Juge selonc le remantant.
Le don fait grant li granz corages
Nient li granz pois, dist uns des sages.             3020
Se vos volez que de toz die
Ne sivrai pas l'ordre Ysaie.
Ysaies voloit descendre,

f° 99 v°          N'osai monteir, volons entendre.                    3024
Esperiz de force reguarda                              *
Sor Pharaon, quant Deus guarda
En la Mer Roge ses amis
Si com avoit anchois pramis,                          3028
E Pharaon, e tote s'ost
Ov lor curre noia molt tost.
Ne lor valut toz lor efforz,
N'en eschapa foibles ne forz.                         3032
Espirz de conseil enseigna                             *
Le jovincel ki demanda
Nostre Seignor par quel mesure
On a vie ki toz jors dure.                            3036
E il li dist que s'il faisoit
Les Deu comanz ja n'i falroit.                         *
Deus par esperit d'entendement
Reguarda sor sa povre gent                            3040
E dist: — Povre par esperit
Sunt a avoir le ciel eslit,
Li suef cuer come d'enfanz
Avront la terre des vivanz.                           3044
Cil ki pleurent de desirrier
Avront confort sains encombrier.

f° 100 r°         Ces paroles, e altre tels,
Leur dist li Sire esperitels.                         3048
U mestier est d'entendement,
Quar il covient que subtilment

*v. 3025, *in left margin*: .iiij. spiritus fortitudinis.
*v. 3033, *in left margin*: .v. spiritus consilii.
*v. 3038, *in left margin*: .vj. spiritus intellectus.

Par set tresels mete purreiz,
Set esperiz, set beneurtez 3052
F. celes set peticions
Que contient la sainte oreisons:
En cez tresels, cui Deus les done,
Dui deservent le tierz corone: 3056
Gracie oreisons sont la deserte
Par cui la tierce est aoverte.
Par esperit de sapience
Conferme Deus cele sentence 3060
Que Sainz Espirs ne se repose
Sor orgueillos por nule chose.
Por cho dona humilité
Ensemble a la virginité 3064
A celi dont il fist sa Mere
Dont nos lisons e fillz e frere.
Deus Nostre Sire ki nos fist,
Quant il por nos nostre char prist, 3068
Bien dut avoir noble maison,

Se nos dire volons raison:
Il meismes l'apareilla,
Il meismes por soi veilla. 3072
Tur i fist de virginité
Halte de grant nobilité,
Que n'i peust nuls avenir
Ki mals vers li volist tenir. 3076
Mais que d'orgueil ne fust soprise,
Ki bien sovent tels casteals brise,
D'umilité i fist un mur
Ki le chastel fait tot seur. 3080
Cist sunt set ueil, que Ysaies
Raconte entre ses profecies.
De toz poüms briement entendre *
Que tel com Deus vuelt l'ome rendre, 3084
Tel le fait lues a un reguart,
Il en seit la maniere e l'art.
Se il li plaist ke jo le crieme,
Sor moi espant l'ueil de sa crieme. 3088

v. 3056, MS.: Doui ('o' *expuncted by the copyist*).
*v. 3083, *in left margin*: altre maniere.

De toz tenez ceste sentence
Dusqu'al sovrain, c'est sapience,
Quanque tu faiz, de bien vuelsz,
Saces tot vient de ces sains uelz.                    3092

f° 101 r°          Colunbine simplicité                         *
Unt cist saint ueil en verité,
Quar en Deu n'a forsen ne ire,
Encore ait on raison de.l dire.                      3096
Tot esguarde paisiblement,
Unques en lui n'eut troblement.
Sur les ruiscels des aiques sunt,                     *
Quar il mainent, e cil s'en vont.                    3100
Sur aus sunt par estableté
E par tot altre dignité.
De lait lavé sunt cist colon,                         *
Cho warde al Incarnacion,                            3104
Quar Deus fait tot par jugement,
Mais puis la fait plus dolcement.
Por en un seul sabat ovreir
Fist il un ome lapideir;                             3108
Mais nos apele a penitence,
Ne quiert de nos altre venjance.


TES JOES SUNT si come airetes                         *
Ki sens fardeir sunt totes netes,                    3112
U les especies sunt molt chieres,
Ainç de meilleurs ne s'aida mieres.
Si com li bon especiarie                              *
f° 101 v°          Le seurent mielz o dire o faire.                     3116
Par deus joes entent deus faces,
Tu ki le sens dusqu'al vif caches,
En la face est la coneissance
De la persone sains dotance.                         3120
Deus faces a Criz, Nostre Sire,
Dont jo vos vueil verité dire.

*v. 3093, *in right margin*: sicut columbe. (*5: 12*)
*v. 3099, *in right margin*: super rivulos aquarum. (*5: 12*)
*v. 3103, *in right margin*: que lacte sunt lote. (*5: 12*)
*v. 3111, *in right margin*: gene illius sicut areole aromatum. (*5: 13*)
*v. 3115, *in right margin*: consitea pigmentariis. (*5: 13*)
v. 3120, MS.: persoine ('*i*' *expuncted by the scribe*).

L'une face est d'umanité,
E l'altre est de devinité.   3124
Vels Deu conoistre come ome
De cho qu'il fist conkell la somme,
Quar il i a mainte merveille
U nuls a lui ne s'apareille.   3128
Come vrais om peut travaillier,
Aleir, parleir, dormir, veillier.
Toz sormomta par pacience,
Par charité, par sapience.   3132
Ainç ne pecha, ne ne volt faire,
Maiz toz a bien volt il atraire.
Por a toz jors nos delivreir
Volt il a mort son cors livrer.   3136
Sa char, son sanc, mangier e boire
Done a toz chaus ki vuelent croire.

f⁰ 102 r⁰  Ceste est une de ses deus faces.
Or te paine ke l'altre saches.   3140
Conois ke Deus terre e ciel fist,
Ne plus n'i eut mais qu'il le dist.
Conois qu'il fist angles e omes,
E quanques nos el mont veommes.   3144
Que n'eut onkes comencement,
Sa naiscence, ne finement,
Qu'il est del peire resplendors,
Sapience, vertuz, honors.   3148
Ceste est l'autre des deus airetes.
Guarde te bien ke tu n'i metes,
E il que li saint, li Deu eslit,
Disent par voiz ou par escrit,   3152
Cist sunt li buen especiare
Ki plantée ont l'une e l'altre aire.
Nient que del lor i metent rien,
Quar en eles sunt tot li bien,   3156
Mais cho qu'il seivent e entendent
Plantent es cuers, e bien ordenent.
Cho vueil dire tot altrement:
Deus mi doinst son enseignement.   3160
Joes solonc l'omanité

f⁰ 102 v⁰  Eut Criz: l'une d'umilité,

E l'autre fu de pacience
Si com estoit en providence.                    3164
Ces li donent teil coneseance
Que fors metent tote dotance.
Humilitez fu sains mesure
Que Deus rechut nostre nature.                  3168
Cil cui li monz Seignor apele
Fu nez en povre maisoncele.
Li Rois ki tot le mont adresce,
Deigna gisir en une creche.                     3172
Cil ki les ciels fist granz e bels,
Fu mis en uns povres drapels.
Est bien par che reconichables
Li buens, li pius, li parmanables.              3176
De sa pacience puis dire
C'onques son cuer ne trobla ire.
De chaus se soffri laidengier
Soi e ses uevres chalengier,                    3180
Cui de legier fesist taisir
S'il li venist bien a plaisir.
Del cous, des cleus, de son martyre
Asseiz en avez oï dire.                          3184

f° 103 r°   Il sofri tot molt dolcement
Por nos, por nostre enseignement.
Don est asseiz ceste sofrance
De Jhesu Crist reconeisance.                    3188
Est nuls ki ne se corichast,
Se om issi le demenast.
Cho faisoient tot li sien
Ki li rendoient mal por bien.                   3192
Or as que par ces deus vertuz
Est Criz sor toz reconeuz.
Por cho bien dis, se tu.s apeles
Joes, u faces, u maisceles,                      3196
Nient proprement, mais par semblance,
Por cho qu'en vient reconisance.
Cez sunt airetes apelees
Ki ne puent estre celees,                       3200
Quar teil odor donent al mont
Que nis les morz revivre font.

Airetes sunt, quar molt petites                               *
Furent al mont, e molt despites,                         3204
Mais especies ja eslites,
Dont nos avoms alquantes dites,
Dont nos n'osons altrement faire                             *
f⁰ 103 v⁰ Que firent li especiaire,                      3208
Li patriarche et li prophete,
Cui armes sunt en grant quiete,
Quar maintesfoiz lor dist om lait
Por cho dire qu'est ore fait.                             3212

Tot cho revueil dire altrement,                              *
E se jo puis, molt plus briement,
De Jhesu Crist membres e chief
Vos vueil faire parole brief.                             3216
Ses maiseles sunt les iglises                                *
Ki premieres furent asises
E fondees en droite foi
Par les baillis del severain Roi.                         3220
Li saint apostle les fonderent
Quant il le mond d'eror torneirent.
Es maisceles monte li sancs
Quant i vient hontes u ahans.                            3224
Honte e ahan li seint sofrirent
Tant que lor sanc en espandirent.
Airetes furent, nient granz aires,                           *
Quar des feaus n'i avoit guaires.                        3228
Mais des especes de vertuz
I avoit il granz, rez e druz.
f⁰ 104 r⁰ Quar cil planté les i avoient,
Ki de buen maistre le tenoient.                          3232
Cil les planterent voirement,
Mais Deus i mist acroisement.

Ses levres sunt, fait la pulcele,                            *
Lilie espandant mirre novele.                            3236
Les levres dunt ele ce dist

*v. 3203, in right margin: areole. (5: 13)
*v. 3207, in left margin: consite a pigmentariis. (5: 13)
*v. 3213, in left margin: altrement.       *v. 3217, in left margin: gene illius. (5: 13)
*v. 3227, in left margin: sicut areole aromatum consite a pigmentariis. (5: 13)
*v. 3235, in right margin: labia eius lilia distillancia mirram primam. (5: 13)

Sunt les paroles Jhesu Crist,
Celes qu'il dist en sa persone,
Nient celes qu'il as altres done.                    3240
Cez sunt as liles comparees,
Quar beles sunt e bien formees,
Blanches defors par innocence,
Dedenz ont or de sapience;                           3244
D'eles decort mirre molt sure
Ki tolt e vers e porreture.
Trois sunt d'armes corrupcions:
En males cogitacions,                                3248
En uevres dignes de venjance
E en malvaise acostumance
Cez sunt trois morz dunt Deus suscite
Quant il les cuers des morz visite.                  3252
L'un en maison, l'altre en la voie,

fo 104 vo    L'altre el sepulcre a greignor joie.
Quar que greindre est nostre grevance,
Plus nos fait liez la delivrance.                    3256
Contre ces trois enfermetez
U morz, se dire le volez,
Covient, se il i a savoir,
Trois manieres de myrre avoir.                       3260
Cele est la premeraine mirre
Ki puet les mals pensez ocirre.
Ceste decort de la parole
Nostre Seignor e de s'escole,                        3264
Quar il dist: — Ki molt m'espoente
Que se la char a cho me tente
Que jo voie femme e covoit,
Par jugement reisnable e droit                       3268
Sui ja colpables d'avoltiere,
E se remaint la chose entiere.
D'une puet bien cist jugemenz
Tolir malvais porpensemenz.                          3272
Or redirai d'on altre guise
Qui de buen maistre m'est aprise.
Les levres sunt doi testament                        *
Ki se joignent avenantment                           3276

*v. 3275, *in left margin*: altrement labia eius. (*5: 13*)

f° 105 r°

E concordent en verité
Solonc sens de moralité.
Lilies les nome la pulcele,
Quar li lilies est flors granz e bele. *3280
Lilies les fait la majestez
Del escriture, e l'onesteiz.
Li grain dedenz ki semblent or
Nos prametent le halt tresor 3284
U par les deus testamenz vienent
Tot cil qui se aiment les tienent.
Mirre en decort, le premeraine
Ki de vertu tres digne est plaine. 3288
Mais del viez curt occultement
Del novel tot apertement.
Quar cil est clos, e cist overz,
Cist li sens clers, e la coverz. 3292
Chascuns en sa maniere dist *
Que li sainz cors que Jhesu prist
Por nostre liberacion
Ne senti pas corrupcion. 3296
Cele mirre soit benoite
Ki si garda la chose droite.
Cele eut la premeraineté

f° 105 v°

E par tans e par dignité. 3300
Cele mirre que nos disons,
Cho fu ceste incorrupcions.
L'autre fu quant ne porri mie
Li cors de la Virgne Marie. 3304
En son sepulcre eut il sejor,
Mais puis al quarantisme jor
Fu il del sepulcre leveiz
E des angles en ciel porteiz. 3308
De cesti mirre nequedent
S'en taisent li doi testament:
Par sainte revelacion
Seit on ceste incorrupcion. 3312
Encore vueil dire altre maniere, *

*v. 3280, *in left margin*: lilia. (*5: 13*)
*v. 3293, *in right margin*: distallancia mirram primam. (*5: 13*)
*v. 3313, *in left margin*: altrement.

E

Quar molt est halte la matiere.
Les leivres Crist son li buen maistre
Ki tot son cors doivent repaistre.                    3316
Son cors sunt cil ki bien ferm croient
Tot altre chose qu'il ne voient
Es sacramenz de Sainte Glise,
Si com le fois lor est aprise.                        3320
Cil sunt dit lilie par figure,
Si vos dirai en quel mesure.

f° 106 r°        Sis foilles a liles defors,
Dedenz set grains teus cum est ors,                   3324
E a chascon sa vergelete
Ki de parfont vient droite e nete.
Li set greinet dont jo ai dit
Sunt set don del Saint Esperit,                       3328
U li bon cuer des sages tendent
E lor vergeles i estendent:
Quels vergeles? Lor volentez,
Lor desirriers, a cho tornez.                          3332
Les foilles unt blanchur plaisant,
Tot dis croiscent en eslaisant.
De sus s'espandent environ,
E tot mostrent a abandon.                              3336
Tot cho par droit nos senefie
Buenes uevres e buene vie.
Blanchors est signes d'onesté
E laece de charité.                                    3340
Li espandres de totes pars
Vuelt que li om ne soit escars,
E que li cuers soit aovers
As Deu feaus e a ses sers,                             3344
A conforter e a bien faire,

f° 106 v°        Bien enorter, del mal retraire.
De sis foilles notez le nombre,
Toz est parfaiz, riens n'i en ombre                   3348
Quar il est faiz de ses parties
Totes ensemble conkueillies,
N'est pas de nul nombre partie
Ki n'i trueve altre a soi unie.                        3352
Mais cele est partie a creant

Ki le tot fait multipliant:
Tels parties sunt de senarie
Sis unitez, e troi binarie,                         3356
E avec cez ternarie doi
De ses parties plus n'i voi.
Le tot seront uns, deus e trois,
Cho.st des parfaiz numbres le lois.                 3360
Parfaiz numbres doit par raison
Seneficr perfection.
Cist acontes del lilie est faiz,
E de petit tenuz granz plaiz                        3364
Por nos maistres demainement
Dont nos avons l'enseignement.
Des lilies tienent la figure
Cil ki des puples unt la cure.                      3368

f° 107 r°

Que lor example e lor buen dit,
Vaillent a chaus qui sunt sogit,
S'il tel ne sunt, ne ne le quierent,
Ja Jhesu Crist levres ne nierent,                   3372
Ja Deus par chaus ne parlera
Cui vie alkes ne li plaira.
Veritez est ke Deus parole
Par chaus ki dient sa parole                        3376
Mais nient par toz, ainz sunt pluiseur
Ki les paroles Deu font leur,
Si parolent, e Deus se taist
Quar leur sermons point ne li plaist.               3380
Vuels savoir quant cho qu'il a dit
Ne puet passer sens grant porfit;
S'altrement est, tot ne valt rien,
Quar li puples ni prent nul bien.                   3384


DE LA MIRRE de penitence                            *
Doivent avoir grant abundance
Tant qu'ele puisse degoteir
Sor lor sogiz, e enboteir                           3388
A faire cho qu'il faire doivent
Que del hanap lor maistres boivent.

*v. 3385, *in right margin*: distillancia mirram primam. (*5: 13*)

Ceste mirre ki va premiere
Par mesure est forz e legiere,                    3392
De cesti bois, se sages ies,
Quar la seconde iert mult plus griés.
Cele iert espurgatories paines,
U tu toi espargnant te maines,                    3396
La tierce iert en dampnacion,
Il ja n'avra redempcion.

SES MAINS, fet ele, sunt tornees                  *
E de jagonces aornees                             3400
E ories sunt. De ceste letre
Ouvrir nos covient entremetre.
Criz a, selon divinité,
Deus mains: largesce e poesté.                    3404
A l'une done largement,
E a l'autre ses dons defent.
Que nols ne toille cho qu'il done,
Se cil ki l'a ne l'abandone.                      3408
Mais se Deus ore uevre ses mains,
E de ses biens ies ore plains,
Se des larmies as a plenté,
E des gracies a volenté.                          3412
Aprés le jor, criemes le nuit,
Que ne te truises de bien vuit.

LES MAINS JESU sunt torneices
Ki sovent font des povres riches,                 3416
E chaus ki sunt de vers le mont
Tornent el val bien en parfont.
Ki tels choses voit avenir
Ne.l doit a legierté tenir.                        3420
Jo cui fols sui m'en esmerveil
Mais tot vient del devin conseil.
Cist sens est vrais, mais nekedent
Cho porriemes dire altrement.                     3424
Uevre a tor faite est liste e plaine,
De cho semblance nos amaine.
Cele ki dist par droite amor

*v. 3399, *in left margin*: manus eius tornatiles auree plene iacinctis. (*5: 14*)

Les mains Jhesu faites a tor, 3428
Quar nuls ne.s puet de rien reprendre,
Se laidement ne vuelt offendre.
Droit va l'ueuvre qe tels mains funt
E sagement, quar ories sunt. *3432
Ors sapience senefie,
De tel or est buene l'envie,
Mais nuls n'avra chose tant bone,
Se la mains orie ne li done. 3436
Jagoncie gracies senefient, *
f⁰ 108 v⁰ Dont ces mains totes resplendient.
Or regardons en l'altre fueill,
Quar altrement parler en vueil. 3440

LES MAINS CRIZ en l'omanité *
Sunt les uevres de pieté.
Par cez ariere fu portee
La berbiete meserré 3444
Ki venue ert en cest desert
U li plus sages sovent pert.
Ces saintes mains enfer prierent
E l'Enemi s'i conreerent 3448
Qe mais vers nos n'a nient de force,
E neporquant molt s'en efforce.
Par ces mains recovra sa dragme
Ke perdue eut cele granz dame 3452
Ki tant le quist a la lumiere
Qe sa perte eut, or l'a molt chiere. *
A tor les forma veritez
Si que n'i a liu vanitez 3456
Ne riens que om puisse blasmer
Ne dont om puist mal aesmer.
De fin or sunt, quar sagement *
Sunt faites e tres purement. 3460
f⁰ 109 r⁰ De jagoncies sunt destinctees: *
C'est de vertuz enluminees

*v. 3432, *in left margin*: auree. (*5: 14*)
*v. 3437, *in right margin*: plene jacinctis. (*5: 14*)
*v. 3441, *in left margin*: manus eius. (*5: 14*)
*v. 3454, *in left margin*: tornatiles. (*5: 14*)    *v. 3459, *in left margin*: auree. (*5: 14*)
*v. 3461, *in right margin*: plene jacinctis. (*5: 14*)

Que Deus faisoit resucitant
Les morz, e les Enfers savant.                3464
D'altrement dire ai volenté
Quar de materie ai grant plenté.

LES MAINS DEU sunt li almosnier            *
Ki sains pechié sunt userier               3468
Quar il prestent, e Deus rendra
Plus de cent tantz q'il n'en prendra.
A tor sunt faites, quar torner             *
Covient sovent, e retorner.                3472
Chaus ki des povres sunt soigneus,
Quar molt i a des bosoigneus,
Cha donent pain, la vesteure,
Primes le drap, puis la custure,           3476
Cez herbergent, e chaus visitent,
Si com divers besoign lor ditent.
D'or sunt ces mains, quar greignor sens    *
Ne puis trover, tant me porpens,           3480
Que Deu amer e Lui servir
E por Lui povres sostenir.
De jagoncies sunt aornees                   *
f° 109 v°         Les mains ki sunt a cho tornees,         3484
C'est de vertuz, ki molt avienent
A chaus ki tel uevre maintienent,
Quar Deus por hospitalité
E por uevres de pieté                      3488
A fait miracles maintes foiz,
Dont confermee est ceste foiz.
Sainz Gregories asseiz en conte,
Sainz Winwalois raison aconte.            3492
Ne conteroie a pose grant
Cho queu jo.n ai trové lisant.

*v. 3467, *in right margin*: manus eius. (*5: 14*)
*v. 3471, *in right margin*: tornatiles. (*5: 14*)
*v. 3479, *in right margin*: auree. (*5: 14*)
*v. 3483, *in right margin*: plene jacinctis. (*5: 14*)
v. 3494: *Two lines left blank.*
v. 3494: *This epilogue is separated from the main text by a space of two blank lines. It is introduced by an initial 'P' which is three lines deep. After it, without a gap, but introduced by initial 'S', is an eighteen-line version of the fabliau* Du Vilain Asnier *which is given overleaf (see notes).*

Por l'oneur Deu premierement,
Aprés por nostre enseignement                    3496
E por celi cui jo present
A Deu, quant jo le sai present,
Ki me pramist k'ele por moi
Deu prieroit, e fait, jo croi,                    3500
Ai de rimer paine soferte.
Or sui venuz a bogne certe.
Ici vueil jo metre ma cire,
Ne m'en orreiz ore plus dire.                    3504
Mais tant requier que cist romanz
Unkes ne viegne en main d'enfant.

Soviegne vos del fol vilain
Ki waegnier deüst son pain,
E il vint rendre le musage
A un estal lez un passage                    4
U om especies remuoit
E laituaires confisoit?
Quant li vilains d'un laituarie
Tres precios senti le flaire,                    8
Ne.l puet sofrir, vint al pasmer.
Ne le savoient dont blasmer,
Quar om cuidoit que par destroit
De mal chaïst, si com om voit.                    12
Mais par conseil d'on bien sage omme
Fu aperchuz, cho.n est la somme:
Porter le fist sor un femier
Bien ort, cui om trova premier.                    16
La fu guariz par la pueur
Cil ki pasmez ert por l'odeur.

# COMMENTARY

vv. 1–8. These lines set the serious tone of the work, and they may be translated as follows:

'The subject matter of this book aims at freeing the whole heart so that there shall be no covetousness in the world, and all may be free of vanity. This is essential, for otherwise it will not be soundly understood; for the book was made about love and drawn from it with great wisdom.'

v. 9. The attribution of the Song of Songs to Solomon is probably a very early one, and was widespread throughout the Middle Ages.

v. 13. The graphy *enz* for the more usual *ainz* or *einz* is either a western dialectal trait (M. K. Pope, § 1326, § iii, p. 501) or possibly a fortuitous spelling since the initial e is separated from the body of the line by a space. In any event, this western levelling is not noted under other circumstances in the text (e.g. *saint*, v. 15). The spelling *ainz* is found at v. 254.

v. 23–34. These lines establish precisely that the major interpretation was that the work is an allegory of the union of Christ and the Church, but other interpretations are not excluded. In v. 1989 the Bride is specifically identified with the Soul:

La saint arme, c'est la pulcele,

as is suggested also in line 28.The Old French writer presents his idea in a more personalized manner but feels it necessary to offer an interpretation of the Bride's outburst.

v. 25. *le parole*: The reduction of unstressed *la* to *le* is characteristic of the northern dialects (M. K. Pope, § 1320, § xii (c), p. 488).

v. 43. The range of different approaches to the work is specifically announced at this point.

v. 56. The Song of Songs opens abruptly. 'Let him kiss me with the kisses of his mouth' (1: 1; 1: 2, in the Latin Vulgate). This presupposes a longing on the part of the Bride, which is here interpreted as provoked by a separation caused by a failing on the part of the Bride. The plea to be reunited with the Beloved inspired St. Bernard to declare:

Praeceps amor, nec judicium
praestolatur, nec consilio temperatur,
nec pudore frenatur, nec rationi
subjicitur: Rogo, supplico, flagito:
osculetur me oscolo oris sui.
(Sermo V in Canticum Canticorum)

vv. 75–80. Richelet's partial edition begins at this point on p. 151. This first extract ends at v. 80. Henceforth we shall indicate the beginning and end of each section transcribed by Richelet.

v. 84. The manuscript reads *si grait plait*. The scribe's eye has clearly wandered from one word to the following word, and his *lapsus* has been corrected.

v. 89. The cause of the Bride's separation from her lover is the biting of the forbidden fruit, 'Le mors de la pome'. In this phrase there is a play on words in 'mors' (biting and death) and it is later used as the title of a poem on the fall of man. Cf. F. Schneegans, 'Le Mors de la Pomme' in *Romania*, vol. xlvi (1920), pp. 537–70, and L. P. Kurtz (editor), *Le Mors de la Pomme*, New York, 1937 (*Institute of French Studies*).

v. 101. The declension system in which the subject case of masculine nouns of the Latin second declension end in -s remains still strong, and a Latin neuter signum is provided by analogy with the masculine nouns with an -s termination. The adjective *cerz* (certus) also shows that the declension system is still strong.

v. 110. *sens*: The spelling of the nasal a could be varied—*en* and *an*. Here the word is the preposition *sans*.

v. 127. Amors vaint, the equivalent of *omnia vincit amor*, becomes a proverbial cliché when it refers to human love. Cf. *Aucassin et Nicolete*, paragraph 2, *Amors qui tot vaint*.

v. 140. The enclisis *ne.l* for *ne le* is common in Old French.

vv. 141–8. Richelet, p. 152.

v. 152. The allusion is too general to permit the precise identification of the written authority to which reference is made.

v. 160. Although an n is clearly written, the scribe surely intended to write *Espeuse*.

vv. 163–8. Richelet, p. 152.

v. 165. *Mameles*: The Latin Vulgate reads 'ubera'. The meaning is in fact the caresses of love. The difficulty of interpretation presented by the reading of the Vulgate is solved here by suggesting that the use of the term is figurative (v. 178).

v. 184. *lait*: In his preface to the sermons on the Song of Songs, St. Bernard also takes up this image of milk.

v. 196. *clofigié*: Fixed with nails, i.e. nailed to the Cross, the Crucified.

v. 197. The poet seems to be suggesting that he wrote for at least two different types of audience.

v. 203. Once more there seems to be an echo of the Bernardine teaching on grace, but the reference is of a general kind.

vv. 212–13. Richelet, p. 152.

v. 215. The name Christ is closely linked with the Greek word for anointing oil: in the Hebrew the sounds of the words for oil recall the name of Solomon. Thus the link between the sound of the word and the name is developed both in the attribution of the Song of Songs to Solomon and in this comment on the meaning of the name of Christ. Cf. also Luke 4: 18, Spiritus Domini super me; propter quod unxit me . . .

v. 223. *Wape*: Empty, insipid. The retention of the initial w is characteristic of northern and western French where Francien uses the consonant g (M. K. Pope, § 1320, § iii (i)).

vv. 231–2. Richelet, p. 153.

v. 239. The manuscript reads clearly *C ehaus*. The separation of the initial letter from the body of the line is doubtless responsible for this *lapsus*.

vv. 239–40. This comment on what is meant by the term *enfant*, namely one who has no experience of love, of divine love that is, forms the basis of the observation in the final line of the work, where is expressed the hope that this 'romance' will not fall into the hands of an infant. A similar point is made in lines 1871–3.

vv. 245–8. Richelet, p. 153.

v. 255. The first person plural form in *-oms* is characteristic of northern and north-eastern dialects.

vv. 255–8. Richelet, p. 153.

v. 265. The room to which the Bride alludes is not so much a nuptial chamber as the private quarters of the master of the household. A cellar or 'celier' is not necessarily a gloomy underground place. In Béroul's *Tristan* the hero is granted refuge in *le bel celier* of Orri (v. 3017).

vv. 265–8. Richelet, p. 153.

vv. 275–84. Richelet, pp. 153–4.

vv. 287–8. Richelet, p. 154.

v. 290. Old Testament scholars consider that this point (*recti diligunt te*) marks the end of the introduction to the Song of Songs. A recent view is that these initial verses in the Hebrew text deal with the theme of exile, and that Israel is expressing the desire, while remaining faithful to Jehovah, to return to Palestine. (Robert, Tournet et Feuillet, *Cant. des Cant.*, p. 68.) Needless to say, the French text, like many other medieval commentaries, does not take this view, and stresses rather the union of the Soul with the Divine Being.

v. 291. The dramatic and narrative nature of the poem is evident at this point.

vv. 295–300. Richelet, p. 154.

v. 297. The dark colouring is a sign of sufferings endured, not only in this interpretation, but elsewhere in the Old Testament, e.g. Lamentationes Jeremiae 4: 8, Denigrata est super carbones facies eorum . . .

v. 313–16. The daughters of Jerusalem are here clearly seen as a very chosen few. They could be either the women of the royal harem, or, more likely in this interpretation, the few who have chosen to dedicate themselves to God. The expression recurs in lines 871–2, where they are the handmaidens of the Bride, i.e. the servants of the Church, and similarly in vv. 825, 1578, and 2368, where their obligations to the Bride are emphasized.

vv. 323–6. Richelet, p. 154.

v. 325. The French text does not develop the final part of verse 4 and the beginning of verse 5 of Canticum Canticorum 1:

> sicut tabernacula Cedar, sicut pelles
> Salomonis. Nolite me considerare quod
> fusca sim, quia decoloravit me sol.

The Bride refers to her mother, but never, in the Song of Songs, to her father.

vv. 329–30. Richelet, p. 155.

v. 330. The vines required a guard to protect the ripened fruit. The image of the vine is a classic one in the Old Testament and it is well developed in Isaiah 5: 1–7. The interpretation here is that the vine represents the faithful believer.

v. 350. *rendre*: The manuscript reads *rēdēt*, which should expand to *rendent*. The sense is that only by dying can the grapes produce wine.

v. 351. This verse is often interpreted as the failure of the children of Israel always to follow the true faith. The French text suggests that not simply the children of Israel but all believers can from time to time lapse.

vv. 351–2. Richelet, p. 155.

v. 363. The French text overlooks the latter part of this verse: 'ne vagari incipiam post greges sodalium tuorum'. This verse is a development of Genesis 37: 16, 'Tell me, I pray thee, where they feed their flocks?', which is the question posed by Joseph when seeking his brothers. The image of the shepherd is, once again, a classic Biblical one.

vv. 363–4. Richelet, p. 155.

vv. 367–8. Richelet, p. 155.

vv. 371–82. Richelet, pp. 156–6.

v. 388. The fear of heresy reflects twelfth-century religious history.

v. 400. The riding of a black horse symbolized, in the twelfth and thirteenth centuries, being carried off by evil. Thus in the *Queste del Saint Graal*, Perceval rides off furiously on a black horse and is saved from sin only by the intervention of God (*Queste*, ed. Pauphilet, pp. 92 et ss.: 'Et lors . . . ameine un cheval grant et merveilleux, et si noir que ce iert merveilles a veoir').

v. 405–16. The Bridegroom takes this opportunity of outlining the dangers of the sin of Pride. For St. Bernard, Pride (*superbia*) was the beginning of all other vices, 'Initium omnis peccati superbia'.

v. 421. The Bridegroom interprets this verse as an example of how the faithful can be delivered from peril.

vv. 431–5. The various categories of good qualities and persons listed in lines 431–4 are gathered together as one in the phrase 'cist pueples' (v. 435).

vv. 437–40. Richelet, p. 156.

v. 439. The Biblical text has presented many difficulties to commentators, but here the comparison with the dove symbolizes absolute fidelity and chastity.

v. 449. The neck is interpreted spiritually as symbolizing the route by which words are pronounced and the manner in which spiritual sustenance is received.

vv. 449–52. Richelet, p. 156.

v. 471. The neck ornaments are a symbol of the work of the saints, St. Jerome the translator, St. Augustine the philosopher, and St. Gregory, probably Gregory of Tours, the historian. Their wisdom and eloquence are celebrated (v. 488).

vv. 471–6. Richelet, pp. 156–7.

vv. 479–82. Richelet, p. 157.

v. 494. An allusion to the disputes of the 'scholars' or theologians which is too general to permit any precise identification.

vv. 501–8. Richelet, p. 157.

v. 502. *Nard* is a plant of Indian origin from which is extracted a costly perfume. In the New Testament it is associated with Christ (Mark 14: 3, 'an alabaster box of spikenard, very precious', and John 12: 3, 'Then took Mary a pound of spikenard, very costly, and anointed the feet of Jesus'). In the French text it is equated with the virtue of 'Caritas'.

v. 523. The Vulgate text reads: 'fasciculus myrrhae dilectus meus'. This is clearly echoed in the French text though not in the Latin marginal note. It symbolizes here the sufferings and Passion of Christ for His Church.

vv. 523–4. Richelet, p. 157.

vv. 541–2. Richelet, p. 158.

v. 547. The 'botrus cypri' refers to a bunch of heavily perfumed cypress flowers which in form resembles a bunch of grapes. It has been understood literally, and a play of words in French (roisin—roisin) is evolved.

vv. 547–54. Richelet, p. 158.

vv. 561–8. Richelet, p. 158.

vv. 566–7. The French text does not develop the Latin prototype but prefers a lyrical and rhetorical outburst in which the author's awareness of the figures of rhetoric such as *frequentatio* becomes apparent.

vv. 561, 567, 569. The beauty of the beloved is systematically seen in terms of spiritual symbolism.

v. 582. *une fordine*: This word seems to be a variant of the more usual *un ferlinc*, a small coin, and the form suggests some influence of the Anglo-Saxon coin which was a fourth part of a larger unit, i.e. the farthing.

v. 583. Richelet reads 'Ke tu ies beals' though the manuscript clearly gives 'Mais tu ies beals'.

vv. 583–6. Richelet, p. 159.

v. 589. The Bridegroom is clearly Christ, of both human and divine nature.

v. 595. The eroticism of the Song of Songs becomes a praise of chastity and divine love.

vv. 595–6. Richelet, p. 159.

v. 611. The cedars, especially the cedars of Lebanon, are frequently associated with the cypress tree in the Old Testament, e.g. Isaiah 14: 8, '. . . the fir trees rejoice at thee and the cedars of Lebanon'; and in the description of the building of Solomon's palaces in 1 Kings, Chs. 5–7, cedars feature prominently.

vv. 611–12. Richelet, p. 159.

v. 614. The reference to *le figure* is surely to figures of rhetoric for the poet explains in the next few lines that material objects help us to understand spiritual things. The poet is referring to himself by the use of *me* in this line.

v. 617. The fact that the physical properties of things correspond to their spiritual values was an idea which was extensively and elaborately developed in medieval symbolism. These points are well illustrated in the *Plantaires*, *Lapidaires*, and *Bestiaires*, and in G. Raynaud, 'Poème moralisé sur les propriétés des choses' in *Romania*, vol. xiv (1885), pp. 442–84.

vv. 645–9. The variant graphies *velt* and *vuelt* in close proximity indicate how hazardous it is to base precise conclusions concerning the dialect of the text on a few forms.

v. 655. The clash of vices and virtues, seen in fact as a battle, is one which saw a separate literary development in works such as the *Bataille d'Enfer et de Paradis* (p.p. A. Guesnon, 1909), or the better-known *Tournoiement Antechrist* of Huon de Méry, ed. G. Wimmer, Marburg, 1888.

v. 667. The reference to chivalry recalls not only the vogue for *Chansons de Geste* and romances of chivalry which flourished from the twelfth century onwards, but also the imagery used by St. Paul and again by St. Bernard of Clairvaux in his *De laude novæ militatis*.

v. 671. In the Song of Songs these words, and those referred to in v. 675, are clearly placed in the mouth of the Bride. They form the opening of Chapter 2 of the Canticum Canticorum. In the French text they are attributed to the

Bridegroom or King. The Flower of the Field here symbolizes the reward which will be won by the victor in the strife between good and evil. The lily of the valley symbolizes the flower which will be watered by the tears of the humble. Neither of these interpretations is the usual one propounded in biblical exegeses. It is more usually argued that the Bride is comparing her own beauty with that of the humble flower as a means of stressing her confusion that the Bridegroom should place her in such an exalted position. This hesitation of the Bride is, however, suggested in v. 680.

vv. 671–6. Richelet, p. 159. This passage marks the opening of Chapitre Deuxième in Richelet, and corresponds to the beginning of the second chapter of the Song of Songs.

v. 687. The 'filles' mentioned are not the 'daughters of Jerusalem' but young women in general.

vv. 687–98. Richelet, p. 160.

v. 700. The author here points clearly to the two levels on which the work can be read, making a careful distinction between the words (*paroles*) and what they imply (*sens*), and suggests that there is a spiritual as well as a human interpretation.

v. 705. The apple is now a rare tree in Palestine. Other Old Testament references to it include Joel 1: 12, though because of the rarity of the apple tree, it has been argued that in fact it is the apricot which is designated here. This image is rapidly developed and the fruit of the trees of Paradise are in fact the works of the Holy Martyrs.

v. 705. Richelet reads *Cele dist.*

vv. 705–12. Richelet, p. 160.

vv. 731, 733. The image of shade often suggests the idea of protection.

vv. 731–48. Richelet, p. 161.

v. 739. The word *celier* is used here as an equivalent of *Cellam vinariam*, whereas in v. 256 (see note) it renders *celaria*. The reference here, v. 739, is to a place where wine is kept. Wine throughout the Canticum Canticorum (1: 2, 4; 4: 10; 5: 1; 7: 10; 8: 2) symbolizes love.

v. 745. The term *adinavit* is interpreted here as 'give instruction in' whereas in fact it is closer to the A.V. rendering 'his banner over me was love'. In adapting the Latin in this way, the French author avoids a somewhat puzzling problem. The sign, or banner, of love is perhaps an extension, according to Renan, for example, of some banner or sign floating above the cellar where wine was distributed. The simpler twelfth-century French interpretation has the advantage of not distracting the reader from the mystical meaning of the text.

vv. 771–3. Richelet, p. 161.

v. 772. The flowers and the apples sustain the Bride who is here speaking to the daughters of Jerusalem.

v. 774. The evidence of the rhyme proves that a line has been accidentally omitted. Scribal errors of this magnitude are comparatively rare in this manuscript.

vv. 775–6. Richelet, p. 162.

v. 793. The erotic nature of the scene is interpreted entirely in mystical terms. The embracing arms of the Bridegroom symbolize the Sacraments of the Church.

vv. 793–4. Richelet, p. 162.

vv. 801–18. Richelet, p. 162.

v. 805. We have corrected what is a simple slip of the pen.

v. 809. The reference to gazelles and hinds, both of them well-known animals in Palestine, has provoked the comment that both, in classical mythology, are associated with the Goddess of Love. They are doubtless chosen here as symbolizing agility.

v. 816. The subtleties of this passage in the Canticum Canticorum in which there are allusions to the Exile are here overlooked in favour of a consideration of the symbolism of animals.

v. 831–2. 'The kid swiftly leaps over the muddy places and all the thorny ones.'

v. 833. The relationship between the stag and the serpent is not new. The evil qualities of the serpent are a commonplace in medieval French literature. In the *Yvain* of Chrétien de Troyes, the serpent, in conflict with the lion, is seen to be the less noble creature. Similarly in the *Queste del Saint Graal*, Perceval intervenes on the side of the Lion which is engaged in mortal conflict with a serpent or dragon (*Queste*, éd. Pauphilet, p. 94). In the medieval French bestiaries, the serpent is described as symbolizing

> Mort et enfer
> (*Bestiaire* de Guillaume le Clerc, v. 1710)

and the stag symbolizes, on the contrary,

> Cels qui a Deu se voelent rendre
> (*Bestiaire* de Guillaume le Clerc, v. 2816)

Again in the *Livre dou Trésor* of Brunetto Latini we find:

> Cerf soient generalment anemis as serpens
> (ed. F. J. Carmody, i, 183, p. 160)

v. 841. Biblical commentators suggest that a new and independent poem begins at Canticum Canticorum 2: 13. Our text marks a new paragraph here, but not a major division of the work. This occurs at v. 1447.

vv. 841–50. Richelet, p. 163.

v. 844–7. The narrative passage in the Old French is an echo of the Biblical text. There is certainly a change of manner at this point, and this is accentuated in the French text by so ordering the narrative that the Bride awakes at this juncture.

v. 852. The verb here is use impersonally: 'and I do not tremble at all'.

v. 855. Richelet reads *Cil resemble*, but the manuscript is clear at this point and reads *e il resemble*. The comparison with the young gazelle enables the French text to develop at length the links between the Old and New Testaments. To make the leaps of the gazelle correspond to stages in the life of Christ—his conception, birth, baptism, temptation, Crucifixion, descent into Hell, Resurrection, and Ascension—is to echo the preaching and teaching of twelfth-century France, especially the teaching illustrated by the basilica of St. Denis as reconstructed by Abbot Suger. Émile Mâle in his *Art Religieux en France au douzième siècle* gives examples from the plastic arts which reinforce this parallelism of the Old and New Testaments.

vv. 855–6. Richelet, p. 163.

vv. 861–2. Richelet, p. 163.

v. 879. The reading *salili* for *sailli* is clearly a *lapsus*.

vv. 893–906. Richelet, pp. 163–4.

v. 895. In the Canticum Canticorum the narrative is rapid. In the French text the sequence of events is very much subordinate to explanation and symbolism. We have not a lover separated from his mistress by a mere wall, but a long exposition of the nature of religious communication. The erotic gives way to the mystical although the language is that of the love lyric or romance.

v. 900. The correction has been made from the evidence afforded by the rhyme word. Richelet also suggests this reading. The error is doubtless caused by the repetition of the group of letters *mes*.

v. 903–4. The separating wall in Canticum Canticorum is a real one: here it is one of flesh, that is the physical barrier which prevents full comprehension of the mystical experience.

vv. 917–34. Richelet, pp. 164–5.

v. 929 et ss. The lover's call to his bride to come out, not for the pleasures of love but to work, since winter has passed and spring is come, does not celebrate merely the pleasures of a Palestinian spring. The Biblical text stresses the phenomena of the seasons, the French text refers to faith and the winter of unbelief.

v. 932. The graphy *muex* (i.e. *mueus*) in the manuscript does not seem to be a dialectal form. It is used nowhere else in this text, and we have permitted ourselves the slight emendation to *mieus*.

vv. 939–42. Richelet, p. 165.

vv. 939 and 942. In both these lines Richelet reads *iviers* but the manuscript clearly gives *ivers*.

v. 959. The Palestinian spring is marked by the brilliance of the flowers. The return of spring was also celebrated in the medieval French lyric, particularly of the 'reverdie' type, e.g. the poem by Colin Muset which begins:

> Quant voi lo douz tens repairier,
> Que li rosignols chante en mai . . .
> (Colin Muset, *Les Chansons*, ed. J. Bédier, Paris (1938),
> p. 13. *Les Classiques français du Moyen Âge*, No. 7)

or, from the fifteenth century, the celebrated *rondeau* of Charles d'Orléans:

> Le temps a laissé son manteau
> De vent, de froidure et de pluie . . .

vv. 959–60. Richelet, p. 165.

v. 967. The reference to the pruning of vines in spring is either poetic licence on the part of the author of the Biblical text, or, more probably, a faulty reading, which has left its mark on the exegesis of this line. Robert and Tournay suggest that the Hebrew text should be read to mean that it is the season of gay songs rather than the season of pruning. However, the French text utilizes the image of pruning to suggest, without much ingenuity, the cutting away of the evil and the leaving of the good. March was the season for pruning in the Middle Ages.

vv. 967–72. Richelet, p. 165.

v. 971. The turtle dove is a migratory bird which returns to Palestine in the spring.

v. 978. *sains* is the stressed form of *sans*. M. K. Pope, § 597, suggests that the stressed form is very rarely found.

v. 981. The text is not clear at this point. Lines 981 onwards as they stand can only be seen as a series of somewhat disconnected observations if it is argued that the last two words of line 981 have been accidentally transposed. The alternative explanation that the scribe has omitted two lines offers a solution, but we are not sufficiently convinced that this is the case, thus we do not note an actual omission in the text.

vv. 981–2. Richelet, p. 166.

v. 985 et ss. The fig tree as a symbol of the Church is not confined to this text. The fig and the vine are part of the Palestinian countryside and symbolize the delights promised to the Children of Israel: e.g. Isaiah 36: 16, 'eat ye everyone of his vine, and everyone of his fig tree'.

vv. 985–6. Richelet, p. 166.

vv. 997–8. Richelet, p. 166.

v. 1001. The Old Testament reference in the Vulgate to the hiding-place of dry stone walling was clearly not meaningful to the Old French commentator who seized this opportunity to allude to the Crucifixion. The harshness of the surroundings suggests the harshness of man who crucified and maimed Christ. The reason why the Hebrew text refers to the rocky plains is twofold: the wild dove of Palestine has its habitat there, and in other places Israel is described as a stupid defenceless dove: Hosea 7: 11, Et factus est Ephraim quasi columba seducta . . ., or Psalm 17: 19, where Israel is described as 'the soul of thy turtledove'.

vv. 1001–2. Richelet, p. 166.

vv. 1017–20. Richelet, p. 166.

v. 1018–35. This passage stresses the power of the beloved's voice. The force of words is well stressed in this section, but it is developed to emphasize the value of the Confession.

v. 1025. Given the reference in v. 1021 to *face* the reading *pace* would appear to be scribal error, possibly induced by the word *por* at the beginning of the line.

vv. 1035–6. Richelet, p. 167.

vv. 1041–6. Richelet, p. 167.

v. 1043. The young foxes whose games destroy the vines, by destroying the new shoots, are in fact the heretics who destroy the Church. The author seems particularly anxious to emphasize the wholly destructive nature of heresy and he approaches the theme in a twofold manner in this section.

v. 1065. The marginal note *altrement en moralité* is in the same hand as the other marginal notes which are passages of the Latin Vulgate. It is possible therefore that this indication should be attributed to the author of the poem. Usually, however, such points are made in the body of the text, e.g. v. 114: *Allegorie nos amaine*.

vv. 1083–6. Richelet, p. 167.

vv. 1089–96. Richelet, pp. 167–8.

v. 1092, 1094, 1101. The author treats very rapidly the poetic and lyric ideas expressed in Canticum Canticorum 2: 16–17, which contrasts markedly with the very full exposition of the symbolism of the little foxes. The link between 2: 15 and 2: 16 is slight, but it is the fact that the beloved responds to the pleas of the Bridegroom and utters expressions of delight. In the French text, the observations are addressed to the Bride's handmaidens. The lilies, for the French writer, symbolize purity: there is no suggestion that the phrase is to be taken literally.

vv. 1101–6. Richelet, p. 168.

v. 116. Though the Bride is helpless without the Groom, the underlying idea is that the Church is helpless without Christ.

vv. 1135–8. Richelet, p. 168.

v. 1137. The reference to Mount Bethel results from a difficulty in the Hebrew text. The word may be a proper name, but it may also refer to a cleft in the mountains, and the allusion could be to the mountains of the Promised Land. The French text stresses that Bethel is the House of God, and that God should come to his House. The image is then developed to show that God is the Head and the people are the members or limbs of the young hinds whose vision is so penetrating. The Bride in this passage is addressing her Beloved. In the following passage (vv. 1169 et ss.) she turns to address her maidens.

v. 1149. *fiee*: This is a characteristically northern or north-eastern form (M. K. Pope, § **422).

v. 1177. The Bride who could not find her Beloved announces, according to Cyril of Alexandria, the woman who, on the morning of the Resurrection, failed to find Christ in the Sepulchre (Luke 24: 3; John 20: 1; Cyril of Alexandria, *apud* Migne, *Patrologia Graeca*, vol. lxix [1864]). The image is, however, an Old Testament one, the darkness and night signifying the long suffering of loyal souls (e.g. Isaiah 5: 30; Psalm 112: 4) and the idea of seeking and not finding is noted in Hosea 5: 6, In gregibus suis et in armentis suis vadent ad quaerendum Dominum, et non invenient; ablatus est ab eis.

vv. 1177–80. Richelet, p. 169. This passage marks the opening of Chapitre Troisième in Richelet, and corresponds to the beginning of the third chapter of the Song of Songs.

vv. 1183, 1195, 1201, 1219. The seeking of the Lord is interpreted both as a narrative in a romance of love and as an allegory of seeking God in the Scriptures. The mother of the Bride is the Holy Church (v. 1219) which is not quite consistent with v. 27,

L'amie, ço est Sainte Eglise.

Needless to say, this symbolism is not found in either the Hebrew text or the Vulgate Canticum Canticorum. The medieval text presents a characteristically twelfth-century rendering of the passage which emphasizes the parallelism of the Old and New Testaments.

vv. 1185–90. Richelet, p. 169.

v. 1188. To interpret the reading *demandoient* as an error of person and number is to amend the text to a greater extent than is strictly necessary. The graphy *ent* for *en* is attested from the eleventh to the fifteenth centuries.

vv. 1193–8. Richelet, p. 169.

vv. 1201–2. Richelet, p. 170.

vv. 1217–18. Richelet, p. 170.

vv. 1227–30. Richelet, p. 170.

vv. 1241–2. This couplet refers to the Bride, though the previous couplet was a generalization.

vv. 1243–6. Richelet, p. 170.

vv. 1245, 1249. These verses in the Hebrew text are identical with Canticum Canticorum 11: 12. They are expanded in vv. 809 et ss. and vv. 816 et ss. above, where similarly the Bridegroom exhorts the handmaiden not to wake the Bride. The phraseology used is quite different in both cases. In this second instance the writer develops even further the value of figurative language. The animal symbolism no longer suggests virtues only. The little foxes represent those who live a clean life, and the stag symbolizes God. This point is made in the *Bestiaires* when the stag which devours serpents is likened to Christ who destroys the Devil (*Bestiaire* de Guillaume le Clerc, vv. 2736–60). For the prose *Lancelot* the stag accompanied by four young lions symbolizes Christ and the four evangelists. Needless to say, such symbolism is quite absent from the Hebrew text.

v. 1248. This couplet re-echoes vv. 81–2:

Icsi covient ententre metre,
La flor entendre de la letre . . .

v. 1255. *buke* is another example of a characteristic northern form.

vv. 1264–6. '. . . for the poison is not slow to act, on the contrary it heats them up and makes the stag seek the living water and this cures it.'

v. 1307. The rhetorical question as a means of emphatic affirmation is a characteristic of the Old Testament (e.g. Isaiah 60: 8, 'Who are these that fly as a cloud and as doves to their windows?'). The symbolism of the column of smoke suggests the travels of the Children of Israel led by a pillar of cloud by day and a pillar of fire by night (Exodus 13: 21, Dominus autem praecedebat eos ad ostendendam viam, per diem in columna nubis, et per noctem in columna ignis).

vv. 1307–10. Richelet, p. 170.

vv. 1323–58. Richelet, pp. 171–2.

v. 1335. The dreaming or vision of the Bride suggests the divine revelation in visions as expounded by Bernard of Clairvaux, among others. In his 31st Sermon on the Song of Songs, § 4, there is a particularly interesting passage, 'Et haec demonstratio non quidem communis, sed tamen foris facta est, nimirum exhibata per imagines extrinsecus apparantes, seu voces sonantes. Sed divina inspectio eo differentior ab his quo interior, cum per seipsum dignatur invisere Deus animam quaerentem se, quae tamen ad quaerendum toto se desiderio et amore devovit. Et hoc signum istiusmodi adventus ejus, sicut ab eo qui expertus est edocemur [Psalm 96: 3]: *Ignis ante ipsum praecedit et inflammabit in circuitu inimicos ejus*. (Quoted from E. Gilson, 'La mystique de la grâce dans la *Queste del Saint Graal*' in *Romania*, vol. li (1925), p. 337, note 1.)

v. 1337. The vision of the Couch of Solomon has provoked many different expositions. It has been agreed that this Old Testament reference to Solomon, like that in Psalm 72: 1 ('Give the king thy judgement, O God, and thy righteousness to the king's son'), is a prophecy which refers to the Messiah. This is indeed the most usual medieval interpretation which is emphasized again in v. 1366.

v. 1366. See below notes to vv. 1507 and 1509.

vv. 1375–84. The meaning of the vision is expounded in terms which were normal in the *lapidaires* and the *plantaires*. In the *Lapidaires* we find

Saphirs est bels et cuvenables . . .
Al ciel resemble kant est purs
(Studer and Evans, *Anglo-Norman Lapidaries*, p. 34, vv. 163 and 165)

and it is linked with chastity:

Mais ki la portet deit estre mult chastes

(ibid., p. 98)

Chastity is frequently represented symbolically by the lily, both in literature and
in the plastic arts in the Middle Ages.

Fleur de lis, c'est la douce dame
Qui bele fu de cors et d'ame . . .
(G. Raynaud, 'Poème Moralisé sur les Propriétés
des Choses' in *Romania*, vol. xiv (1885), p. 459)

v. 1376. The form *forche* in which the group t plus jod initial of a syllable
shifts to t plus pre-alveolar fricative is characteristically northern dialect. See
M. K. Pope, § 1320, § i.

v. 1391. The rose as a symbol of martyrdom is conventional.

v. 1404. The reference to the *chançon d'amor* is doubtless to the Canticum
Canticorum and it is the only allusion in the French poem which re-echoes the
title of the Old Testament work.

vv. 1408–16. The symbolism of numbers is ancient. It is not simply a question
of a round number, or, as has been suggested by Riciolti, that the twelve tribes
of Israel each had five representatives, but a careful linking of the twelve apostles
who spread Christianity, and the five senses by which men make perceptions.
The numerical apothegm is popular in oriental literature and in the wisdom
literature of the Middle Ages. Cf. Isidore of Seville, *De numeris* in *Patrologia
Latina*, lxxxiii, pp. 179 ff.

v. 1425. Cf. the Epistle to the Ephesians 6: 17, 'The sword of the spirit, which
is the Word of God'.

v. 1437. The end of the *digressio* is marked by the formula 'repairies velt a ma
matere'. The *digressio* is a recognized pattern of literary composition, as laid
down by Geoffroi de Vinsauf in *Documentum de modo et arte versificandi*:
'Digressio similiter ampliat et decorat materiam' (E. Faral, *Les Arts poétiques
du XIIᵉ et du XIIIᵉ siècle, en France* ii, 2, 17, p. 274.)

v. 1446. The division into two 'books' does not correspond to a division in
the Canticum Canticorum. Moreover it is not marked in the manuscript by any
indication different from the large initial two lines deep which indicates the
beginning of a new 'paragraph'.

v. 1447. This proverbial expression is not to be found in the lists published
by J. Morawski, *Proverbes français antérieurs au XVᵉ siècle*, Paris (*Cfmâ*, no. 47),
1925.

v. 1463. The Latin term *ferculum* signifies a litter, or chair, which is carried,
and is the translation of a Hebrew term which is found in this context only:
it is in fact a *hapax legomenon*.

vv. 1463–8. Richelet, pp. 172–3. Richelet takes no account of the fact that the
Old French text divides the work into two books at this point.

vv. 1471, 1475, 1485. This description of the throne of Solomon echoes that which is found in 1 Kings 10: 18–19, Fecit etiam rex Salomon thronum de ebore grandem, et vestivit eum auro fulvo nimis. Qui habebat sex gradus; et summitas throni rotunda erat in parte posteriori . . . (*Liber Tertius Regum*, x. 18–19).

vv. 1481–4. The paratactical construction of these lines heightens the force of the description: '. . . but the gemstones and the enamel set in this work with great labour, and this makes it more costly than all the gold, indeed more than a rich treasury'.

vv. 1485–94. Richelet, p. 173.

v. 1499. In order to restore the rhyme the reading *tuit* would be more appropriate than *tot*. Since the sense would be unchanged we have preferred to respect the graphy of the manuscript which doubtless signified in this context a pronunciation to rhyme with *nuit*.

vv. 1503–4. This equating of the throne of Solomon with the Holy Church is characteristic of twelfth-century exegesis.

v. 1507. The name of Christ is linked with the word *Chrism* or Holy oil. This oil was used for the anointing of kings, priests, and prophets. Etymologies of this kind are widespread in the Middle Ages. See also above, v. 1366.

v. 1509. The name Solomon is probably associated with the Hebrew word *salôm*, which means peace. Solomon was considered to be a peace-maker: 1 Chronicles 22: 9, where Solomon is described as a peace-maker from his very birth: Filius qui nascetur tibi erit vir quietissimus; faciam enim eum requiescere ab omnibus inimicis suis per circuitum; et ab hanc causam Pacificus vocabitur. Such exploiting of etymology is a particular form of the figure *interpretatio*.

v. 1545. The many figures of rhetoric are expounded in detail by Geoffroi de Vinsauf in his *Poetria Nova*, vv. 1094–1229, published by E. Faral, *Les Arts poétiques du XIIᵉ et du XIIIᵉ siècle en France*, pp. 231–5. The symbolic interpretations are made specific and not left to each reader to determine for himself. Geoffroi de Vinsauf expresses the matter succinctly, 'Est autem interpretatio color quando eamdem sententiam per diversas clausulas interpretamur' (*Documentum de Arte versificandi*, ii. 2, 89; Faral, op. cit., p. 277), or again cf. Evrard the German in his *Laborintus*,

Vestio rem verbis variis: non est tenor idem
Verborum, sed quod significatur idem.

(vv. 309–10, published by E. Faral, op. cit., p. 347)

v. 1562. The redness of the steps suggests the blood of martyrdom.

v. 1568. Personification can readily become allegory, a device specifically favoured by the author of this poem: 'Allegorie nos amaine' (v. 114, *supra*).

vv. 1585–6. The rhyme *vaisseaus*: *bels* is acceptable if we assume that the scribe is using the older orthography for *beaus* rather than attempting to produce a phonetic spelling. According to M. K. Pope (op. cit., § 383) all prae-consonantal l- sounds were vocalized to u before the middle of the twelfth century. The graphies *bels* and *beals* are the normal ones in this manuscript, but the apparent clash of rhyme and orthography occurs only in this couplet.

vv. 1587–1600. Richelet, pp. 173–4.

vv. 1591 et ss. The crown of Solomon is the symbol of supreme authority, and for long had been symbolic in this way (see 2 Kings, 11: 12, 'And he brought

COMMENTARY 1

forth the King's son and put the crown upon him'). A secondary symbolism is that the crown was the traditional headdress of Bride and Groom, and the poem develops this theme by likening Solomon to Christ, and the Bride is, of course, the Church, so once more the allusion is to Christ and the Church.

v. 1605. There is no precise statement in the Bible that Solomon bore the face of Christ, though medieval commentaries on Canticum Canticorum often make this point.

v. 1609. *Deus ki tot set* is a proverbial expression. See Morawski, *Proverbes français*, no. 587: *Deus set tot.* The ultimate source is 1 John 3: 20, major est Deus corde nostro, et novit omnia.

v. 1623. *Rubin:* An alternative name for the carbuncle. It is noteworthy for its redness, 'Ruby veint tutes les peres vermeyles de beauté . . . ço est la gemmes des gemmes . . . Ele deit estre mise en bon or' (*Lapidaries*, ed. Studer and Evans, pp. 126–7). *Sardines:* Similarly a red-coloured stone, 'sardine. . . ruge est' (ibid., p. 39, vv. 291–3).

v. 1624. *Grenat:* Another red stone, 'la granate a ruge colur' (ibid., p. 168, v. 369). *Alemandines:* This stone is listed in the lapidaries as *alabandica,* then it is described as follows:

Alemandina est vaillante
Forment chaude et resplendissante
(ibid., p. 210, vv. 189–90)

It resembles the *sardine*

E a sardine si ressembles
Ke por un poinne sont ensemble
(ibid., p. 48, vv. 509–10)

v. 1628. *Topace:* The chilling properties of this stone are vividly described sa

Desboillir fait l'eue boillant
(ibid., p. 41, v. 333)

It is associated in the lapidaries with the emerald:

Topace . . . resemble
. . . esmeralde par vigir
(ibid., p. 82, vv. 323, 329, 330)

Its association with abstinence is thus described in the 'Second Prose Lapidary':

Ele refreidit homme et le rent plus chaste et moins luxurius
(ibid., p. 123, vi, ll. 6–7)

v. 1632. *Esmeraugdes:* the qualities which make this stone appropriate are:

Les oylz salve et l'esgardeüre
E tout tempeste et luxure
(ibid., p. 88, vv. 515–16)

v. 1634. *Perle o margeries:* the link between the Confessors and the pearl is not made in the lapidaries. The attribution of certain qualities to certain gems is given here a specifically mystical interpretation. A series of similar, though different, mystical interpretations is to be found in the *Apocalyptic Lapidary*. See Studer and Evans, op. cit., pp. 260–76.

vv. 1649 et ss. This reference to a source book is too general to permit a precise identification. Nevertheless, the grouping of Prudence, Temperance, Strength, and Justice is reminiscent, for example, of the *Summa de Virtutibus* by Guillielmus Paraldus (see *Brunetto Latini, Livre dou Trésor*, 'Les Ensegnemens des Visces et des Vertus', éd. F. J. Carmody, pp. 224 et ss.). On this subject St. Bernard, Cicero, and Aristotle all made their contribution to what became a traditional medieval grouping of the virtues.

v. 1720. After a digression of some 370 lines—or more than one-tenth of the whole poem—the author returns to the biblical text. The long 'commentary' is situated at the end of Chapter III and before the beginning of Chapter IV of Canticum Canticorum. The work is taken up again and the theme of the lover praising his Bride becomes dominant once more. This rapidly becomes transformed to a description of the Church and the Trinity.

vv. 1721–2. Richelet, p. 174. This passage marks the opening of Chapitre Quatrième in Richelet, and corresponds to the beginning of Chapter 4 of the Song of Songs.

vv. 1735–40. Richelet, p. 174.

vv. 1735–6. The rhyme *valt: haut* raises the same considerations as those presented at vv. 1585–6. See notes thereto.

v. 1750. This etymologizing is another example of *interpretatio*.

v. 1778. The clear sight of the goat is emphasized in the bestiaries, e.g.

> Mult de clere veue sont:
> Quant sont la sus en som le mont,
> Mult veient de loing et halt et cler.
>
> (Guillaume le Clerc, *Bestiaire*, ed. cit., vv.1743–5)

This makes the goat able to see his enemy from afar:

> a l'essample de Deu afert
>
> (ibid., v. 1752)

The comparison with the sinner is not found in Guillaume le Clerc's bestiary, nor in, for example, Brunetto Latini.

vv. 1789–90. This vigorous call to end the digression is a lively formula of transition.

vv. 1793–6. Richelet, pp. 174–5.

v. 1871. The need to be of sufficient spiritual maturity in order to benefit from a reading of this poem is emphasized by this line which compares the use of words by the unskilled to a knife. The author has made a similar point already in vv. 239–40 and returns to the theme in the final lines of the poem.

v. 1910. The copyist has corrected *le roine* to *la roine*. This would suggest that a francien copyist confronted by the north-eastern dialect form of the feminine definite article (*le*) 'corrected' it to *la*.

v. 1915. The comparison of the neck of the Bride with the Tower of David is a warlike image which has puzzled some commentators who find it difficult to reconcile with a love poem. The Old French interpretation is ingenious: the white neck symbolizes the Holy Scripture which unites God with the Church, and the weapons of the tower are used to destroy evil.

vv. 1915–22. Richelet, pp. 175–6.

v. 1959. The meaning of the name of David, who stands for and is our Lord, as being the equivalent of strong in arm or desirable to look upon, both go back to 1 Samuel 16: 12, pulcher aspectu, and St. Jerome, 'iste puer qui interpretatur fortus manu in die qua liberavit eum Dominus de manu Saul', Migne, *Patrologia Latina*, xxiv, col. 607, § 715. The interpretation of the etymologies of Hebrew names was codified by St. Jerome in *Les Liber de nominibus hebraicis*, and later by St. Augustine, but above all by Isidore of Seville in his *etymologiarum libri*. It is doubtless the influence of this latter—the 'basic book of the Entire Middle Ages' (E. R. Curtius, *European Literature and the Latin Middle Ages*, p. 496)—which is most discernible in our text.

vv. 1971–8. Richelet, p. 176.

v. 1980. *puischons*: This form of the present subjunctive of *pouvoir* is typically northern. M. K. Pope, § 1320, § xvi.

v. 1981. In the Bible the breasts are not usually a symbol of fertility, except perhaps in Genesis 49: 25, and even there the symbolism is doubtful. The usual interpretation is literal—suppliers of milk—rather than figurative. Here the allusion to milk for children (*enfants*, v. 1985) is clearly related to the spiritual interpretation of *enfants* which characterizes this text. The two breasts are interpreted as love and pity (v. 2001) whereas Guillaume de Saint Thierry sees them as representing the Old and New Testaments (op. cit., ch. 46, p. 135) which seems to be reflected in v. 2008.

vv. 2019–2164. Richelet, p. 177.

vv. 2024 et ss. 'Who feedeth a flock and eateth not of the milk of the flock?', 1 Corinthians 9: 7. The use of the figure of comparison is referred to by Geoffroi de Vinsauf thus:

> aut aliter, quando res comparo, secum
> Contendunt positae rationes, saepius ex re
> Dissimili similem traho.
>
> (ed. Faral, pp. 235–6, vv. 1253–5)

v. 2041. The reference to the lilies and their comparison with the flowers of the Holy Scripture is possibly echoed also in Hosea 14: 6, where the age of salvation is announced: Ero quasi ros; Israel germinabit sicut lilium, et erumpit radix ejus ut Libani.

vv. 2044, 2051. These two passages are a rendering of a Latin text which in Canticum Canticorum 3: 6 is repeated from 2: 17. When the poet handles this phrase for a second time his interpretation is quite different from that offered on the earlier occasion, vv. 1101 et ss. There is a marked evolution of thought towards a greater knowledge of God.

vv. 2071–4. Richelet, p. 176.

v. 2072. The Old Testament refers to incense only in a liturgical context and doubtless here the allusion in Canticum Canticorum is to the hill of the Temple in Jerusalem. The twelfth-century poet develops the allusion quite differently and sees the myrrh as a prophetic allusion to the New Testament and to the

Passion in particular. The interpretation of incense as a symbol of prayer is made specific in Psalm 140: 2, Dirigatur oratio mea sicut incensum in conspectu tua!

v. 2079. The subject of this sentence is the 'Bride of Christ' named in the previous line. 'When she reflects that he suffered, without having done wrong himself, and entirely for her sake, and that he endured such hard blows and bonds, she considers to be hers the nails which transfixed his feet, and there pierce her heart the nails which fixed his hands: the whole Cross causes great distress in her heart.'

vv. 2139–44. Richelet, pp. 176–7.

v. 2141. This summary of the beauty of the Bride is reinforced by the line

En Toi n'a maile ne putie

which medieval commentators attacked with zeal. Bede saw this as perfection in charity, or love, and later St. Anselm was to stress the view that the *macula* or *maile* referred to *peccatum criminale*. St. Bernard stressed the mystical union between the individual soul and God, and many writers saw in this phrase an allusion to Mary, mother of Christ.

v. 2145. See 1 Epist. John 1: 8, Si dixerimus quoniam peccatum non habemus, ipse nos seducimus, et veritas in nobis non est.

v. 2149. Cf. 1 Epist. John 3: 20, Deus . . . novit omnia, which is reflected in the Old French proverb 'Deus set tut' (Morawski, *Proverbes*, no. 587).

vv. 2159 et ss. The author is not concerned with the geographical details of Lebanon: his interpretation is symbolic. The equation Lebanon = whiteness is inspired by the snows of Lebanon mentioned by Jeremiah 18: 14, Numquid deficiet de petra agri nix Libani?

v. 2201. The pride of the lion and the cruelty of the leopard become almost proverbial from the bestiaries. The characteristics here attributed to them are found also in the Bible where the lion signifies pride, strength, and valour (Proverbs 28: 1, justus autem quasi leo confidens). The leopard, with unchangeable spots (Jeremiah 13: 23), is in Revelation, the symbol of the Antichrist (Revelation 13: 2, Et bestia, quam vidi, similis erat pardo).

v. 2208. These lines echo part of Paul's account of his conversion spoken to Agrippa: Acts 26: 18, ut convertantur . . . de potestate Satanae ad Deum.

v. 2211. The linking of the terms Bride and sister is a way of emphasizing an expression of endearment: no incestuous union is implied. Such a linking was not unusual in Egyptian lyric poetry according to E. Erman, *The Literature of the Ancient Egyptians*, London (1927), pp. 242–51.

vv. 2211–18. Richelet, p. 177.

v. 2217. The allusion to the breasts of the Bride is found in the French text as well as in the Vulgate. The Hebrew text refers more generally to the charms of the Bride.

v. 2225. *cil ki nient ne ment*, cf. qui non mentitur Deus, Epist. ad Titum 1: 2.

v. 2226. The wounds made by love are reminiscent of courtly romance and theories of courtly love, some of which in their turn derive from the writings of Ovid.

v. 2260. The arrows of love similarly recall courtly theories.

v. 2283. The reference to honey on the lips of the Beloved suggests Proverbs 5: 3, Favus enim distillans labia meretricis, et nitidius oleo guttur eius.

COMMENTARY

vv. 2283–90. Richelet, p. 186 (*sic*). At this point there is a fault in the pagination of Richelet which passes directly from p. 175 to p. 186.

v. 2289. The phrase milk and honey recalls the terms used to describe the promised land in the Pentateuch. Here the words symbolize sweet and refreshing speech.

v. 2297. The perfume of the clothing re-echoes Psalm 44: 9, Myrrha et gutta et casia a vestimentis tuis . . .

vv. 2297–8. Richelet, p. 186.

v. 2303. The comparison of the Bride with an enclosed garden suggests protection as well as affirming the right of property.

vv. 2303–22. Richelet, pp. 186–7.

vv. 2315 et ss. The author, curiously enough, does not follow the model of the 'herbiers' and expound at length the symbolism of these various plants.

vv. 2319–20. At this point the French text relies very heavily on the Latin for the names of the various plants of the garden. The forms used are slightly gallicized versions of the Latin. Their English equivalents, according to the Authorized Version, are as follows: 'camphire, with spikenard, spikenard and saffron; calamus and cinnamon, with all trees of frankincense; myrrh and aloes, with all the chief spices' (Song of Songs, 4: 13–14).

vv. 2331–8. Richelet, p. 187.

vv. 2331–7. The image of living waters is not infrequent in the Old Testament, e.g. Leviticus 24: 5–6, 50–2; Numbers 19: 17, etc. The mount of Lebanon suggests the mount on which stands the Temple, and thence the author thinks of this as a source of wisdom, which in turn implies, for him, Christ. A chain of thought of this nature is not unusual in twelfth-century exegesis.

vv. 2345–56. Richelet, pp. 187–8.

v. 2347. The symbolism of the north wind representing adversity and the south wind representing prosperity is extended in a particularly personal way, and the author makes an allusion to his patroness:

cele por cui jo travail (v. 2367)

with whom he has, apparently, frequently discussed this equation of the south wind with the Holy Spirit. The closing lines (2376–8) seem to imply that he has attempted to persuade her to adopt the life of a religious. (See Introduction, p. xx–xxi.)

v. 2383. *l'arbre de sapience*: The tree of knowledge of good and evil (Genesis 2: 9) is called thus as it is the knowledge of good and evil which comes of the eating of its fruit.

v. 2385. *ysope*: Hyssop was a very widely known herb, and it was often used as a means of purification, e.g. Psalm 50: 9, Asperge me hyssop, et mundabor; lavabis me, et super nuvem delababor.

v. 2386. *l'arbre de charité*: This is an expression which is not to be found in the Old Testament: *caritas* is a term which occurs in the New Testament.

vv. 2399–2404. Richelet, p. 188.

vv. 2400 et ss. The fact that the north wind symbolizes evil and the Devil (Nostre Enemis, v. 2405) and the south wind represents the Holy Spirit is not a unique interpretation, though it is fully developed in this text, no doubt from the suggestions in, for example, Jeremiah 6: 1, . . . malum visum est ab aquilone.

et contritio magna, where the north is a source of evil, and Habacuc 3: 3, Deus ab austro veniet, in which the south is seen as the place from which God comes. Thus the symbolism is not merely an extension of the types of climate associated with the north and south winds, but has a literary and Biblical counterpart.

v. 2408. Cf. Isaiah 14: 12–13, Quomodo cecidisti de caelo Lucifer . . . qui dicebas in corde tuo . . . sedebo . . . in lateribus Aquilonis.

vv. 2421–30. Richelet, pp. 188–9.

vv. 2423 et ss. The symbolism of the garden and its enclosure proves particularly attractive and is expounded by the personages in the poem rather than directly by the author. It is the spiritual nature of the garden which is stressed and no naturalist explanation is considered.

vv. 2431–44. Richelet, p. 189. This passage marks the opening of Chapitre Cinquième in Richelet, and corresponds to the beginning of the fifth chapter of the Song of Songs.

v. 2448. myrrh: Associated with aloes in Canticum Canticorum 4: 6 (vide v. 2072) and 4: 14 (vide v. 2315), is used for the·anointing of the body of the crucified Christ (John 19: 40, mixtura myrrhae et aloes).

v. 2452. The spices of this verse also seem to look forward to the same passage in John 19: 40, acceperunt ergo corpus Jesu, et ligaverunt illud cum aromatibus . . .

vv. 2455–6. The sweetness of honey is not simply representative of the love of our Lord: there is here doubtless an allusion to Luke 24: 42, when the risen Christ appears before the disciples who give to him a honeycomb and honey: et illi obtulerunt ei . . . favum mellis.

vv. 2457–62. Wine and milk represent spiritual blessings in, for example, Isaiah, 55: 1, omnes sitientes . . . venite, emite . . . vinum et lac.

vv. 2485–2544. Richelet, pp. 190–2.

v. 2489. This line emphasizes the importance of visions, see above, note to v. 1335.

v. 2492. The use of the terminology of feudal relationships to describe either human or spiritual love is not unusual, and is to be found elaborated in the opening scenes of the Mystère d'Adam, where God says to Eve:

> Moi aim e honor ton creator,
> E moi reconuis a seignor.
>
> (Le Mystère d'Adam, éd. P. Aebischer, vv. 29–30)

vv. 2495 et ss. This is the only passage in the whole poem in which several verses (5: 2–7) of Canticum Canticorum are transcribed as continuous text.

v. 2498. The dew was felt to be a beneficent gift from Heaven, e.g. Deuteronomii 30: 28, caelique colligabant rore.

v. 2510. It is notable that the Old French avoids any erotic interpretation at this point.

v. 2544. This scene is compared with a honeycomb—full of sweet meaning. All the interpretations are didactic: none are erotic. The door at which the Groom knocks symbolizes the ears which hear the word of God, etc.

v. 2619. eswaree is the northern dialectal form: the retention of the sound 'w' is characteristic. M. K. Pope, § 1320, § iii (1).

v. 2621. The darts or arrows of love are usually found in the context of courtly romance. In this case the author uses a normally profane literary image in a religious context.

v. 2631. This phrase, adjuro vos filie Jerusalem (Canticum Canticorum 5: 8), is almost a refrain. It is found also at 2: 7, 3: 5, as well as 8: 4. At vv. 810 et ss. (2: 7) and v. 1245 (3: 5), it is rendered in terms quite different from those used here. The author was clearly avoiding the impression of providing a refrain.

vv. 2631–6. Richelet, p. 192.

v. 2636. The illness which is love is found frequently in courtly romance, where it derives ultimately from Ovid. In this passage the source of the analogy is Canticum Canticorum.

vv. 2637–8. *Jerusalem* depends on *filles*: 'The fact that she calls them daughters of Jerusalem is not new.'

v. 2648. The reference to the Jews recalls the detail that in the Middle Ages the Jews were often criticized for failing to understand the allegorical meanings in the Old Testament.

v. 2649. This question does not follow the preceding discussion so much as it prepares the subsequent description of the Bridegroom.

vv. 2649–68. Richelet, pp. 192–3.

v. 2656. The symbolism of the colouring of the Bridegroom is not expounded in Canticum Canticorum. The lengthy development which is here put forward is characteristic of the parallelism of the Old and New Testaments which is such a feature of twelfth-century thinking.

vv. 2659–60. 'Others have virtues, but bestowed by his hand: he has them without their having been given from without.'

vv. 2713–14. These two lines are a repetition of vv. 2655–6 and 2683–4. They mark not only a refrain, but a wholly abstract interpretation of the colour symbolism. As a repeated leitmotiv, they occur anew at vv. 2719–20.

v. 2718. The lion, king of beasts, was also equated with Christ in some of the bestiaries, but such a symbolism no doubt stems from Apocalypse 5: 5, ecce vicit leo de tribu Juda, radix David, aperire librum, et solvere septem signacula ejus.

v. 2739. The dragon of the vision is that of the Apocalypse (chs. 12 and 20) and is the Devil.

v. 2741. The strange metaphor that the head of the Bridegroom is of pure gold has presented difficulty to Old Testament critics. The Old French poet ingeniously suggests that we are in the presence of a description of divine wisdom.

vv. 2743–5. Richelet, p. 193.

v. 2755. *Ceste* refers back to divine sapience (vv. 2747 and 2751): 'The head is divine wisdom'.

v. 2765. Again the suggestion that the hair of the Bridegroom is like the fronds of the palm is a puzzling image, but once more the poet convincingly makes this suggest Christ's victory over the powers of darkness and death.

vv. 2817–18 repeat word for word vv. 2795–6 and introduce a further interpretation of the meaning and symbolism of the hair of the beloved.

vv. 2851–4. Richelet, pp. 193–4.

v. 2854. The eyes of the Bride have earlier been likened to doves (1: 14, v. 568 and 4: 1, v. 1733). This elaborate exposition of the eyes of the Bridegroom is a fine example of the twelfth-century extraction of every possible element of value from a text.

v. 2901. In the Bible, the dove plays a threefold important role: the dove which brought back the olive branch to Noah (Genesis 8: 11), the dove of the Psalms (54: 6), and the Spirit of God descended in the form of a dove (Matthew 3: 16; Mark 1: 10; Luke 3: 22; John 1: 32).

v. 2925: *ki* is the generalizing relative: 'whoever is so proud is not a dove, he is rather a hawk or a sparrow-hawk'.

v. 2957. The reference is not to Judas Iscariot, but to Judas, son of Jacob (Genesis 49: 11, Lavabit in vino stolam suam).

v. 2989. In giving his source as Isaiah, the author is mistaken: the reference is to Zechariah 3: 9, Quia ecce lapis quem dedi coram Jesu: super lapidem unum septem oculi sunt. That the author intended to write Ysaies is confirmed by vv. 3022–3 and 3081. F. Ohly (op. cit., p. 286), followed by H. R. Jauss (*Grundriss*, vi, 2, p. 211), refers, but without precision, to Isaiah.

v. 2994. The likening of Christ to a stone is expounded in the First Epistle of Peter.

v. 2997. The seven 'graces', corresponding to the seven eyes, are carefully listed, with marginal indications in Latin, as follows:

(1) spiritus timoris (v. 2997)
(2) spiritus pietatis (v. 2999)
(3) spiritus scientie (v. 3005)
(4) spiritus fortitudinis (v. 3025)
(5) spiritus consilii (v. 3033)
(6) spiritus intellectus (v. 3038)

A seventh is not in fact listed in the margin but it is the *esperit de sapience*, v. 3059.

v. 3001. Peter's threefold denial of Christ is told in Matthew 26, Mark 14, Luke 22, and John 18.

vv. 3005 et ss. The sacrifices made by Cain and Abel are related in Genesis 4. This narrative was dramatized superbly in *Le Jeu d'Adam*, an Anglo-Norman play, probably of the twelfth century.

v. 3012. The incident of the widow's two mites cast into the temple treasury is related in Mark 12: 43 and Luke 21: 2, 3. In the twelfth-centuy French text the money is described by contemporary names, marks, pounds sterling, and farthings. The Latin Vulgate describes the coins as 'aera minuta' or 'duo minuta, quod est quadrans'.

vv. 3027 et ss. For the incident of Pharaoh's attempt to cross the Red Sea, see Exodus 14.

v. 3033. The narrative of the man who asked Christ how to inherit eternal life is recounted in Matthew 19: 16 et ss., Mark 10: 17 et ss., and Luke 10: 25, but it is only in the version of Matthew that the questioner is described as a young man (*adolescens*).

vv. 3041 et ss. These lines are an adaptation of the first Beatitudes—Matthew 5: 2–5.

vv. 3093, 3099, 3103. After a long digression, based on the vision of Zechariah, the poet returns to Canticum Canticorum 5: 12, at the point he had already reached above, v. 2851.

v. 3104. The prophetic nature of the work is specifically emphasized at this point.

v. 3111. Although the meaning of this verse of Canticum Canticorum is allegorical rather than literal, the interpretation here offered that the cheeks represent the dual nature of Christ, human and divine, is not to be found in the biblical commentators.

vv. 3111–16. Richelet, p. 194.

v. 3137. This is a clear allusion to the Last Supper. The nature of the Mass, and the mystery of transubstantiation, was much debated by theologians during the latter half of the twelfth century. The doctrine is also discussed in secular works such as Robert de Boron's *Roman de l'Estoire dou Graal* and the *Queste del Saint Graal.*

v. 3159. An alternative explanation that the two cheeks represent humility and patience is introduced by the oft-repeated sentiment that the power of exposition is God-given. Cf. Marie de France, *Les Lais*, Prologue, vv. 1–4:

> Ki Deu ad duné escïence
> E de parler bone eloquence
> Ne s'en deit taisir ne celer,
> Ainz se deit voluntiers mustrer

The theme becomes a commonplace in medieval literature, and it owes its origin no doubt to the parable of the talents (Matthew, 25: 14–32), and even earlier to Ecclesiasticus, 20: 32, and especially Proverbs, 5: 16, Deriventur fontes tui foras; et in plateis aquas tuas divide.

v. 3213. The author carefully expounds, in yet a different way, the symbolism of the cheeks, which are now said to represent the Churches founded by Christ and his Apostles.

v. 3235. The lily is, in the Bible, used as a symbol of purity and innocence. Curiously enough, the flower is named principally in Canticum Canticorum and elsewhere in the New Testament in Matthew 6: 28 and Luke 12: 27 ('consider the lilies of the field'). The elaboration of the symbolism of the lily is for the most part medieval.

vv. 3235–6. Richelet, p. 194.

vv. 3252 et ss. The three cases of Christ's raising people from the dead are (i) the daughter of the ruler (Matthew 9: 18 et ss., Mark 5: 22, Luke 8: 41), (ii) the dead son of the widow of Nain (Luke 7: 12 et ss.), and (iii) Lazarus, raised from the tomb (John 11).

vv. 3265 et ss. This is an adaptation of Matthew 5: 27 et ss.

v. 3275. The likening of the two lips to the two Testaments is quite in keeping with the twelfth-century parallelism of the Old and New Testaments.

v. 3296. This point that Christ's body did not experience corruption is based on Acts 2: 31, neque caro ejus vidit corruptionem.

v. 3305. In the New Testament nothing is stated about the latter years of Mary's life, nor even when or where she died. Apocryphal writings, especially the fifth-century *Transitus Mariae*, provide the starting-point for the widely developed cult of Mary. It became an article of faith to believe that her body was taken up into heaven: the author clearly emphasizes the apocryphal nature of these beliefs in v. 3310, but he believes that this is at the same time a divinely revealed truth. Curiously enough, it was as recently as 1950 that Pope Pius XII gave the stamp of authenticity to what Catholics had believed for centuries.

vv. 3321 et ss. The development of the symbolism of the lily is an interesting mixture of biblical and later influences. The seven seeds represent the seven Graces of the Holy Spirit, described above (vv. 2997 et ss.), but the six petals have a perfection of form which is not so much spiritual as mathematical. The account of the perfect 'roundness' of the number six which is developped in vv. 3347 et ss. is very close to the account given by Isidore of Seville. In the third book of his *Etymologies*, which is entitled *De quatuor disciplinis mathematicis*, Chapter V, 'De prima divisione parium et imparium', there is a definition and example of the perfect number:

> 'Perfectus numerus est qui suis partibus adempletur, ut senarius, habet enim tres partes, sextam, tertiam et dimidiam; sexta enim ejus est unum, tertia duo, dimidia tres. Hae partes in summam duetae; id est unum, et duo, et tria, simul eumdem consummant perficuntque senarium. Sunt autem perfecti numeri intra denarium VI, intra centarum XXVIII, intra millenarium CCCCXCVI.'

> (Migne, *Patrologia Latina*, Tome 82, cols. 157–8)

It is noteworthy that the perfect numbers are so few.

v. 3385. Myrrh was used by Joseph of Arimathea to anoint the body of Christ (John 19: 39).

v. 3399. The interpretation of the hands of the Bridegroom is once more expressed in terms of the New Testament.

vv. 3399–3400. Richelet, p. 194.

v. 3433. The lapidaries suggest that the setting of the jacinth should be of gold, e.g.

> Jagunces sunt mot riches peres,
>
> .    .    .    .    .    .
>
> En or se provent sans argent.
>
> (Verse adaptation, ed. Studer and Evans, *Anglo-Norman Lapidaries*, p. 83, vv. 361–80)

The stone has the power of edifying and protecting the wearer.

v. 3439. This reference to another leaf could either suggest the written source from which he was working, or it could be a literary *trompe l'œil*.

v. 3451. The parable of the widow who lost, and later recovered, her piece of silver is related in Luke 15: 8, where the coin is described as a *drachma*.

v. 3466. The abundance of material for commentary, to which the author alludes, may well be in written form, for in lines 3439–40 above he states that an alternative explanation is to be found on another leaf. Also in v. 3494 he refers to his reading.

v. 3468. To lend money at interest (usury) was considered to be sinful throughout the Middle Ages.

v. 3491. In view of the references in the immediately preceding lines to works of piety and to miracles, the St. Gregory here mentioned could be one of several saints of that name. Since one of these saints wrote on the Song of Songs, it is almost certainly to Pope Gregory that our author alludes. The *Excerpta ex libris Sancti Gregorii Papae super Cantica Canticorum* were edited by J. P. Migne in *Patrologia Latina*, vol. clxxx, pp. 441–74. On the other hand the hagiographical writings of Gregory of Tours were always popular in France, and the write may have had this Gregory in mind.

The adaptation of Canticum Canticorum ends at this point, which is not the end of a chapter, nor even of a section or verse, of the biblical text. As the commentary lengthens, and as the range of possible interpretations widens, so the author of the poem deems it wise to bring his romance to a close.

v. 3492. St. Winwalois, or, as he is more often known, especially in Brittany, St. Guenolé, is a relatively minor figure. For the light which this reference to a little-known saint may throw on the authorship of the work, see Introduction, pp. xix–xx, and *Histoire Littéraire de la France, III* (1829), pp. 183–5.

vv. 3495–3506. Richelet transcribes this passage in his three-page Introduction to the French text (pp. 148–9) where he describes it as 'une espèce d'épilogue' without making any further observations about it.

v. 3497. The name of the patron for whom the poet is writing is nowhere mentioned in the unique manuscript. On this passage see Introduction, pp. xx et ss.

v. 3501. The difficulties of literary composition are stressed in prologues and epilogues. Chrétien de Troyes observes at the beginning of his *Lancelot*:

> Comance Crestïens son livre;
> . . . et il s'antremet
> de panser, que gueres n'i met
> fors sa painne et s'antancïon.
>
> (Chrétien de Troyes, *Lancelot*, ed. M. Roques, vv. 25–9; Paris, 1958, *Cfmâ*, No. 86).

v. 3507. This short version of the *Fabliau de vilain Asnier* follows the text without a break. It perhaps suggests the refreshing qualities inherent in an edifying work. The placing of comic anecdotes in the context of a pious work is not unusual. In its longer version this *fabliau* is found in MS. B.N. fr. 19152, a volume which contains not only *fabliaux*, but also romances of chivalry and pious works. Carefully prepared anthologies of this kind were a feature of medieval libraries. See T. B. W. Reid, *Twelve Fabliaux*, Manchester University Press, 1958, pp. 1–2, and E. Faral, *Le Manuscrit 19152 du fonds français de la Bibliothèque Nationale*, Paris, 1934, ff. 56a–56c. H. R. Jauss sees in this short version of the *fabliau* a comment on the understanding of texts of an allegorical nature. This possibility is reinforced by the fact that the presentation of the Divine Word to men is illustrated in the poem by the idea of *odeur* (vv. 168, 171, 256, 257, 505, 507, 551, 620, 707, 725, 774, 997, 1297, 1304, 1310, 1852, 1913, 2299, 2303, 2316, 2229, 3203) to which is often coupled the idea of *especies* and *especiaire* (vv. 2326, 2334, 2329, 2331, 2334, 2437, 3115, 3117, 3155, 3207, 3231, 3210, 3513). It is clear that this interpretation is well developed in the last part of the poem. No doubt either the poet, or the scribe, and it is impossible to decide which, regarded this *fabliau* as an *exemplum* which would summarize one aspect of the Song of Songs, and in particular vv. 1851–2 of the French poem.

# BIBLIOGRAPHY

## (a) Edition

RICHELET, Charles, *Le Cantique des Cantiques attribué à Salomon, traduit de l'Hébreu; accompagné d'une version latine littérale, suivi de notes et d'une traduction en vers du XIII<sup>e</sup> siècle*, Paris (Techener), 1843, 1 vol., xx+200 (*sic*) pp. (The pagination is faulty, numbers 176–85 inclusive are omitted.) Pp. 150–94 contain a transcription of long extracts from the poem contained in MS. Le Mans, Bible. mun. 173. A *Glossaire* of Old French words is on pp. 195–200. The extracts chosen by Richelet are for the most part those passages which correspond most closely to the Latin Vulgate. He consistently suppresses all the commentaries, whether they be allegorical or not, and all the interventions of the author of the French poem are eliminated. The reader is not fully aware of the extent of the suppressions for the lines are not numbered. Missing passages are indicated by dots, and instead of the last 104 lines of the poem are the words *alia desunt*. In the Commentary we give a full list of the passages which are transcribed by Richelet, together with the indication of the pages of his edition on which they are to be found.

## (b) Critical Works

BERGER, Samuel, *La Bible Française au Moyen Âge, étude sur les plus anciennes versions de la Bible écrites en prose de langue d'oïl*, Paris (Champion), 1884, 1 vol., xvi+450 pp. [Reprinted Geneva (Slatkine), 1967.]

BERNARD (Saint), *On the Song of Songs, Sermones in Cantica Canticorum*, translated and edited by a Religious of C.S.M.V., with an Introduction and Notes, London (Mowbray), 1952, 1 vol., 272 pp.

Biblia Sacra, *Vulgatae Editionis Sixti V Pontificis Maximi jussu recognita et Clementis VIII auctoritate edita, Nova editio accuratissime emendata*, Paris (Garnier), 1922, 1 vol., xxviii+1376 pp.

BONNARD, Jean, *Les Traductions de la Bible en vers français au Moyen Âge*, Paris (Champion), 1885, 1 vol., pp. ii+243. [Reprinted Geneva (Slatkine), 1967.]

CAPELLANUS, Andreas, *The Art of Courtly Love, with Introduction, Translation and Notes* by John Jay Parry, New York (Columbia University Press), 1941 (*Records of Civilisation*), 1 vol., xi–218 pp. [Reprinted New York (Ungar), 1959, 1964.]

CURTIUS, Ernst Robert, *European Literature and the Latin Middle Ages*, translated from the German by Willard R. Trask, London (Routledge and Kegan Paul), 1953, 1 vol., xv+662 pp.

DAVY, M.-M., *Théologie et Mystique de Guillaume de Saint-Thierry, I, La Connaissance de Dieu*, Paris (Vrin), 1954, 1 vol., xiii+431 pp.

DROUART DE LA VACHE, *Li Livres d'amours, publié d'aprés le manuscrit unique de l'Arsenal* par R. BOSSUAT, Paris, 1926, 1 vol.

GILSON, Étienne, 'La mystique de la grâce dans la *Queste del Saint Graal'* in *Romania*, Tome li (1925), pp. 321–47.

JAUSS, Hans Robert, *Grundriss der Romanischen Literaturen des Mittelalters. Volume VI. La Littérature didactique, allégorique et satirique*, Heidelberg (Carl Winter), 2 vols., 1968, 1970, xvi+315; 496 pp. Tome 1 (*Partie historique*), pp. 52, 154–5; Tome 2 (*Partie documentaire*), pp. 210–11, No. 4116.

—— 'La transformation de la forme allégorique entre 1180 et 1240: d'Alain de Lille à Guillaume de Lorris' in *Humanisme Médiéval*, publié par Anthime Fourrier, Paris (Klincksieck), 1964, pp. 105–46.

LOT-BORODINE, Myrrha, *De l'amour profane à l'amour sacré, études de psychologie sentimentale du Moyen Âge*, Paris (Nizet), 1961, 1 vol., xii+191 pp.

OHLY, F., *Hohelied Studien, Grundzüge einer Geschichte der Hohenlied-Auslegung des Abendlandes bis um 1200*, Wiesbaden, 1958, 1 vol., esp. pp. 40–1, 107, 151, 155, 280–302, 307–8, 314.

POPE, M. K., *From Latin to Modern French with an especial consideration of Anglo-Norman, Phonology and Morphology*, Manchester (University Press), 1934, 1 vol., xxix+571 pp. (Publications of Manchester University, No. CCXXIX, French Series No. 6).

POUGET, G., and GUITTON, J., *Le Cantique des Cantiques, nouvelle édition*, Paris (Gabalda), 1948, 1 vol., 187 pp. (*Études Bibliques*).

*Queste del Saint Graal, La*, Roman du XIIIᵉ siècle édité par Albert PAUPHILET, Paris (Champion), 1923, 1 vol. (*Les Classiques français du Moyen Âge*, No. 33).

RENAN, Ernest, *Le Cantique des Cantiques, traduit de l'hébreu avec une étude sur le plan, l'âge et le caractère du poème*, Paris (Michel Lévy), 1860, 1 vol., xiv+212 pp.

ROBERT, A., P.S.S., et TOURNAY, R., O.P., avec le concours de A. FEUILLET, P.S.S., *Le Cantique des Cantiques, traduction et commentaire*, Paris (Gabalda), 1963, 1 vol., 465 pp. (*Études Bibliques*).

ROWLEY, H. H., *The Servant of the Lord and Other Essays on the Old Testament*, London (Lutterworth Press), 1952, 1 vol., xii+327 pp. Chapter 6, 'The Interpretation of the *Song of Songs*', pp. 187–234. First published in the *Journal of Theological Studies*, xxxviii, Oxford, 1937, pp. 337–63; now embodying material published also in the *Journal of the Royal Asiatic Society*, London, 1938, pp. 251–76.

SAINT-THIERRY, Guillaume de, *Exposé sur le Cantique des Cantiques, texte latin*, introduction et notes de J.-M. DECHANET, O.S.B., traduction française de M. DUMONTIER, O.C.S.O. Paris (Éditions du Cerf), 1962, 1 vol., 418 pp. (*Sources Chrétiennes, Nº 82, Série des Textes Monastiques d'Occident, Nº VIII*).

SMALLEY, Beryl, *The Study of the Bible in the Middle Ages*, Oxford (Blackwell), 1 vol., xxii+406 pp. 2nd edition, 1952.

# INDEX OF NAMES

References are to the lines of the poem: personal names are in SMALL CAPITALS, place names are *italicized*.

ABEL; Abel, brother of Cain and son of Adam, the first man, 589, 3005, 3007.
ALLEGORIE; Personification of Allegory, 114.
APOSTLE, APOSTLES, APOSTOILE; apostle, of the twelve apostles, 1615, 3221; 1412, 2026, 2937; 993.
Auster; the south wind, 2350, 2351, 2358, 2401, 2411.
*Betel*; Mount Bethel, 1138, 1155.
CAYM; Cain, brother of Abel and son of Adam, the first man, 3008.
CONFESSOR; the Confessors, 1633.
CRIST, CRIZ; Jesus Christ, 23, 196, 215, 530, 1366, 1506, 1606, 1652, 2078, 2249, 2343, 2774, 2794, 2800, 2859, 2993, 3188, 3215, 3238, 3314, 3372; 2741, 2819, 3121, 3162, 3194, 3403, 3441.
Croiz; the Cross on which Christ was crucified, 879, 883, 2085.
DAME; the Lady, or Bride, in the Song of Songs, 53, 83, 1503, 1856, 3452.
DAMOISELE; the Lady, or Bride, in the Song of Songs, 35, 209, 1233, 1323, 2173, 2876, 2431.
DAVID; King David, 1915, 1953, 1955.
DEABLES; the Devil, 876.
DEU; God (oblique case), 90, 97, 105, 269, 295, 343, 428, 512, 542, 589, 649, 697, 749, 759, 779, 785, 1155, 1157, 1168, 1184, 1206, 1210, 1284, 1304, 1324, 1425, 1438, 1547, 1622, 1681, 1785, 1816, 1824, 1935, 2058, 2175, 2175, 2228, 2360, 2449, 2473, 2631, 2765, 2877, 2912, 3038, 3095, 3125, 3151, 3344, 3378, 3467, 3481, 3495, 3500.
DEUS; God (nominative case), 10, 93, 111, 121, 179, 183, 264, 334, 489, 765, 767, 960, 1157, 1158, 1249, 1273, 1398, 1411, 1609, 1615, 1627, 1875, 1884, 1981, 1984, 2157, 2227, 2246, 2259, 2287, 2291, 2364, 2419, 2548, 2721, 2733, 2734, 2750, 2855, 2873, 2894, 2988,

2995, 3000, 3006, 3016, 3017, 3026, 3039, 3055, 3060, 3084, 3105, 3117, 3121, 3139, 3141, 3149, 3160, 3168, 3193, 3234, 3251, 3285, 3373, 3375, 3379, 3409, 3463, 3469, 3487.
DEX; God (nominative case), 520, 540, 654, 747, 1362, 2365.
DIABLE, DIABLES; the Devil, 1430, 2829; 1069.
DOMOISELE; the Bride, 1083.
Dragme; drachma (coin), 3451.
Eglise; the Church, 27, 116, 716, 797, 1515, 1551, 1809, 1935, 2454, 2897.
*Egypte*; Egypt, 422.
ENEMIS; the Devil, 2405.
Escriture, Escritures; Holy Scripture, 45, 178, 1546, 1606, 1801, 2008, 2043, 2618, 2927, 3282; 1640, 2056, 2944.
ESPERIT; the Holy Spirit, 2372, 2413, 2991, 3328.
ESPEUSES, ESPOSE, ESPOSSE; the Bride, 1631; 1990; 1598.
*Espurgatories*; Purgatory, 3395.
*Galaad*; Mount Gilead, 1739, 1745, 1747.
*Galilee*; Galilee, 2688.
Glise; the Church, 987, 1504, 3319.
GREGORIES; St. Gregory, 3491.
HEBRIUE; the Hebrew people, 1636.
HERODE, HERODES; King Herod, 2689; 2695.
Iglise, Iglises; the Church, 1219; 1055, 1057, 3217.
Incarnacion; the Incarnation of Christ, 3104.
JEROMES; St. Jerome, 477.
*Jerusalem*; Jerusalem ,313, 811, 825, 1578 , 2638.
JESU, JHESU, JHESUS; Jesus Christ, 2249, 2741, 3415; 530, 1506, 1652, 2343, 2613, 2774, 2794, 2895, 3188, 3215, 3238, 3294, 3372, 3428; 1696, 1757, 2128.
JOHANS; St. John the Evangelist, 2145.
*Jordain*; the River Jordan, 872.

JUDAS; Judas, son of Jacob, 2957.
JUIUS; the Jews, 1513, 2648, 2686.
*Liban, Libans*; Mount Lebanon, 1471, 2159, 2160, 2321, 2338, 2343; 1519, 2169.
MARIE; Our Lady, the Virgin Mary, 1758, 2819, 3304.
*Mer Roge*; the Red Sea, 3027.
*Paradis*; Paradise, 721, 2314.
Passion, Passions; the Passion of Our Lord, 535, 881, 1763, 1843; 386, 2814.
PATRIARCHE; the Patriarchs, 3209.
PEIRRES; Saints, 2559.
PHARAON; Pharaoh, 423, 3026.
PIERRON; St. Peter, 3001.
PILATE; Pilate, 2687, 2701.
POLS; St. Paul, 192.
Pome; the Forbidden Fruit, 89, 91.
PROPHETE; the Prophets, 3209.
Redempcion, Redempcions; the Redemption, 536, 882, 1764, 3398; 2798.
Revelacion; the Revelation, 3311.
ROI; the King, Bridegroom, or Christ, 51, 275, 1477, 1594, 1636, 1752, 1831, 2378, 2689, 2691, 2694, 3220.
ROINE; the Queen or Bride, 1716, 1910.
ROIS; the King, Bridegroom, or Christ, 265, 501, 555, 645, 680, 739, 803, 808, 1125, 1233, 1288, 1349, 1463, 1493, 1505, 1509, 1537, 1543, 1596, 1704, 1715, 1791, 1825, 1853, 1902, 1907, 1955, 1969, 2139, 2174, 2204, 2211, 2282, 2379, 2400, 2400, 2431, 2467, 2563, 2685, 2694, 2708, 3171.

SALEMON, SALEMONS; Solomon, 1594; 9, 1349, 1365, 1509, 1605.
SATHANAS; Satan, 2209.
SEIGNEURS, SEIGNOR, SEIGNORS; Our Lord, 2698, 2986; 1172, 1420, 1460, 1517, 2102, 2181, 2238, 2277, 2456, 2645, 3035, 3169, 3264; 173.
*Sepulcre*; the Burial place of Our Lady, 3305, 3307.
SIRE; Our Lord, 30, 187, 1066, 1300, 1392, 1559, 1610, 2060, 2134, 2149, 2224, 2462, 2549, 2604, 2741, 2894, 2988, 3048, 3067, 3121.
SIRE; the Bridegroom, 211, 225, 577, 609, 709, 744, 1042, 1115, 1125, 1148, 1159, 1162, 1539, 1990, 2527, 2644.
SIRE; King David, 1955.
SIRES; Our Lord, 873.
SIRES; the Bridegroom, 393.
Surrection; the Resurrection, 545.
*Syon*; Zion, 1592.
*Temple*; the Temple in Jerusalem, 3013.
Testament; the New Testament, 184.
Testament; the Two Testaments, 3275, 3285, 3310.
TRINITEZ; the Trinity, 1755.
UNITÉ, UNITEZ; the Three in One, 1059, 1756; 3356.
VIRGNE; Our Lady, Saint Mary, 1643, 1703, 1758, 2810, 3304.
WINWALOIS; St. Guenolé or Winwalois (see notes), 3492.
YSAIAS, YSAIE, YSAIES; the Prophet Isaiah, 2989; 3022; 3023, 3081.

# GLOSSARY

The Glossary contains those words which are no longer current in modern French, or whose modern equivalents differ in either form or meaning from their twelfth-century counterparts. Words are listed in alphabetical order: the only occasional departures from this order are in the case of verbs whose forms are given alphabetically with cross-reference to the infinitive. Usually the first two line references are given for each form and meaning. The abbreviations used include: *sf.* feminine noun; *sm.* masculine noun; *adj.* adjective; *adv.* adverb; *conj.* conjunction; *prep.* preposition; *num.* numeral; *vb.* verb; *pr.* present; *pft.* perfect (preterite, past definite); *fut.* future; *imper.* imperative; *impf.* imperfect; *cond.* conditional; *subj. part.* subjunctive; *past* past participle; *pres. part.* present participle. The persons of the verb are numbered from one to six.

ABANDON, *sm.* A ABANDON, generously, without reserve, 3336.

ABEVREE, *past part.*, ABOIVRE, to give to drink, 740.

ABUISSEMENT, *sm.* stumbling-block, 1870.

ABUNDE, *pr.* 3, ABUNDER, *vb.* abound, 1660, 2340.

ACLIN, ACLINE, ACLINS, *adj.* submitted to, 182; 107; 1754.

ACOISONS, *sf.* opportunity, 2409.

ACONTE, *pr.* 3, ACONTER, *vb.* tell, relate, 3492.

ACONTES, *sm.* account, description, 3363.

ACORANT, *pres. part.*, ACORIR, *vb.* run, 2338.

ACOSTER, *vb.* used as *sm.* approach, be close to, 384.

ACOTA, *pft.* 3, ACOTES, *pr.* 2, ACOTER, be by the side of, 501; 594.

ACRAVENTER, *vb.* crush, destroy, 2974.

ACRUI, *sm.* hardening, hardness, 661.

ADÉS, *adv.* instantly, with interruption, 1682, 1739.

ADEVICIEZ, *past part.*, ADEVICIER, *vb.* separate from, divide from, 2580.

ADRESCE, *pr.* 3, ADRESCER, *vb.* rule, govern, 279, 3171.

AEGUENT, *pr.* 6, AEGUER, *vb.* become equal to, ressemble, 1787.

AEMPLIR, *vb.* accomplish, 1112.

AERT, *pr.* 3, AERDRE, *vb.* clasp, grip, adhere to, 153.

AESMER, *vb.* estimate, evaluate, 3458.

AFEET, *sm.*, AFFECTE, *sf.* qualities, characteristics, 433; 1652.

AFICHENT, *pr.* 6, AFICHIER, *vb.* affirm, 254.

AFOLE, *pr.* 5, AFOLER, *vb.* trip, crush, 1526, 1868.

AGREVER, *vb.* weigh down, burden, 2916.

AGRIECE, *sf.* misfortune, 1246.

AGUES, *adj. f. pl.* sharp, pointed, 1946.

AHAN, *sm.* suffering, 3225.

AIDEUR, *sm.* helper, 1113.

AIGNEALS, *sm.* lamb, 383.

AIGUE, AIGUES, *sf.* water, 2523, 2854.

AIM, *pr.* 1, AMER, *vb.* love, 132, 135, 408, 762.

AINÇ, *adv.* ever, with NE, never, 95, 103, 502.

AINS, AINZ, *conj.* but, rather, 254, 1232; AINS KE, before, 1206.

AIQUE, AIQUES, *sf.* water, 2336; 2852.

AIRE, AIRES, *sf.* place, area, 3154; 3227.

AIRETES, *sf.* dim. of AIRE, (flower) bed, 3227.

AIUE, *sf.* help, aid, 2571.

AIUT, *pr. subj.* 3, AIDIER, *vb.* help, aid, 2988.

AIVE, *sf.* water, 1265.

AJUR, *pr.* 1, AJURÉ, *past part.*, AJURER, *vb.* beseech, make to swear on oath, 1244; 1257.

AL, *prep.*, A and LE, 3, 78, etc.
ALCON, *pron.* and *adj.* any, 2104.
ALEGIER, *vb.* make light, 2964.
ALEMANDINES, *sm.* a precious stone, see commentary, 1624.
ALETTIES, *past part.*, ALETTIER, *vb.* suckle, nurse, 191.
ALIVE, *pr.* 3, ALEVER, *vb.* raise up, 1531.
ALKES, *adv.* somewhat, 125, 912.
ALMOSNE, *sf.* alms, 1583.
ALMOSNIER, *sm.*, alms-giver, 3467.
ALO, ALOE, ALOEIN, *sm.* aloes, 2320; 2362; 2354.
ALOSÉ, *past part.*, ALOSER, *vb.* praise, 362.
ALQUANTES, *pron.* some, 3206.
ALQUES, *adv.* somewhat, 1980.
ALS, *pron.* them, 575.
ALTER, *sm.* altar, 1053.
ALTRE, *pron.* and *adj.* other, 33, 447.
ALTREMENT, *adv.* otherwise, 5, 67.
ALTRESI, ALTRETANT, *adv.* in just the same way, 2154; 1414.
ALTRUI, *pron.* another, 319, 484.
AMAINE, *pr.* 3, AMENER, *vb.* lead towards, bring, 114, 416.
AMBESDEUS, *pron.* both, 2217.
AMER, *vb.* love, 236, 240, 243.
AMESUREE, *past part.*, AMESURER, *vb.* measure, 1572.
AMEZ, *past part.*, AMER, *vb.* love, 747, 760.
AMINE, *pr.* 3, AMENER, *vb.* bring, lead towards, 2558.
AMOLZ, *pr.* 3, AMOLOIER, be gentle, 1847.
AMONESTEZ, *past part.*, AMONESTER, *vb.* advise, counsel, admonish, 2652.
AN, *prep.* in, on, 879, 1446.
AN, *sm.* year, 2322.
ANCESSOR, *sm.* ancestor, 785.
ANCHOIS, *adv.* before, 3028.
ANÇOIS KE, *conj.* before, 1374.
ANEME, *sf.* soul, 2525, 2767.
ANGELE, ANGELES, ANGLES, *sm.* angel, 1280; 1080; 1305.
ANGOISE, *pr.* 3, ANGOISSIER, *vb.* torment, 19.
ANME, *sf.* soul, 2256.
ANNUI, *sm.* vexation, 662, 1094.
ANTANT, *pr.* 3, ANTANDRE, *vb.* hear, 1233.
AORNEE, AORNEES, *past part.*, AORNEER, *vb.* adorn, 495; 565; 490, 3400.
AOVERS, *past part.*, AOVRIR, *vb.* open, 3343.
APAIE, *pr.* 3, APAIER, appease, 1873.
APAREIL, *sm.* preparation, equipment, 471, 605.

APAREILLE, *pr.* 3, APAREILLIER, *vb.* make ready, prepare, equip, 1373, 2921.
APAROLE, *pr.* 3, APARLER, *vb.* address, speak to, 1042.
APARRA, *fut.* 3, APAROIR, appear, 2403.
APENT, *pr.* 3, APENDRE, *vb.* to be related to, 2000.
APARENT, *pr.* 6, APERT, *pr.* 3, APAROIR, *vb.* appear, 959; 444.
APERT, *adj.*, EN APERT, *adv.* clearly, 876.
APERTE, *adj.* evident, manifest, 2266.
APERTEMENT, *adv.* clearly, manifestly, 3290.
APOIER, *vb.* support, 789.
APOSTOLE, APOSTOILE, *sm.* apostle (usually, though not here, pope), 1615; 993.
APOTEKE, *sm.* apothecary, healer, 2979.
APPAREILLEMENT, *sm.* ornament, decoration, 1476.
APRESTE, *pr.* 3, APRESTEE, *past part.*, APRESTER, *vb.* make ready, prepare, 50; 1354, ARDANT, *pres. part.*, ARDE, *pr.* 3, ARDOIR, *vb.* burn, 210; 918; 1321.
ARMARIE, *sf.* press, cupboard, 2291.
ARME, *sf.* soul, 1803.
AROISONER, *vb.* address, speak to, instruct, 2602.
ART, *pr.* 3, ARDOIR, *vb.* burn, 18, 1292.
ART, *sm.* art, skill, 3086.
ARTIFIERE, *sm.* artisan, 1347.
AS, *prep.*, A and LES, to the, 185, 292.
AS, *pr.* 2, AVOIR, *vb.* have, 439, 443.
ASEMBLER, *vb.* bring together, 109.
ASOAGE, *pr.* 3, ASOAGIER, soothe, comfort, 217.
ASPRES, *adj.* harsh, 948, 2193.
ASPRETÉS, *sf.* harshness, 1523.
ASSALT, *sm.* attack, 1919, 1939.
ASSEIZ, *adv.* much, a great deal, sufficient, 3184, 3491.
ASSEZ, *adv.* much, a great deal, sufficient, enough, 537, 2529.
ASSIDUEL, *adj.* assiduous, continual, 2195.
ASSIGNEE, *past part.*, ASSIGNER, *vb.* assign to, 1590.
ASTER, *sm.* the south wind, 2372.
ASUAGEMENT, *sm.* soothing, healing, comfort, 2715.
ATALENTENT, *pr.* 6, ATALENTER, *vb.* please, give desire to, 2215.
ATANS, ATANT, *adv.* then, at that time, 2555; 1969.
ATEMPRANCE, *sf.* moderation, 1659, 1667, 1669, 1671.

ATEMPRÉ, ATEMPREE, *past part.*, ATEMPRER, *vb.* temper, put in accord with, 468; 286, 1668.

ATOCHE, *pr.* 3, ATOCHIER, *vb.* touch, 78, 730.

ATORNEE, *past part.*, ATORNER, *vb.* make ready, prepare, 566.

ATRAIRE, *vb.* attract, complete, achieve, 273, 1762.

AUCTORITÉ, *sf.* authority, 2968.

AUMBRE, *pr.* 3, AUMBRER, *vb.* shade, protect, 2815.

AUS, *pron.* them, 2675, 3101.

AUSI COME, *adv.* just as, 2257.

AUSTER, *sm.* the south wind, 2350, 2351.

AVAL, *adv.* below, 2294.

AVALEES, *past part.*, AVALER, *vb.* descend, 676.

AVEIR, *sm.* wealth, possessions, 731.

AVENANTEMENT, AVENENTEMENT, *adv.* in a suitable manner, becomingly, 3276; 1656.

AVENEMENT, *sm.* arrival, coming, 2415.

AVEVRE, *vb.* fill, stock, 2291.

AVIERRE, *sm.* opinion, 2289.

AVISENT, *pr.* 6, AVISER, *vb.* recognize, aim at, 2456.

AVOIE, *impf.* 1, AVOIENT, *impf.* 6, AVOIR, *vb.* have, 503; 194.

AVOIER, *vb.* go astray, wander, 1414.

AVOLTIERE, *sm.* adultery, 3269.

AVOMES, AVOMMES, *pr.* 4, AVOIR, *vb.* have, 115, 277; 2865.

AVRA, *fut.* 3, AVRAI, *fut.* 1, AVRAS, *fut.* 2, AVROIT, *cond.* 3, AVRONT, *fut.* 6, AVOIR, *vb.* have, 669, 692; 79, 801; 474, 2164; 6, 2482; 722, 2561.

BAERIE, *sf.* covetousness, 3, 1839.

BAILLE, *past part.*, BAILLIR, *vb.* give, control, govern, 1087, 2282.

BAILLIE, *sf.* jurisdiction, 1902.

BAILLIS, *sm.* officers, here especially apostles, 3220.

BALSMES, *sm.* balm, healing substance, 552.

BARAT, *sm.* ruse, deceit, 346.

BASTIR, *vb.* build, 1645.

BATIRENT, *pft.* 6, BATTRE, *vb.* beat, 2540.

BEALS, *adj.* beautiful, handsome, fair, 225, 384.

BEISIERS, BEISIER, *sm.* kiss, 86, 99; 107.

BELTÉ, *sf.* beauty, 641, 1239.

BENDE, *sf.* band, strip, 1820, 1837.

BENEURTEZ, *sf.* happiness, 3052.

BENOITE, *adj.* blessed, 3297.

BERBIETE, *sf.* small sheep, 3444.

BERBIS, BERBIZ, *sf.* ewe, sheep, 1817; 1793.

BESOIGNE, *sf.* task, 2040.

BESOIGNEUS, *adj.* needy, 2015, 3474.

BEVEZ, *pr.* 5, BOIVRE, *vb.* drink, 2439.

BINARIE, *adj.* binary, 3356.

BISCETES, *sf.* small hind, 1160, 1163.

BISE, *sm.* the north wind, 2347, 2351.

BISSES, BISSETES, *sf.* (small) hind, 1257; 1139.

BLANCES, BLANCS, *adj. m. nom. sing.* white, 2719; 2655, 2665.

BLANDISSEMENT, *sm.* flattery, 2975.

BLANS, *adj.* white, 1520.

BLASTENGIER, *vb.* blame, 1436.

BOCHE, *sf.* mouth, 77, 729.

BOEUS, *adj.* muddy, 831.

BOGNE, *sf.* limit, 3502.

BOLIST, *pr.* 3, BOLLIR, *vb.* boil, 1265.

BORDEALS, *sm.* hovel, hut, 1048.

BOSOIGNOS, *adj.* needy, 2841.

BOTE, *pr.* 3, BOTER, *vb.* push, 2470, 2549.

BRACHEZ, *sm.* hunting dogs, hounds, 1140.

BRIVE, *adj.* deceitful, 2274.

BUEN, BUENE, BUENES, *adj.* good, 516; 1200; 580.

BUES, *sm.* oxen, 415.

BUKE, *sf.* mouth, 1255.

BUT, *past part.*, BOIRE, *vb.* drink, 1267.

BUTER, *vb.* push, 664.

CACHES, *pr.* 2, CACHIER, *vb.* hide, 3118.

CACIES, *past part.*, CACIER, *vb.* hunt, chase, 1139.

CAMBRIERES, *sf.* chambermaid, servant, 599.

CANELE, *sf.* calamus (and cinnamon, Song of Songs 4: 14), 2319.

CANT, *adv.* when, 220.

CASTE, *adj.* chaste, 440.

CASTEALS, *sm.* fortified place, 3078.

CASTEÉ, *sf.* chastity, 975.

CASTIEMENZ, *sm.* warning, advice, 1802.

CAVAIN, *sm.* cellar, ditch, 1004.

CAVEL, *sm.* (head of) hair, 2803.

CEALS, *pron.* those, 1804.

CELESTIEL, *adj.* heavenly, celestial, 365, 1380.

CELEZ, *sm.* canopy, tester, baldachin, 1333.

CELI, *pron.* that, that one, 866, 1991.

CELIER, cellar, 266, 740.

CELS, *pron.* that, that one, 188, 973.

CEMBEL, *sm.* call, provocation, 572.

CERS, *sm. nom.*, CERF, *sm. acc.* stag, 813; 1245.

CERTE, *adj. f.* sure, certain, 499, 1626.

CERTES, *adv.* surely, certainly, 211, 1093.

CERVECEL, *sm.* young (she-) goat, kid, 861, 1137.

CERZ, *adj.* sure, certain, 101.

CEST, CESTE, CESTI, *adj.* this, 1, 10; 15, 21; 2093, 3309.

CESTUI, *adj.* and *pron.* this, this one, 1275, 1845, 2111.

CEVERLAUS, *sm.* 2041.

CEVRELS, *sm.* goat, 1244, 1259.

CEVROLET, *sm.* young goat, kid, 1135.

CEVRON, *sm.* rafter, 611.

CEZ, *adj.* these, 284, 291.

CHA, *adv.* here, 773, 900.

CHACE, *pr.* 3, CHACIER, *vb.* pursue, 1170.

CHAIENZ, *adv.* within, in here, 925.

CHAIST, *pr. subj.* 3, CHEOIR, *vb.* fall, befall, p. 97, l. 12.

CHAITIS, CHAITIVE, *adj.* wretched, 2686; 2519.

CHALENGE, *sf.* calumny, shame, 2140.

CHALENGIER, *vb.* attack, dispute, 3180.

CHALOR, *sf.* heat, warmth, 2047.

CHANS, *sm. pl.* fields, 363.

CHAPEL, *sm.* chaplet, wreath, garland, 504.

CHAPERON, *sm.* hood, bonnet, 2922.

CHAR, *sf.* flesh, 661, 904.

CHARNEL, CHARNEUS, *adj.* of flesh, fleshly, 470, 1220; 315, 1821.

CHARTRE, *sf.* prison, 123.

CHASCUN, *adj.* and *pron.* each, each one, every, everyone, 190, 258, 1996, 2996.

CHASTEÉ, *sf.* chastity, 984, 1384.

CHASTIER, *vb.* warn, admonish, 2954.

CHAUS, *pron.* those, 239, 1529.

CHAUT, *adj.* and *sm.* hot, heat, warm, warmth, 372, 1976.

CHAVELURE, *sf.* (head of) hair, 2565, 2567.

CHE, *pron.* this, 2181, 2201.

CHEVALCHIE, *sf.* troop of mounted men, 421.

CHEVALERIE, *sf.* troop of horsemen, 667.

CHEVALIER, *sm.* armed men (Song of Songs 3: 8: 'valiant men'), 1421.

CHEVEL, *sm.* hair, 1737, 2499.

CHEVERLAZ, CHEVREL, *sm.* young goat, kid, 2003; 813, 855.

CHIEF, *sm.* head, 793, 1477.

CHIER, CHIERE, CHIERES, CHIERS, *adj.* dear 474, 1483; 34, 1304; 600, 810; 225, 462.

CHIERTÉ, *sf.* affection, love, 228.

CHIÉS, *sm.* head, 795, 1742.

CHIEVRE, *sf.* goat, 383, 1782.

CHIEZ, *sm.* head, 2745.

CHIST, *pt.* 3, CHASER, *vb.* establish, 2426.

CHO, *pron.* this, 46, 63.

CHOU, *pron.* this, 1693.

CI, *adv.* here, 173, 1025.

CIEL, *sm.* heaven, 272, 520.

CIEL, *sm.* sky, 1379.

CIÉS, *sm.* head, 1161.

CIL, *pron.* this one, these, he, 132, 207.

CILS, *adj.* this, 1317.

CINC, *num.* five, 1410, 1413.

CIPRES, *sm.* cypress, 2311.

CIRE, *sf.* wax, METRE MA CIRE, put the seal on, i.e. conclude, 3503.

CIST, *adj.* this, 26, 49.

CLAIME, *pr.* 1, CLAMER, *vb.* proclaim, call, 1460, 2521; 2174, 2260.

CLAMOR, *sf.* judicial complaint, 133, 2491.

CLER, CLERE, CLERS, *adj.* clear, 267, 570; 298, 2253; 1328, 3292.

CLEUS, *sm.* nails, 3183.

CLINE, *pr.* 3, CLINER, *vb.* bow, 1543.

CLOFIGIÉ, *past part.*, CLOFIGIER, *vb.* fix with nails, crucify, 196.

CLOS, *sm.* nails, 2085.

CLOS, *past part.*, CLORE, *vb.* close, enclose, 2383, 3291.

CLOT, *pr.* 3, CLORE, *vb.* enclose, 453.

CO, *pron.* this, that, 27, 47.

COE, *sf.* tail, 2019, 2739.

COGITATIONS, *sf.* meditation, thought, 1743, 3248.

COIE, *adj.* tranquil, quiet, 2610.

COINNIES, *sf.* axe, 1525.

COIS, *adj.* tranquil, retiring, 1622.

COIS, *sm.* tranquillity, 1544.

COLEE, *sf.* blow on the neck, buffet, 300.

COLON, COLONS, *sm.* pigeon, 2887, 3103; 568, 1733.

COLOR, *sf.* colour, 1626, 1833.

COLPABLES, *adj.* guilty, 3269.

COLPE, *pr.* 3, COLPER, *vb.* cut, 341; 336, 968.

COLTEAUS, *sm.* knife, 1871.

COLTEL, *sm.* knife, 1875.

COLTIVES, *past part.*, COLTIVER, *vb.* cultivate, 1078.

COLUMBELE,   COLUMBELES,   COLUMBELS,

COLUMBES, *sf.* turtle-dove, 933; 1475; 2907; 1549.

COLUNBINE, *adj.* dove-like, 3093.

COLUNS, *sm.* pigeon, dove, 2849, 2899.

COM, *conj.* and *adv.* as, like; SI COM, just as, 1368, 1813; TANT COM, as long as, 1100.

COMANT, *sm.* order, command, 754, 1159.

COMBIEN, *adv.* how much, 135.

COMES, *sf.* hair, 2809, 2823.

COMPAIGNES, *sf.* companions, 779; 1234.

COMPERE, *past part.*, COMPEREIR, COMPERER, *vb.* compare, 2911, 2899; 2860; 1778.

COMPEREMENT, *sm.* comparison, 1954.

COMPERISON, *sf.* comparison, 2024, 2867.

COMPLISSEMENZ, *sm.* fulfilment, 778.

COMPS, *sm.* blows, 2081.

CON, *conj.* and *adv.* as, like, 413, 2214.

CONCORDENT, *pr.* 6, CONCORDER, *vb.* agree, be in harmony, 3277.

CONEISANCE, CONEISSANCE, CONESEANCE, *sf.* knowledge, 402; 1580; 3167.

CONEISTRE, *vb.* know, 1345.

CONESSANCE, *sf.* signs, symbols, 1907.

CONFERME, *pr.* 3, CONFERMER, *vb.* confirm, strengthen, 1771.

CONFISOIT, *impf.* 3, CONFIRE, *vb.* prepare, make, 3512.

CONFORTEMENT, *sm.* comforting, 1134.

CONISTRA, *fut.* 3, CONEISTRE, *vb.* know, 2327.

CONJUR, *pr.* 1, CONJUREZ, *pr.* 5, CONJURER, *vb.* entreat, beseech, 810; 2651.

CONKELL, *pr.* 1, CONKELT, *pr.* 3, CONKUEIL-LIES, *past part.* CONKUEILLIR, *vb.* gather up, gather together, 3126; 2906; 3350.

COMPAIGNES, *sf.* companions, 496.

CONREERENT, *pr.* 6, CONREER, *vb.* equip, prepare, 3448.

CONSACHABLE, *adj.* knowledgeable, conscious of, 2310.

CONT. *pr.* 1, CONTEIR, *vb.* tell, relate, 2177; 2796.

CONVERSACION, *sf.* way of life, 2936.

CONVI, *sm.* invitation, banquet, 2441.

CORAGE, *sm.* heart, state of mind, 210, 218, 3017.

CORANT, *pres. part.*, CORRE, *vb.* run, 814, 2852.

CORBEL, CORBELS, *sm.* crow, 2804; 2777.

CORICHAST, *impf. subj.* 3, CORICHER, *vb.* grow angry, 3189.

CORONA, *pft.* 3, CORONER, *vb.* crown, 1703.

CORONE, *sf.* crown, 529, 653.

CORPOREILMENT, *adv.* bodily, 2090.

CORPOREL, CORPORELS, CORPOREUS, COR-POREZ, *adj.* of the body, bodily, 2015; 617; 1998; 2023.

CORRE, *sm.* chariots, 424.

CORRE, *vb.*, CORT, *pr.* 3, run, 3011; 1138.

CORT, *sf.* court, 2786.

CORTILZ, *sm.* enclosure, garden, 2331.

COST, *pr.* 3, COSTIER, *vb.* be alongside, 459.

COSTUME, *sf.* custom, 2076, 2913.

COTE, *sf.* surcoat, tunic, 2506.

COTE, *sf.* share, portion, 2583.

COUS, *sm.* neck, 1915, 1927.

COUS, *sm.* pl. blows, 3183.

COVENANT, *pres. part.*, COVENROIT, *cond.* 3, COVENIR, *vb.* be necessary, behove, 1522; 2547.

COVERTE, COVERZ, *adj.*, *past part.*, COVRIR, *vb.* cover, 2623; 2769. .

COVOIT, *pr. subj.* 3, COVOITER, *vb.* desire, covet, 3269.

COVOITISE, *sf.* excessive desire, covetousness, 575, 2898.

CRAS, CRASSE, *adj.* fat, well-fed, 1796, 2021; 508.

CREANCE, *sf.* belief, 2807.

CRECHE, *sf.* cradle, 867, 2812.

CREMEZ, *pr.* 5, CREMER, *vb.* fear, 779.

CRESME, *sf.* (holy) oil, 1052.

CRIEM, *pr.* 1, CRIEMENT, *pr.* 6, CRIEMES, *pr.* 2, CRIENT, *pr.* 3, CREMER, *vb.* fear, 388, 851; 624; 3413; 1919, 1939.

CRIEME, *sf.* fear, 1664, 1680.

CRIN, CRINE, CRINS, CRINZ, *sm.* hair, 2223, 2251; 2257, 2263; 1792, 1829; 2254.

CROC, *sm.* crocus, saffron, 2320.

CROISCENT, *pr.* 6, CROISTRE, *vb.* grow, 635; 398.

CROIZ, *sf.* the Cross, 879, 833, 2085.

CUER, CUERS, *sm.* heart, 2, 15; 108, 140.

CUEVRENT, *pr.* 6, COVRIR, *vb.* cover, 2803.

CUI, *pron.* whom, which, 10, 121.

CUIDE, *pr.* 1 and 3, CUIDES, *pr.* 2, CUIDEZ, *pr.* 5, CUIDOIT, *impf.* 3, CUIDIER, *vb.* think, 1236; 126, 1184; 420; 1359; 3517.

CUILLIR, *vb.* gather up, 2928.

CUM, *adv.* how, 2241, 2706.

CURE, *sf.* care, trouble, protection, 242, 290.

CURENT, *pr.* 6, CORRE, *vb.* run, 2945.

CURIEUSE, *adj.* anxious, concerned about, 2192.

CURRE, *sm.* chariots, 3030.

CURT, *pr.* 3, CORRE, *vb.* run, flow, 3289.

CUSTURE, *sf.* care, protection, shelter, 3476.

CYPRE, *sm.* cypress-tree, 547, 612, 635.

DAMACHE, DAMACHES, DAMAGE, *sm.* harm, 319, 380; 1806; 406, 978.

DAMNENT, *pr.* 6, DAMNEZ, *pr.* 5, DAMNER, *vb.* condemn, damn, 1051; 1047.

DAMPNENT, *pr.* 6, DAMNER, *vb.* condemn, damn, 1787.

DARZ, *sm.* spears, darts, 1945, 2621.

DEABLES, *sm.* devil, 876.

DEBONAIRE, *adj.* of good race, noble, gentle, 30, 259.

DECEVEEUR, *sm.* deceiver, 2148.

DECORRE, *vb.* DECORT, *pr.* 3. run, run from, 2521; 3245, 3263.

DECRIER, *vb.* become out of order, upset, 2391.

DEDUIENT, *pr.* 6, DEDUIRE, *vb.*, SE DEDUIRE, amuse oneself, 1146.

DEFAILLE, *pr. subj.* 3, DEFAILLIR, *vb.* lack, 1088.

DEFENSION, *sf.* defence, 1943.

DEFFERRE, *pr.* 3, DEFFERMER, *vb.* set free, open, 960.

DEFINEMENT, *sm.* end, completion, 1888.

DEFORS, *adv.* outside, 297, 563.

DEGOTA, *pft.* 3, DEGOTERENT, *pft.* 6, DEGOTEIR, *vb.* flow, drip from, 2784; 2515; 3387.

DEGRE, DEGREZ, *sm.* step, 1561; 757, 1485.

DEGUTERENT, *pft.* 6, DEGOTEIR, *vb.* flow, drip from, 2591.

DEIGNA, *pft.* 3, DEIGNES, *pr.* 2, DEIGNIER, *vb.* deign, 1637, 1643; 364.

DEITÉ, *sf.* godliness, 2984.

DEITEIZ, *sf.* the Deity, 2793.

DEKEURT, *pr.* 3, DEKOROIT, *impf.* 3, DEKORRE, *vb.* run off, flee, 2525; 2614.

DEI, *art.* and *prep.* of the, from the, 12, 93.

DELICIES, *sf.* pleasure, charm, delight, 1213.

DELIS, DELIT, *sm.* pleasure, charm, delight, 1184; 1186, 1398.

DELIT, *pr. subj.* 3, DELITE, *pr.* 3, DELITOIT, *impf.* 3, DELITIER, *vb.* rejoice, take pleasure in, delight, 2429; 1097; 1350; 1466.

DELIVRE, *adj.* resolute, free, 2; *sm.* A DELIVRE, freely, immediately, 1453.

DELIVRE, *pr.* 5, DELIVREIR, DELIVRER, *vb.* set free, 16, 1961; 3135; 2680.

DELIVREMENT, *adv.* freely, promptly, 657.

DELIZ, *sm.* pleasure, delight, 660, 2198.

DELS, *sm.* grief, sorrow, 1243.

DELT, *pr.* 3, DELEIR, *vb.* grieve, sorrow, 646.

DEMAINEMENT, *sm.* conduct, 3365.

DEMENAST, *impf. subj.* 3, DEMENEZ, *past part.*, DEMENER, *vb.* ill-treat, 3190; 533.

DEMENTEMENT, *sm.* lamentation, complaint, 560.

DEMOERA, *fut.* 3, DEMOREIR, DEMORER, *vb.* dwell, live, 541; 2074; 934, 1067.

DEMORANCE, *sf.* stay, delay, 1566, 2482.

DEMOSTRE, *pr.* 3, DEMOSTRER, *vb.* show, 1023.

DENS, DENT, DENZ, *sf.* tooth, teeth, 2064; 1793, 1811; 1803.

DEPART, *pr.* 3, DEPARTI, *pft.* 3, DEPARTIR, *vb.* separate from, 924; 93.

DERAINS, *adj.*, A DERAINS, in the end, at last, 2703.

DESCHARGE, *pr.* 3, DESCHARGIER, *vb.* unburden, remove, 1263.

DESCOLOREE, *past part.*, DESCOLORER, *vb.* make pale, 299.

DESCOVRIR, *vb.* reveal, 2314.

DESCRIRE, *vb.* describe, 128, 2900.

DESCUEVRE, *pr.* 5, DESCOVRIR, *vb.* uncover, reveal, 1451.

DESDIRE, *vb.* deny, 2674.

DESERS, DESERT, *sm.* desert, wilderness, 814, 1317; 875, 1313, 3445.

DESERTE, *sf.* deserts, 500, 1625, 2431, 3057.

DESEURE, *adv.* above, 1607.

DESIR, *pr.* 1, DESIRAI, *fut.* 1, DESIRE, *pr.* 3, DESIRRAI, *fut.* 1, DESIRRE, *pr.* 3, DESIRREIZ, DESIRREZ, *past part.*, DESIRRIER, *vb.* desire, 141, 150, 926; 731; 1565; 734; 524, 1108; 2050; 100, 893.

DESIRRIER, DESIRRIERS, *sm.* desire, 73, 417; 1567, 3332.

DESJOINDRE, *vb.* used as *sm.* come apart, separation, 110.

DESOR, *adv.* upon, 304, 387.

DESPIRE, *vb.*, DESPIST, *pr.* 3, DESPITE, DESPITES, *past part.*, despise, 272; 556, 3008; 557; 3204.

DESPLACE, DESPLAISE, *pr. subj.* 3, DESPLAISES, *pr.* 3, DESPLAISIR, *vb.* displease, 295; 1242, 1284; 420; 126.

DESPOILLIES, *past part.*, DESPOILIR, *vb.* deprive of, 1820.

DESROI, *sm.* disorder, disarray, fault, 326 945.

DESSEMBLANTZ, DESSEMBLANZ, *adj.* dissimilar, 1880; 2109.

DESTINCLEES, *past part.*, DESTINCLOIENT, *impf.* 6, DESTINCLER, *vb.* sparkle, 1614; 1335.

DESTINCTEES, *past part.*, DESTINCTER, *vb.* distinguish, 3461.

DESTORBER, *vb.* trouble, prevent, disturb, 1070.

DESTRAINT, *pr.* 3, DESTRAINDRE, *vb.* constrain, oppress, 19, 1427.

DESTRE, *adj.* and *sf.* right (hand), 794, 800, 2508.

DESTRECE, DESTRESCE, *sf.* distress, severity, 869; 437, 742.

DESTROIT, *sm.* difficulty, constraint, domination, 64, 131, 146.

DESTROIZ, *sm. pl.* sufferings, constraints, 880, 1020.

DESTRUIRE, *vb.*, DESTRUIZ, *past part.* destroy, 1947, 2244; 2775.

DESUZ, *adv.* above, 732.

DESVOIE, *pr.* 3, DESVOYER, *vb.* lead astray, 1070.

DEUS, *num.* two, 109, 111, 179, 489, 1280, 1884, 1973, 1981, 2227, 2364, 2721, 3734, 3016, 3117, 3121, 3139, 3149, 3193, 3285, 3359, 3404.

DEUS, *sm.* God, 10, 93 (for full list of references, see Index of Names).

DEUST, *pft.* 3, DEVOIR, *vb.* to be obliged to, 3508.

DEVASTANT, *pres. part.*, DEVASTER, *vb.* lay waste, 1045.

DEVIN, DEVINE, *adj.* divine, 3422; 206, 587.

DEVINITÉ, *sf.* divinity, the quality of being divine, 3124.

DEVISE, *pr.* 3, DEVISER, *vb.* separate, distinguish, 903, 1756.

DEZ, *var. of* DES, *art.* of the, 2461.

DI, *pr.* 1 and 3, DIE, *pr. subj.* 1 and 3, DIENT, *pr.* 6, DIRE, *vb.* say, tell, 322, 902; 562, 1020; 254, 1203; 127, 175.

DIRES, *sm.* from DIRE, *inf.* telling, speaking, 1850.

DIS, *sm.* day, TOTDIS, *adv.* always, 722, 3334.

DISCEPINES, *sf.* punishment, chastisement, 1524.

DITENT, *pr.* 6, DITIER, *vb.* instruct, 3479.

DIZ, *sm. pl.* sayings, 291, 1039.

DOBLE, *adj.* double, twofold, 181, 626.

DOCES, *adj.* sweet, 366.

DOCTRINE, *sf.* instruction, teaching, 181.

DOI, *pr.* 1, DEVOIR, *vb.* to be obliged to, 761, 1095.

DOI, *num.* two, 1769, 3275, 3310, 3357.

DOIE, *pr. subj.* 3, DEVOIR, *vb.* to be obliged to, 1921.

DOIGNE, *pr. subj.* 1, DOINST, *pr. subj.* 3, DOIZ, *pr.* 2, DONNER, *vb.* give, 2039; 149; 1439.

DOLCE, *adj.* sweet, gentle, 159, 561.

DOLCEMENT, *adv.* gently, 119, 738.

DOLCERS, DOLCEUR, DOLCEURS, DOLCHOR, DOLÇOR, DOLÇORS, *sf.* sweetness, 2296; 2288, 2455; 2287, 2857; 730; 807, 1912; 1909.

DOLE, *pr.* 3, DOLEIR, DOLER, *vb.* cut, trim, 1530; 1525; 1521.

DOLEROSEMENT, *adv.* grievously, 1008.

DOLEUR, *sf.* grief, 2677, 2780.

DOLEZ, *pr.* 5, DOLOIR, *vb.* grieve, 1148; 71, 537.

DOLOR, DOLORS, *sf.* grief, 160, 2622; 543, 2088.

DOLZ, *adj.* sweet, gentle, 147, 165.

DONEIR, *vb.* give, 2036, 2929.

DONERRE, *sm.* giver, donor, 585.

DONKES, *adv.* then, 829.

DONT, *adv.* then, 787.

DONTER, *vb.* tame, 660.

DORM, *pr.* 1, DORMIR, *vb.* sleep, 2489; 808, 3130.

DOTA, *pft.* 3, DOTE, *pr.* 3, DOTES, *pr.* 2, DOTER, *vb.* fear, 502; 2469, 2582; 1002; 679.

DOTANCE, *sf.* doubt, fear, 62, 401.

DOUS, *num.* two, 780, 1285.

DOZ, *adj.* sweet, gentle, 2820.

DOZAINE, *sf.* twelve, 1418.

DOZE, *num.* twelve, 1412, 1413.

DRAGME, *sf.* drachma (coin), 3451.

DRAPELS, *sm.* cloth, 3174.

DRAS, *sm.* cloth, clothes, 1344, 1348.

DRECIER, *vb.*, DRESCE, *pr.* 3, set up, place, 2408; 428.

DROIZ, *sm.* right, 50, 1662.

DRUZ, *adj.* vigorous, 3230.

DUCE, *adj.* sweet, 21.

DUI, *num.* two, 2871, 3056.

DUIT, *past part.*, DUIRE, *vb.* lead, train, 332.

DUKE, *conj.* up to, as far as, until, 1740.

DULCES, *adj.* sweet, 166.

DULCEUR, *sf.* sweetness, gentleness, 118, 167.

DULZ, *adj.* sweet, 2951.

DUNC, *adv.* then, 71, 98.

DUNT, *adv.* whence, 14, 87; *rel. pron.* of which, whose, 228, 282.

DURESCE, *sf.* hardness, harshness, 285.

DUSK, *prep.* as far as, 872.

DUSQUE, *prep.* and *conj.* until, as far as, 96, 104, 348, 866.

E, *conj.* and, 4, 8, etc.

EAUES, *sf.* waters, 676.

EIRT, *impf.* 3, ESTRE, *vb.* be, 1343, 2406.

EISCHUES, *past part.*, ISSIR, *vb.* come out of, go out of, 1794.

EISIL, *sm.* exile, 88.

EISSI, *pft.* 3, EISSUZ, *past part.*, ISSIR, *vb.* issue from, 1012; 2300.

EL, *prep.* and *art.* in the, to the, 117, 184.

ELE, *pron.* she, 84, 87.

EM, *prep.* in, 970, 2578.

EM, *pron.* of it, 1198.

EMBATISSENT, *pft.* 6, EMBATRE, *vb.* come upon, strike against, 1355.

EMPOISE, *pr.* 3, EMPESER, *vb.* weigh upon, grieve, 1142.

ENBOTEIR, *vb.* force, oblige, 3388.

ENBRACHEMENZ, *sm.* embraces, 906.

ENCLINE, *pr.* 3, ENCLINER, *vb.* incline, lean towards, 1845.

ENCLOS, ENCLOSE, *adj.* shut up, enclosed, 2303, 2346; 125.

ENCOMBRIER, *sm.* obstacle, encumbrance, 418, 3046.

ENCRAISCENT, *pr.* 6, ENCRAISSE, *pr.* 3, ENCROISTRE, *vb.* grow, 2042; 511.

ENDITE, *past part.*, ENDITIER, *vb.* instruct, prescribe, 1196.

ENDURER, *vb.* suffer, endure, 68.

ENEKEDENT, *adv.* notwithstanding, 1563.

ENEMI, *sm.* the devil, 2405, 3448.

ENFANT, ENFANZ, ENFENT, *sm.* child, one uninstructed in divine matters, 237, 3506; 239, 979; 1871, 1873.

ENFERMETEZ, *sf.* weaknesses, ailments, infirmities, 1524, 3527.

ENFES, *sm.* child, 2811.

ENFICHIEZ, *past part.*, ENFICHIER, *vb.* fix into, 2084.

ENGELEE, *past part.*, ENGELER, *vb.* completely freeze, 945.

ENGLUME, *sf.* anvil, 526.

ENGREIGNE, *pr.* 3, ENGREIGNIER, *vb.* increase, make greater, 2418.

ENHORTE, *pr.* 3, ENHORTER, *vb.* exhort, 260.

ENIVERERENT, *pft.* 6, ENIVRA, *pft.* 3, ENIVRE, *pr.* 3, ENIVREE, *past part.*, ENIVRER, *vb.* intoxicate, 2457; 741; 15, 551; 122, 266.

ENNUI, *sm.* irritation, hardship, 70, 156, 305, 2711.

ENOINT, ENOINTES, ENOINZ, *past part.*, ENOINDRE, *vb.* anoint, 266; 2217; 215, 227.

ENORS, *sm.* honours, 485.

ENORTE, *pr.* 3, ENORTER, *vb.* exhort, 1086, 2550; 3346.

ENSAIE, *pr.* 3, ENSAIER, *vb.* try, attempt, 22.

ENSEMENT, *adv.* thus, equally, 52, 719.

ENSENS, *sm.* incense, 2298.

ENSENT, *pr.* 3, ENSEIGNIER, *vb.* instruct, teach, 1502, 1609.

ENSERRE, *past part.*, ENSERRER, *vb.* enclose, 962.

ENSIVENT, *pr.* 6, ENSIVRE, *vb.* follow, 1418; 318, 378.

ENSORQUETOT, *adv.* above all, 1959.

ENT, *adv.* away, thence, 931, 1003.

ENTAMEE, *past part.*, ENTAMER, *vb.* cut into, harm, 1862; 448.

ENTENTE, *sf.* thought, effort, intent, intention, 1247, 2860.

ENTENTIU, *adj.* attentive, 2949.

ENTENTRE, *sm.* thought, attention, 81.

ENTRE, *prep.* between, among, 198, 324.

ENTRE, *pr.* 3, ENTRER, *vb.* enter, 2446; 1446.

ENTREMETRE, *vb.* be occupied with, interrupt, 650, 3402.

ENTREPRESURE, *sf.* enterprise, surprise attack, difficulty, 1274, 1488, 2236, 2578, 2950.

ENVENIMEE, *past part.*, ENVENIMER, *vb.* poison, 622.

ENVIE, *pr.* 3, ENVIER, *vb.* send, 261, 1601.

ENVIE, *sf.* envy, jealousy, 629, 1602.

ENVIRON, *adv.* around, near, 612, 1917.

ENZ, *conj.* but, rather, 13, 584, 2361.

ENZ, *adv.* within, 1001, 1926, 2161, 2264.

ERE, *impf.* 1, ERENT, *impf.* 6, ERT, *impf.* 3, ES, *pr.* 2, EST, *pr.* 3, ESTOIENT, *impf.* 6, ESTOIT, *impf.* 3, ESTRA, *fut.* 3, ESTRE, *vb.* be, 323; 996, 2458; 668, 945; 2143; 7, 12; 1090, 1351; 37, 201; 2050; 74, 85.

ERITEALS, *sm.* heretic, 1047.

EROR, *sf.* error, wrong, 3224.

ERRANZ, *sm.* those who have gone astray, 2556.

ERT, *impf.* 3, ESTRE, *vb.* be, 668, 945.

ES, EN and LES, *art.* in the, 554, 847.

ESCARS, *sm.* scorn, contempt, 3342.

ESCHAMEL, *sm.* small stool, 1535.

ESCHAPA, *pft.* 3, ESCHAPER, *vb.* escape, 3032.

ESCLARCIST, *pft.* 3, ESCLARIR, *vb.* enlighten, 1103.

ESCLINE, *pr.* 3, ESCLINER, *vb.* incline, 834.

ESCOLE, *sf.* school, 58, 206.

ESCOLIER, *sm.* scholar, 494.

ESCORCHE, *sf.* bark, 1891.

ESCOULES, *past part.*, ESCOULER, *vb.* lead astray, seduce, 2920.

ESCRIN, *sm.* box, chest, 1499.

ESCRIPTURE, *sf.* writing, scripture, 464.

ESCRIT, ESCRITE, *past part.*, ESCRIRE, *vb.* write, 116, 152; 2682.

ESCRIT, *sm.* writing, written document, 2220, 3152.

ESCRITURE, ESCRITURES, *sf.* writing, scripture, the Scriptures, 45, 178; 1640, 2056.

ESCU, *sm.* shield, 1917, 1943.

ESCUS, *past part.*, ESCORRE, *vb.* shake (off), 991.

ESCUZ, *sm.* pl. shields, 1941.

ESCUSEMENZ, *sm.* excuse, 854.

ESEVERS, *past part.*, ESSEVER, *vb.* pour out, 2046.

ESFORST, *pr. subj.* 3, ESFORCER, *vb.* make effort, 2130.

ESFROIENT, *pr.* 6, ESFREER, *vb.* fear, frighten, 2888.

ESGUARDE, *imper.* 2, *pr.* 3, ESGUART, *pr.* 1, ESGUARDER, *vb.* look at, 900, 911, 2241; 1886; 329, 1165.

ESHAITE, *pr.* 3, ESHAITIER, *vb.* please, comfort, heal, 665, 1506.

ESKARAT, *sm.* vine-prop, support, 345.

ESKARCHONER, *vb.* support with vine-props, 336.

ESKELT, *pr.* 3, ESKELER, *vb.* sound, resound, 1255.

ESLAISANT, *gerund*, ESLAISIER, *vb.* enlarge, dilate, 3334.

ESLAVER, *vb.* wash out, wash away, 874.

ESLEECHIEZ, *past part.*, ESLEECHIER, *vb.* make happy, 914.

ESLEVERA, *fut.* 3, ESLEVEZ, *past part.*, ESLIEVE, *pr.* 3, ESLIEVENT, *pr.* 6, ESLEVER, *vb.* raise up, 673; 2933; 514, 919; 627.

ESLIRRE, *vb.*, ESLISENT, *pr.* 6, ESLIST, *pr.* 3, ESLIT, ESLITE, ESLITEZ, ESLIZ, *past part.* choose, select, prefer, 2514; 573; 10, 1615; 570, 1230; 558, 1098; 3205; 2742.

ESLOIGNENT, ESLONGENT, *pr.* 6, ESLONGIES, *past part.*, ESLONGNIER, *vb.* make distant from, be distant from, 1831; 2807, 2885; 1140.

ESMAIE, *pr.* 3, ESMAIER, *vb.* astonish, frighten, 293, 392.

ESMAIL, *sm.* enamel, 1481.

ESMARIE, ESMARIZ, *past part.*, ESMARIR, *vb.* disconcert, 2537, 2607; 47.

ESMERAUGDES, *sf.* emeralds, 1632.

ESMERE, *adj.* pure, refined, 2645.

ESMERVEIL, *pr.* 1, ESMERVEILLEROIT, *cond.* 3, ESMERVEILLER, *vb.* marvel, wonder, 2672, 3421; 2369.

ESMET, ESMUET, *pr.* 3, ESMUEVENT, *pr.* 6, ESMOVOIR, *vb.* move, 1858; 1009, 1306; 2888.

ESPANDANT, *pres. part.*, ESPANDENT, *pr.* 6, ESPANDIRENT, *pft.* 6, ESPANDRES, *inf.* used as *sm.*, ESPANDUE, ESPANDUZ, *past part.*, ESPANT, *pr.* 3, ESPANDRE, *vb.* pour out, 3236; 3335; 3226; 3341; 2572; 214, 1507; 901, 1000.

ESPARGNANT, *pres. part.*, ESPARGNIER, *vb.* spare, 3396.

ESPECES, *sf.* kind, sort, 2332, 3229.

ESPECIAIRE, ESPECIARE, ESPECIARIE, *sm.* pl. spice growers, herbalists, 3208; 3153; 3115.

ESPECIE, ESPECIES, *sf.* spice, herb, 2329; 2324, 2327.

ESPEE, ESPEES, *sf.* sword, 666, 1353; 1425, 1431.

ESPENEIR, *vb.* expiate, 2450, 2596.

ESPERANCE, *sf.* hope, 603, 1182.

ESPERIT, *sm.* spirit, 151, 569.

ESPERITALS, ESPIRITEL, ESPIRITELS, ESPERITEUS, spiritual, 2445; 1363, 1386; 618, 3048; 1997.

ESPERIZ, *sm.* spirit, 155, 3025.

ESPERVIERS, *sm.* sparrow-hawk, 2926.

ESPEUSE, ESPEUSES, *sf.* bride, 49, 57; 1631.

ESPEVENTEMENT, *sm.* terror, 2716.

ESPEVENTER, *vb.* terrify, frighten, 2973.

ESPINES, *sf.* thorns, 690.

ESPINEUS, *adj.* thorny, 832.

ESPIRES, *past part.*, ESPIRER, *vb.* breathe into, inspire, 121.

ESPIRITELS, ESPIRITEUS, *adj.* spiritual, 1519, 1988.

ESPIRS, ESPIRZ, *sm.* breath, spirit, 657, 1896; 1394, 2091.

ESPLOIT, *sm.* vigour, rapidity, 2341.

ESPOENTE, *pr.* 3, ESPOVENTER, *vb.* terrify, 3265.

ESPOIR, *adv.* perhaps, 181.

ESPOIT, *pr.* 1, ESPERER, *vb.* hope, expect, 353.

ESPOSAILEE, *sf.* betrothal, marriage, 2809.

ESPOSE, ESPOSEE, ESPOUSE, *sf.* the Bride, 259, 1990; 292, 1791; 311.

ESPOSSE, *past part.*, ESPOSER, *vb.* marry, 1597.

ESPRENT, *pr.* 3, ESPRIS, *past part.*, ESPRIST, *pft.* 3, ESPRENDRE, *vb.* catch fire, seize, 18; 1569, 2656; 3007.

ESPURGATORIES, *adj.* purgatorial, purifying, 3395.

ESPUSE, *sf.* the Bride, 180.

ESSEMENT, *adv.* thus, equally, 1681, 1998.

ESTABLETE, ESTABLITE, *sf.* stability, 3101; 2863.

ESTAINDRE, *vb.* extinguish, 1071.

ESTAL, *sm.* stall, p. 97, l. 5.

ESTÉ, *sm.* summer, 953, 985.

ESTENDENT, *pr.* 6, ESTENDRE, *vb.* extend, hold out, 3330; 1776.

ESTER, *vb.* stand, 895, 2924.

ESTERKIST, *pft.* 3, ESTERKIR, *vb.* draw oneself up, 2923.

ESTERLINS, *sm.* money (sterling), 3015.

ESTOIENT, *impf.* 6, ESTRE, *vb.* be, 1090, 1351.

ESTOILES, *sf.* stars, 1335, 1381.

ESTOIT, *impf.* 3, ESTRE, *vb.* be, 37, 201.

ESTOR, *sm.* equipment, 494.

ESTOR, *sm.* battle, 656.

ESTORIE, *sf.* history, story, 2459.

ESTRA, *fut.* 3, ESTRE, *vb.* be, 2050.

ESTRAIGNE, *adj.* foreign, strange, 248.

ESTRAINT, *pr.* 3, ESTRAINDRE, *vb.* hold back, 1839.

ESTRAITE, ESTRAIZ, *past part.*, ESTRAIRE, *vb.* draw from, extract, 1516; 8.

ESTRANGE, *adj.* strange, 2165.

ESTRE, *vb.* be, 74, 85.

ESTRES, *sm.* being, state, condition, 900.

ESTROIT, *cond.* 3, ESTRE, *vb.* be, 355.

ESTROIT, ESTROITE, *adj.* tight, narrow, restricted, 1232; 1191.

ESTRUIRE, *vb.* instruct, 2133.

ESTUET, *pr.* 3, ESTOVOIR, *vb. impers.* behove, be necessary, 335, 352.

ESVEILLAI, *fut.* 1, ESVEILLE, *pr.* 3, ESVEILLEZ, ESVEILLIEZ, *pr.* 5, ESVELT, *pr. subj.* 3, ESVEILLIER, *vb.* awaken, 2501; 164, 841; 815; 840, 1245; 1290.

ESWAREE, *past part.*, ESWARER, *vb.* wander, lose one's way, 2619.

EURE, *sf.* hour, time, 848.

EVRE, *imper.* 2, EVRER, *vb.* work, 2495.

EVRES, *sf.* works, 2465.

EXPERIMENT, *sm.* test, trial, experience, 2879.

FABRICHER, *sm.* making, manufacture, fabrication, 480.

FACE, FACES, *sf.* face, 296, 1018.

FACE, *pr. subj.* 3, FAIRE, *vb.* make, do, 1874, 2484.

FAI, *pr.* 1 and *imper. sing.*, FAIRE, *vb.* make, do, 1135; 1148, 1151.

FAIL, *sf.*, TOTE DE FAIL, wholly lost, 130.

FAILENT, *pr.* 3, FAILLE, *pr. subj.* 1, FAILOIENT, *impf.* 6, FAILLIR, *vb.* fail, be lacking, 1211; 851; 1336.

FAIMS, *sf.* hunger, 2839.

FAINDRE, *vb.* hesitate, 1169.

FAIS, *sm.* burden, weight, care, trouble, 139, 591.

FAISANZ, *pres. part.*, FAIRE, *vb.* make, do, 1510; 260, 274.

FAISCELET, *sm.* small basket, 539.

FAISELS, *sm.* bunch, 523.

FAISOIENT, *impf.* 6, FAISOIT, *impf.* 3, FAISOMES, FAISONS, *pr.* 4, FAIT, *pr.* 3 and *past part.*, FAITES, FAIZ, *past part.*, FAIRE, *vb.* make, do, 3191; 1030, 2600; 2958; 608, 609; 24, 83; 405, 426, 3428, 3460; 7, 92; 310, 312.

FAITURE, *sf.* form, fabrication, creation, 1329, 1487.

FALDRAI, *fut.* 1, FALROIT, *cond.* 3, FALT, *pr.* 3, FAILLIR, *vb.* fail, be lacking, 1225; 3038; 636, 767.

FALSE, *adj.* false, 2274.

FAMILLEUS, *adj.* hungry, avid, 2930.

FARDEIR, *vb.* paint over, 3112.

FAULZ, *adj.* false, 331.

FAUT, *pr.* 3, FAILLIR, *vb.* be lacking, 956.

FAVERKIÉ, *past part.*, FAVREKIER, *vb.* make, fabricate, 303.

FAZ, *pr. subj.* 1 and 3, FAIRE, *vb.* make, do, 354; 2491.

FEAUS, *adj.* faithful, loyal, 2228, 3228.

FEEL, FEELS, *adj.* and *sm.* faithful, loyal, 2550; 886.

FEIT, *pr.* 3, FAIRE, *vb.* make, do, 1502.

FEL, *adj.* perfidious, impious, 466.

FELENIE, FELONIE, *sf.* wickedness, treachery, 630, 2901; 2917.

FELON, FELONS, *sm.* and *adj.* wicked, perfidious, treacherous, 1013; 2687, 2717.

FEMER, *vb.* manure, 335.

FEMIER, *sm.* dung-hill, p. 97, l. 15.

FERDINS, *sm.* small coin of minute value, farthing, 3016.

FERIE, *past part.*, FERIRENT, *pft.* 6, FERIR, *vb.* strike, fight, join battle, 668; 2621.

FERM, FERME, *adj.* firm, secure, 3317; 102, 1217.

FEROIES, *cond.* 2, FEROMS, *fut.* 4, FERONT, FERUNT, *fut.* 6, FAIRE, *vb.* make, do, 579; 471; 974; 2352, 2562.

FERUZ, *past part.*, FERIR, *vb.* strike, 2787.

FESIS, *pft.* 2, FESISENT, *pft.* 6, FESIST, *pft.* 3, FAIRE, *vb.* make, do, 712; 1356; 3181.

FESTE, *sf.* rejoicing, feast, 579.

FET, *pr.* 3, FAIRE, *vb.* say, speak (make, do), 744, 3399.

FEUS, *pft.* 2, ESTRE, *vb.* be, 373.

FIE, FIEE, FIEES, *sf.* time, 55; 1147; 192.

FIEL, *sm.* gall, 2898, 2901.

FIENS, *sm.* dung, dirt, 340, 2081.

FIERE, FIERS, *adj.* terrible, fierce, proud, 678; 2774, 2925.

FIERENT, *pr.* 6, FIERT, *pr.* 3, FERIR, *vb.* strike, 2539; 1426.

FIERTÉ, *sf.* fierceness, pride, 2199.

FIERT, *pr.* 3, FERIR, *vb.* strike, 1426.

FIEZ, *pr.* 2, FIER, *vb.* trust, 594.

FIGIERS, *sm.* fig-tree, 987, 989.

FIGURE, *sf.* representation, figure, figure of speech, face, 177, 614.

FIGURE, *pr.* 3, FIGURERENT, *pft.* 6, FIGURER, *vb.* represent, 835, 1782; 637.

FIL, FILG, FILLZ, FILS, FILZ, *sm.* son, 713, 1618; 2640; 3066; 324, 2839; 105, 710.

FILLES, *sf.* daughters, girls, 313, 687.

FIN, FINE, *adj.* fine, pure, 476, 1104; 2135.

FINE, *pr.* 3, FINEES, *past part.*, FINER, *vb.* finish, end, 2152, 2978; 1118; 2153.

FINEMENT, *sm.* end, death, 3146.

FIRENT, *pft.* 6, FIS, *pft.* 1, FIST, *pft.* 3, FAIRE, *vb.* make, do, 720, 724; 395, 483; 9, 529; 332, 403.

FISTLE, *sf.* calamus (herb), 2320.

FIUS, *sm.* lands, 415.

FLAIRANZ, *pres. part.* used as *adj.*, FLAIRE, *vb.* fragrant, 596.

FLAIRE, *inf.* used as *sm.* fragrance, scent, 3514.

FLECHIST, *pres.* 3, SE FLECHIR, *vb.* rise like a spire, 2119.

FLOR, FLORE, FLORS, *sf.* flower, bloom, flower of rhetoric, 82, 998; 3280; 669, 671.

FLORIE, FLORIZ, *past part.*, FLORIST, *pr.* 3, FLORIR, *vb.*, blossom, flower, garnish with flowers, 2172; 596; 1076; 2392.

FOI, *pr.* 1, FOIR, *vb.* flee, escape from, 139.

FOI, *sf.* faith, 438, 946.

FOIBLES, *sm.* from *adj.* feeble, weak, 1491; 1572.

FOIBLETÉ, *sf.* weakness, 3000.

FOILLES, *sf.* leaves, petals, 3323, 3333.

FOIR, *vb.* dig, cultivate, 335.

FOIS, *pr.* 2, FOIR, *vb.* flee, escape, 666.

FOIS, *sf.* faith, 1759, 3320.

FOIZ, *sf.* time, times, 1415, 1416.

FOL, *adj.* mad, foolish, 484, p. 97, l. 1.

FOLC, *sm.* flock, herd, troupe, 2028.

FOLE, FOLS, *adj.* mad, foolish, 12, 976; 470, 2663.

FOLIE, *sf.* madness, 2407.

FONTAINE, *sf.* source, spring, 1129, 1983.

FOR, *prep.* except, 2850, 3495.

FORAIN, *adj.* external, from outside, 2660.

FORCHE, *sf.* strength, force, 1376.

FORDINE, *sf.* small coin of minute value, farthing, 582.

FORMENT, *adv.* strongly, 254, 2042, 2106.

FORREURE, *sf.* fur, 2543.

FORS, *adv.* out, outside, 411, 458; *prep.* except, 74, 2646.

FORS, *adj.* strong, 731; *adv.* strongly, 1892.

FORSEN, *sm.* fury, anger, 3095.

FORT, FORZ, *adj.* and *sm.* strong, strong man, 1352, 1403; 232, 1405.

FOUNS, *sm.* young ewe, lamb, 1823.

FOUS, *adj.* mad, foolish, 1916.

FRANCS, *adj.* noble, 644.

FRARINE, *sf.* wretch, miserable person, 581.

FRECHES, FRESCES, *adj.* fresh, 1342; 601.

FROIDURE, *sf.* cold, 943, 1629.

FRUCTEFIER, *vb.* fruit, produce fruit, 2392.

FRUIZ, *sm.* fruit, fruits, 707, 727.

FRUNT, *fut.* 3, FAIRE, *vb.* make, do, 478.

FU, *pft.* 3, ESTRE, *vb.* be, 8, 63.

FU, *sm.* fire, 18, 1321.

## GLOSSARY

FUEILL, *sm.* leaf, petal, 3439.

FUER, *sm.* price, A NUL FUER, on no account, 627.

FUET, *pr.* 3, FOIR, *vb.* dig, cultivate, 337.

FUI, *imper. sing.* and *past part.*, FUIE, *pr. subj.* 1, FUIENT, *pr.* 6, FUIRET, *cond.* 3, FUIT, *pr.* 3, FUIR, *vb.* flee, escape, 1003, 2401; 860; 2845; 1396; 2188.

FUMERETE, *sf.* thin spiral of smoke, 1727, 2118.

FUMES, *pft.* 4, ESTRE, *vb.* be, 1790.

FUMIERE, *sf.* light smoke, vapour, 1303, 1309.

FUNT, *pr.* 6, FAIRE, *vb.* make, do, 1416, 3431.

FUS, *pft.* 2, FUSENT, *pft.* 6, FUST, *pft.* 3, ESTRE, *vb.* be, 213; 1522; 86, 304.

FUS, *sm.* fire, 1292, 1900.

FUST, FUSTZ, *sm.* wood, tree-trunk, 2321; 1470, 1471.

FUZ, *pft.* 3, ESTRE, *vb.* be, 2629.

G', *pers. pron.* I, 450, 475.

GABBEZ, *past part.*, GABBER, *vb.* rail at, mock, 2787.

GABOIS, *sm.* mockery, railing, 2697.

GARDEIR, *vb.* guard, keep, protect, 2017.

GARDES, *sm.* guards, 2538.

GARDIN, *sm.* garden, 2345, 2353.

GART, *pr. subj.* 3, GARDER, *vb.* observe, see to, 1874, 1876.

GAS, *sm.* mockery, railing, 2706.

GE, *pers. pron.* I, 2304.

GELEE, *sf.* frost, freezing, cold, 941, 961.

GENERACION, *sf.* procreation, 315.

GENT, GENZ, *sf.* people, race, 198, 658; 1279, 1285.

GENTIS, *adj.* noble, beautiful, 2332.

GETÉ, GETEZ, *past part.*, GETER, *vb.* throw, 986; 826; 357.

GIS, *pr.* 2, GISENT, *pr.* 6, GISOIE, *impf.* 1, GISOIT, *impf.* 3, GIST, *pft.* 3, GISIR, *vb.* lie, recline, 594, 2304; 2163; 1177; 1349; 1499; 3172.

GISTES, *sf.* habitations, homes, 2202.

GLISE, *sf.* the Church, 987, 1504, 3319.

GLOIRE, GLORIE, *sf.* glory, 996; 360, 630.

GLOREFIONS, *pr.* 4, GLOREFIER, *vb.* glorify, 1744.

GLORIOS, GLORIOSE, *adj.* glorious, 710; 262, 1843.

GOMMES, *sf.* resins, 2356.

GOTES, *sf.* dark patch, 2500, 2570.

GOVERNEIR, GOVERNER, *vb.* look after, govern, 2896; 1409.

GRACE, GRACES, GRACIE, GRACIES, *sf.* grace, 203, 229; 271; 1001, 2588; 2856, 2991.

GRAIN, *sm.* grain, seeds, 357, 573.

GRAINDRE, *adj.* greater, 2108.

GRAINS, *sm.* seeds, grains, 2318, 2928, 3324.

GRANATE, *adj.*, POMME GRANATE, pomegranate (i.e. fruit with seeds), 1877.

GRANDE, *adj.* big, great, 1011.

GRANDESCE, *sf.* size, grandeur, 2238.

GRANS, GRANT, GRANZ, *adj.* big, great, large, 1393, 1806; 8, 70; 186, 194.

GREF, *adj.* irksome, painful, 1763.

GREGNOR, GREIGNOR, GREIGNORS, GREINDRE, GRENOR, *adj.* greater, greatest, 3254; 1824, 2047; 2162, 2461; 3255; 1781.

GREINET, *sm.* small seed, 3327.

GRELLETS, *adj.* slender, delicate, 1302.

GRENAT, *sm.* garnet (precious stone).

GRENATE, *adj.* with seeds, 2318; POMME GRENATE, pomegranate, 1862.

GREVANCE, GREVEMENCE, *sf.* pain, burden, difficulty, 2569, 3255; 2589.

GREVEZ, *adj.*, *past part.*, GREVER, *vb.* weigh down, grieve, 990, 2735.

GRIECE, GRIECES, GRIESCE, *sf.* misfortune, difficulty, pain, 1574; 2791; 663.

GRIEF, GRIÉS, *adj.* painful, heavy, sad, 1559, 2088; 2730, 3394.

GRIET, *pr. subj.* 3, GRIEVE, *pr.* 3, GRIEVENT, *pr.* 6, GREVER, *vb.* weigh down, grieve, 1670; 2360; 691.

GUAAIGNE, *sf.* gain, 2678.

GUARDA, *pft.* 3, GUARDE, *pr.* 3, *imper. sing.* GUARDEE, *past part.*, GUARDENT, *pr.* 6, GUARDERA, *fut.* 3, GUART, *pr.* I, GUARDER, *vb.* protect, watch over, guard, look at, see that, 984, 1662; 406; 1077, 2574; 1421; 1228; 1159, 1972; 340, 1164.

GUARDE, *sf.* guard, protection, 714, 983.

GUARDEOR, GUARDEUR, *sm.* guardian, protector, guard, 1419; 1399.

GUARDES, *sf.* watchmen, guards, 1195, 1201, 2615.

GUEREDONE, *pr.* 3, GUEREDONER, *vb.* reward, 2204.

GUERPI, *pr.* 3, GUERPIE, GUERPIZ, *past part.*, GUERPIR, *vb.* abandon, give up, 63; 38; 1281.

GUISE, *sf.* manner, way, fashion, 798, 2095.

GUTES, *sf.* dark patch, 2566.

HA, *interject.* Ha! 843.
HALT, *adj.* high, 371, 619; *sm.* high, 436, 635.
HALTE, *adj.* high, noble, exalted, 2171, 2905.
HALTEMENT, *adv.* in a high, loud, voice, 197.
HALTESCE, *sf.* height, 2237.
HALZ, *sm.* heights, 849.
HALZ, *adj.* high, 2190.
HANAP, *sm.* goblet, 3390.
HARDEMENT, *sm.* audacity, 144.
HARDIE, *adj.* bold, 146, 1289.
HARDIEMENT, *adv.* boldly, 2643.
HASTE, *pr.* 2, HASTER, *vb.* hurry, hasten, 935, 1017.
HAUCENT, *pr.* 6, HAUCER, *vb.* raise, 909.
HAUZ, *adj.* high, 1151, 1555.
HAZ, *pr.* 6, HAER, *vb.* hate, 924.
HEBRIUE, *adj.* hebrew, 1636.
HEENT, *pr.* 3, HAER, *vb.* hate, 2847.
HERBERGENT, *pr.* 6, HERBERGIER, *vb.* harbour, lodge, 3477.
HERITEL, HERITES, *sm.* heretic, 1061; 388.
HET, *pr.* 3, HAER, *vb.* hate, 2150.
HOM, *sm.* man, 319, 826; *impers. pron.* one, 239, 464.
HOMAINE, HOMAINS, *adj.* human, 104, 202; 1082.
HOME, HOMES, HOMME, HON, *sm.* man, 93, 345; 176, 314; 356; 1882.
HONESTE, *adj.* pure, honest, 580.
HONEURENT, *pr.* 6, HONOREE, HONOREZ, *past part.*, HONORER, *vb.* honour, 715; 2454; 748.
HONOR, HONORS, *sm.* honour, 10, 506; 2207, 3150.
HONTE, HONTES, *sf.* shame, dishonour, 2728, 2729; 3224.
HOSTEL, *sm.* resting-place, 369.
HUMANITÉ, *sf.*, PRIST HUMANITÉ, became man, 2246.
HUMANITEZ, *sf.* humanity, the quality of being human, 111.

I, *adv.* there, in that place, to that, 54, 94.
ICELE, *adj.* that, 981.
ICIL, *adj.* this, these, 99, 331.
ICO, *pron.* this, 392.
ICSI, *adv.* here, 81.
IERE, *fut.* 1, IERENT, *fut.* 6, IERES, *fut.* 2, IERT, *fut.* 3, IES, *pr.* 2, ESTRE, *vb.* be, 1093, 2505; 1118, 1684; 2163; 354, 486; 165, 227.

IGLISE, IGLISES, *sf.* church, 1219; 1055, 1057.
IGNELE, *adj.* gentle, smooth, 2496, 2571.
IGNELS, *adj.* light, rapid, swift, 831.
IGNOCENCE, *sf.* innocence, 2737.
ILEVEMENT, *sm.* outline, main features, 746.
ILUEC, *adv.* there, in that place, 867, 875.
INFER, *sm.* Hell, 885.
IRE, *sf.* wrath, anger, 1807, 2902.
IRIÉ, *adj.* angry, 56.
IROMS, *fut.* 4, ALEIR, *vb.* go, 255.
IRRISION, *sf.* derision, 2780.
ISCIR, *vb.* go out of, leave, 2553.
ISSE, ISSI, *conj.* thus, as, so, 1966; 744, 858.
ISSI, *adv.* here, 1546, 1639.
ISSIES, ISSIEZ, *imper. pl.*, IST, *pr.* 3, ISSIR, *vb.* go out of, emerge, 1591; 1593; 169, 457.
ITEL, ITELS, *adj.* such, 717; 54.
ITENT, *adv.* then, straightaway, 2705.
IULS, IULZ, *sm.* eyes, 1496; 1733.
IVER, IVERS, *sm.* winter, 942; 939, 943.
IVRESCE, *sf.* intoxication, 269, 741.

J', *pers. pron.* I, 1501, 2510.
JA, *adv.* already, ever, 61, 766; JA TANT LOINZ, however far, 69.
JADIST, *adv.* formerly, 2493.
JAGONCES, JAGONCIE, JAGONCIES, *sf.* ruby, 3400; 3437; 3461, 3483.
JARDIN, JARDING, JARDINS, *sm.* garden, 2313, 2402; 2380, 2425; 2303, 2397.
JO, *pers. pron.* I, 132, 135.
JOES, *sf.* cheeks, 439, 441.
JOIGNE, *pr.* 1, JOIGNENT, *pr.* 6, JOINST, JOINT, *pr.* 3, JOINTES, *past part.*, JOINDRE, *vb.* joint, 151; 3276; 1512; 1935, 2826; 1639; 109.
JOR, JORS, *sm.* day, 1598, 1765; 856, 860.
JOUNES, *adj.* young, 1575.
JOVENCE, *sf.* youth, 293.
JOUVENCELES, JOVINCELES, *sf.* young maiden, 231, 235; 1577.
JOVINCEL, *sm.* young man, 3034.
JUCE, *pr.* 3, JUCIER, *vb.* judge, 1021.
JUCEMENZ, *sm.* judgement, 1538.
JUGE, *pr.* 3, JUGIEZ, *past part.*, JUGIER, *vb.* judge, 1028, 2018; 2787; 2963.
JUISE, *sm.* judgement, 2473.
JUIUS, *sm.* Jew, 1513, 2648, 2686.
JUNER, *vb.* fast, 1627.
JUNES, *sf.* fast, fasting, 1523.
JUS, *adv.* down, below, 2585.

JUSTE, JUSTES, *adj.* and *sm.* just, right, 431, 1532; 1681, 2735.

JUSTICE, JUSTISE, *sf.* justice, 598, 1662; 1673, 2724.

JUT, *pft.* 3, GÉSIR, *vb.* lie, 884.

K', *conj.* that, 162, 233.

K', *rel. pron.* whom, which, that, 324, 820.

KALEUR, *sf.* heat, 735, 946.

KANK', KANKE, KANQUES, *neut. pron.* whatever, whatsoever, 1857; 328; 763, 1372.

KANT, *adv.* when, 544, 581.

KAR, *conj.* for, 98, 115.

KE, *conj.* that, 36, 41.

KE, *rel. pron.* whom, which, that, 92, 115; what, 59.

KEL, *rel. adj.* whichever, whatever, 1173, 1174; *interrog. adj.* which ?, 1358.

KELE, KELS, *rel. adj.* which, 1608; 864.

KEURE, *pr.* 3, COURRE, *vb.* run, flow, 1608.

KI, *rel. pron.* who, whoever, which, what, whatever, 42, 53, 78, 85, 106, 188, 688.

KIEVRES, *sf.* goats, 413.

KUEVRENT, *pr.* 6, COVRIR, *vb.* cover, 2052.

LABORER, *vb.* work, toil, 967.

LACHEURE, *sf.* enclosure, palissade, 613, 639.

LAECE, *sf.* rejoicing, happiness, 3340.

LAIDENGIER, *vb.*, LAIDENGIEZ, *past part.* insult, ill-treat, 3179; 532.

LAIDOR, *sf.* ugliness, 859.

LAIDURES, *sf.* shame, outrage, evil, 301, 947.

LAIENS, LAIENZ, *adv.* within, therein, 1076; 638, 1537.

LAIRA, *fut.* 3, LAIRAI, *fut.* 1, LAIS, *pr.* 1, LAISCHENT, *pr.* 6, LAISSE, *pr.* 3, LAISSEZ, *imper. pl.*, LAISCIER, LAISER, LAISSIER, *vb.* let, leave, allow, 71, 1231; 145, 1094; 398; 2805; 342, 59; 1608; 2555; 2326; 970.

LAISE, *interject.* alas, 129.

LAIT, LAIZ, *adj.* ugly, shameful, 1870, 3211; 857, 1805.

LAIT, LAIZ, *sm.* milk, 2008, 2022; 185.

LAITUAIRES, LAITUARIE, *sm.* electuary, p. 97, ll. 6, 7.

LAMPROIETES, *sf.* fringe, edging (Song of Songs 1: 10: 'borders (of gold)').

LANCE, *sf.* spear, 1015.

LAPIDEIR, *vb.* stone (to death), lapidate, 3108.

LARGEMENT, *adv.* generously, 922, 3405.

LARGESCE, *sf.* generosity, 3404.

LARMIES, *sf.* tears, 3411.

LAS, *adj.* weary, 1545.

LASQUE, *adj.* relaxed, indolent, 1193.

LASTE, *sf.* hardship, 936.

LAVEIR, *vb.* wash, 2951, 2953.

LAVOIR, *sm.* washing-place, dip, 1794.

LEECE, *sf.* rejoicing, happiness, 219, 280.

LEGERIE, *sf.* slightness, triviality, 4.

LEGIER, *adj.* easy, smooth, 1494; DE LEGIER, *adv.* easily, 3183.

LEGIERE, LEGIERS, *adj.* light, nimble, easy, 2012, 3392; 1568, 2189.

LEGIEREMENT, *adv.* easily, lightly, 1564.

LEGIERTÉ, *sf.* triviality, slightness, 3420.

LEIVRES, *sf.* lips, 3315.

LERE, *adj.* thieving, robbing, 667.

LEST, *pr. subj.* 3, LAISSIER, *vb.* leave, 2091.

LETRE, *sf.* letter, written work, 82, 1248.

LEVEIZ, *past part.*, LEVER, *vb.* raise up, get up, lift, 3007; 1977.

LEZ, *sm.* side, 1010, 2790.

LEZ, *adv.* beside, p. 97, l. 12.

LI, *art.* the, 7, 9.

LI, *pers. pron.* he, him, it, 32, 39.

LIBERACION, *sf.* delivrance, 3295.

LIÉ, LIEZ, *adj.* happy, joyful, 422, 1148; 1556, 3256.

LIEMENT, *adv.* joyfully, 889.

LIENS, *sm.* bond, thong (for tying vines), 343.

LIER, *vb.* tie back, 336.

LIEVE, *imper. sing.* 2 and 3, LEVER, *vb.* rise up, 933, 2351.

LIEZ, *past part.*, LIER, *vb.* bind, 533, 2786.

LIGE, *sm.* vassal, liege, 2210.

LILES, LILIE, LILIES, LILLES, *sf.* lily, 368, 601; 690, 1389; 1975, 3279; 2668.

LISTE, *adj.* smooth, 3425.

LIU, *sm.* place, 856, 884.

LIUPART, *sm.* leopard, 2164, 2200.

LIUS, *sm.* places, 757, 831.

LIZ, *sm.* bed, 595, 602.

LO, *art.* the, 1202, 2733.

LO, *pr. subj.* 1, LOE, *pr.* 1 and 3, LOÉ, LOEE, *past part.*, LOES, *pr.* 2, LOER, *vb.* praise, 1722; 556, 1461; 361; 1792, 2379; 2063; 581; 271, 1459.

LOENGES, *sm.* praise, 1069.

LOALMENT, *adv.* loyally, 670.

LOIER, LOIERS, *vb.* used as *sm.* reward, payment, 1388, 2205; 353, 678.

LOINS, LOINZ, *adv.* far, afar, 1165; 69, 216, 1000.

LONCES, *sf.* spears, 1945.

LONGE, *adj.* long, 1650.

LONGEMENT, LONGES, *adv.* for a long time, 60, 168; 1022, 2412.

LONS, *adj.* long, 1132.

LOR, *pron.* to them, of them, 286, 1788; *poss. adj.* their, 350, 384.

LOS, LOUS, *sm.* praise, 2221; 2315.

LUEC, LUES, *adv.* immediately, at once, 897; 3085.

LUIUS, *sm.* place, 2811.

LUMERE, LUMIERE, *sf.* light, 1332; 2414, 3453.

LUXURE, *sf.* lechery, lust, 630.

MAILE, *sf.* spot, stain, 2142.

MAILENTEZ, *past part.*, MAILENTER, *vb.* stain, dirty, soil, 2504.

MAIN, *sf.* hand, 404, 574.

MAIN, *sm.* morning, 538.

MAINE, *pr.* 3, MAINENT, *pr.* 6, MAINES, *pr.* 2, MAINT, *pr. subj.* 3, MENER, *vb.* bring, lead, display (grief, joy, etc.), 84, 1528; 1272; 3396; 256.

MAINENT, *pr.* 6, MAINT, *pr.* 3, MAINDRE, *vb.* rest, remain, dwell, 3100; 1898, 2563.

MAINT, MAINTE, MAINTES, *adj.* many, 418, 494; 300, 798; 2371, 3491.

MAINTENIR, *vb.*, MAINTENUZ, *past part.*, MAINTIENENT, *pr.* 6, MAINTIENT, *pr.* 3, uphold, sustain, defend, 656, 1158; 836; 3486; 984.

MAINTESFOIZ, *adv.* frequently, often, 3489, 3211.

MAIS, *conj.* but, 20, 40; *adv.* any more, any longer, 67, 642.

MAISCELES, MAISELES, *sf.* temples, upper part of the cheek, 2061, 3196; 1864, 3219.

MAISNIE, *sf.* household, retinue, 423.

MAISONCELE, *sf.* small house, 3170.

MAISSELE, MAISSELES, *sf.* temple, upper part of the cheek, 1859; 1903, 1905.

MAISTRE, MAISTRES, *sm.* master, lord, guide, teacher, 1198, 1551; 3365, 3390.

MAIZ, *conj.* but, 1987, 3134.

MAJESTEZ, *sf.* majesty, 3283.

MAL, *adj.* evil, wicked, 571, 2272.

MALBAILLIE, *past part.*, MALBAILLIR, *vb.* ruin, deal harshly with, 2608.

MALDIÇON, *sf.* curse, 978.

MALDIT, *past part.*, MALDIRE, *vb.* speak ill of, curse, 973.

MALE, small coin of little value, 1878.

MALES, *adj.* evil, wicked, 689, 3248.

MALTALENT, *sm.* wrath, anger, 76.

MALVAIS, MALVAISE, *adj.* and *sm.* bad, evil, wicked, 328, 341; 1947, 2630.

MALVAISTIÉ, *sf.* badness, wickedness, 1312.

MAMELES, *sf.* breasts, 165, 175.

MANGIER, MANGIERS, *inf.* used as *sm.* eat, eating, food, 2437, 3137; 461, 2441.

MANIAI, *pft.* 1, MANIER, *vb.* hold, 2513.

MANJUE, *pr.* 3, MANJUST, *pft.* 3, MANGIER, *vb.* eat, 1261; 2424.

MANSION, *sf.* resting-place, dwelling, 2072, 2444.

MANTEL, *sm.* cloak, 2541, 2623.

MARGERIES, *sf.* pearl, 452, 1634.

MARIZ, *sm.* bridegroom, 48.

MARS, *sm.* mark (coin), 3015.

MARTELS, *sm.* hammer, 526.

MARTIRE, MARTYRE, MARTYRES, *sm.* martyrdom, 1391; 995, 1560; 1393.

MARTYR, *sm.* martyr, 717, 993.

MAT, *adj.* afflicted, 2054.

MATERE, MATIERE, *sf.* matter, subject-matter, 1, 1437; 3314.

MATERIE, *sf.* material, cause, 2107, 3466.

MAUS, *sm.* evils, 87.

MEÇLE, *pr.* 3, MESLER, *vb.* mix with, mingle, 1886.

MECINE, MEDECINE, *sf.* medicine, antidote, 2977; 510.

MEESMENT, *adv.* similarly, especially, 2187.

MEFFAIT, MEFFAIZ, *sm.* misdeed, sin, 2080; 91.

MEILLEUR, MEILLEURS, MEILLOR, MEILLORS, *adj.* better, 2670; 3116; 553, 573; 208, 283.

MEIME, MEIMES, *adj.* same, very, self, 1114, 1278; 1697.

MEIN, *sf.* hand, 454.

MEINS, *adv.* less, 251.

MEINTENIR, *vb.* sustain, 2970.

MEISME, MEISMES, *adj.* and *pron.* same, very, self, 451, 915; 364, 410.

MEISON, *sf.* house, 1332.

MEL, *adj.* bad, 2924.

MELLE, *pr.* 3, MELLERUNT, *fut.* 6, MELLER, *vb.* mix, mingle, 1656, 1897; 481.

MEMBRE, *pr.* 3, MEMBRER, *vb. impers.* recall, 1162.

MEMBRE, MEMBRES, *sm.* limb, limbs, 1161, 1906; 1162, 2063.

MEMELES, *sf.* breasts, 1981, 1999.
MEMORIE, *sf.* memory, remembering, 339.
MEN, *poss. adj.* my, 172, 217.
MENBRA, *pft.* 3, MENBRE, *pr.* 3, MENBRER, *vb. impers.* recall, remember, 2520; 442, 2744.
MENBRE, MENBRES, *sf.* limb, limbs, 441, 2722; 2102.
MENEUR, MENEURS, *adj.* smaller, 2125; 850.
MENEZ, *past part.*, MENER, *vb.* lead, bring, treat, 1760, 2786.
MENISTRES, *sm.* minister, 1253, 1928.
MENTEEUR, *sm.* liar, 2147.
MERCI, *sm.* pity, mercy, 65, 66.
MERIDIENNE, *sf.* noon, midday, 375.
MERRE, *sf.* mother, 1218, 1219.
MERVEILLOS, *adj.* wondrous, 32.
MES, *nom. sing. m. poss. adj.*, my, 66, 135.
MESCINES, *sf.* young servant girl, 1089.
MESCREANZ, *sm.* unbeliever, 2870.
MESERRÉ, *past part.*, MESERRER, *vb.* go astray, 3444.
MESFAIZ, *sm.* misdeeds, 958.
MESIERE, *sf.* wall, 1004.
MESIST, *impf. subj.* 3, METRE, *vb.* put, place, 2468.
MESSAGES, *sm.* messengers, 2693.
MESTIER, MESTIERS, *sm.* need, necessity, 1450, 2571; 682.
MESURE, *sf.* measure, moderation, 190, 583.
MET, *pr.* 3, METE, *pr. subj.* 3, METEIZ, *pr.* 5, METENT, *pr.* 6, METES, *pr. subj.* 2, METRAI, *fut.* 1, METRE, *vb.* put, place, 340, 487; 1671, 2105; 2112; 2808, 3155; 3152; 475; 81, 454.
METE, *sf.* food, 3051.
MEURS, *sf.* customs, morals, 580, 1411.
MI, *stressed form pers. pron.*, me, 71, 529.
MI, *sm.* middle, centre, 1948, 2968; *adv.* in the middle of, through, 2083.
MIE, *sf.* beloved, 23, 808.
MIE, *neg. particle*, not, 145, 243.
MIEL, MIELS, *sm.* honey, 2284, 2437; 366, 2287.
MIELEE, *adj.* honeyed, sweet, 2286.
MIELZ, *adv.* most, 3002.
MIELZ, *sm.* best, 203, 695.
MIEN, MIENS, *poss. adj.* my, 164, 524; 60, 486.
MIERES, *sm.* physician, 3114.
MIEUS, MIEZ, *adv.* better, 932; 2067.
MIL, *num.* thousand, 1917, 1941.

MILLIER, MILLIERS, *sm.* thousand, 1770; 2742.
MIRRE, *sf.* myrrh, resin, 525, 2071.
MIS, MISE, *past part.*, MIST, *pft.* 3, METRE, *vb.* place, put, 184, 226; 88, 131; 1182, 1348.
MOI, *pers. pron. obj. of prep.* and *dative case*, me, 66, 75; 1039.
MOIE, *poss. adj.* my, 536.
MOLS, *adj.* gentle, soft, 2349, 2358.
MOLT, *adv.* much, very, 56, 201; *adj.* many, numerous, 757.
MOLTES, MOLTZ, *adj.* many, 1753, 1004; 731, 871.
MOLZ, *adv.* greatly, 736.
MONCEALS, MONCEL, *sm.* mound, hillock, 1748, 1749; 1767, 1773.
MOND, MONS, MONT, *sm.* world, 2344, 3222; 1317, 2203; 213, 272.
MONT, *sm.* hill, mount, mountain, 1471, 1745.
MONTEE, *sf.* ascent, 1489, 1571.
MONTEIR, *vb.* ascend, 3024.
MONTEPLOIER, *vb.* multiply, 1413.
MONTEX, *past part.*, MONTEIR, *vb.* mount, 400.
MONZ, *sm.* world, 449, 1844, 3169.
MONZ, *sm.* mountains, 847, 1138.
MONZ, *adj.* clean, pure, 1151.
MORALITÉ, *sf.* moral lesson, 117, 3278.
MORS, *sm.* biting, 89.
MORSELS, *sm.* fragment, morsel, 465.
MORT, *sf.* death, 350, 883.
MORT, *adj.*, *past part.*, MORIR, *vb.* die, dead, 430, 884.
MORT, *pr.* 3, mordre, *vb.* bite, 1804.
MORTEL, MORTEUS, *adj.* mortal, 1364; 2279.
MORTZ, *sf.* deaths, 2559.
MORZ, *sf.* death, 718.
MORZ, *sm.* dead person, 3202, 3251.
MOSTEISONS, *sf.* vine-harvest, 348.
MOSTRE, *imper. sing.* and *pr.* 3, MOSTRÉ, MOSTREE, MOSTREZ, *past part.*, MOSTRENT, *pr.* 6, MOSTRER, *vb.* show, 363, 377; 1380, 1384; 1326; 1033, 2308, 2740; 3336; 34.
MOT, MOTZ, MOZ, *sm.* word, 805, 1294; 1802; 891.
MOVRA, *fut.* 3, MOVEIR, *vb.* move, 542.
MUABLETÉ, *sf.* changing condition, instability, 2864, 2890.
MUCHANT, *pres. part.*, MUCHIER, *vb.* hide, 1048.

MUE, *pr.* 3, MUER, *vb.* change, 1262, 1268.

MUEL, MUELE, *adj.* sinner, 1441; 1128.

MUEVE, *pr. subj.* 3, MOVEIR, *vb.* move, 1210.

MULT, *adv.* much, very, 619, 1722.

MULTIPLIANT, *pres. part.*, MULTIPLOIER, *vb.* multiply, 3354.

MULZ, *adj.* many, 2387.

MUNDAINES, *adj.* worldly, mundane, 2583.

MUSAGE, *sm.* trickery, deceit, p. 97, l. 3.

MYRRE, *sf.* myrrh, 523, 2079.

NAIR, *adj.* black, 400.

NAISCENCE, *sf.* birth, 3146.

NAISCENT, *pr.* 6, NAISTRE, *vb.* be born, 688, 2258; 1643, 1703.

NARD, NARDE, *sm.*, *sf.* nard, spikenard, 503; 2319.

NATURALS, NATUREIL, *adj.* natural, 1654; 2955.

NAVRE, *pr.* 3, NAVRÉ, NAVRES, *past part.*, NAVRER, *vb.* wound, 2212; 2251; 2261.

NE, *conj.* and *neg. particle*, neither, nor, not, 14, 68; 14, 22.

NEKEDENT, NEQUEDENT, NEQUIDENT, *adv.* however, 544, 1215; 2064, 2389; 20.

NEPORQUANT, *adv.* however, nevertheless, 527, 3450.

NETE, NETES, *adj.* pure, clean, 598, 1272; 1164, 3114.

NETEÉ, *sf.* purity, cleanness, 370.

NEZ, *past part.*, NAISTRE, *vb.* be born, 2811, 3170.

NI, *sm.* nest, 2906.

NIENT, *pron.* nothing, 2153, 2247; *adv.* not at all, 176, 253.

NIENTAGE, *sm.* nothingness, emptiness, 2264.

NIERENT, *pr.* 3, NIER, *vb.* deny, 3372.

NIS, *adv.* not even, 165, 1053.

NIVE, *adj.* fragile, 2273.

NO, *pron.* us, 1404; *poss. adj.* our, 896.

NOBILITÉ, *sf.* rank, nobility, 3074.

NOIA, *pft.* 3, NOIER, *vb.* drown, 3030.

NOIENT, *sm.* nothing, 2695.

NOIER, NOIR, NOIRE, NOIRS, *adj.* black, 2833; 2777, 2779; 297; 2759, 2778.

NOIRTUME, *sf.* blackness, 2792, 2835.

NOISE, *sf.* din, noise, 1141.

NOL, *adj.* no, none, 628.

NOLS, *pron.* no one, 41, 818.

NOM, NOMS, *sm.* name, 1616; 214, 215.

NOM, *pr.* 1, NOME, *pr.* 3, NOMEE, *past part.*,

NOMER, *vb.* name, call, 441, 823; 313, 3279; 1641.

NOMEEMENT, *adv.* namely, specifically, 1953.

NON, *adv.* not, 141, 234.

NON, NONS, *sm.* name, 2125, 2219; 219, 222.

NORETURE, NORRETURE, *sf.* food, nourishment, 1933; 463, 1985.

NORISSENT, *pr.* 6, NORRI, *past part.*, NORRIST, *pr.* 3, NORRIR, *vb.* feed, nourish, 1796; 1854; 204, 456.

NORRISEMENZ, *sm.* food, nourishment, 1925.

NOS, *pron.* we, us, 114, 155; *poss. adj.* our, 987, 2148.

NOSKE, *sf.* clip, brooch, collar, 450, 467.

NOSTRE, *poss. adj.* our, 187, 281; *pron.* ours, 981, 2874.

NOTE, *pr.* 3, NOTENT, *pr.* 6, NOTES, *imper. sing.*, NOTEZ, *imper. pl.*, NOTEIR, *vb.* denote, note, take note of, 1944; 2593; 1949, 3347; 2033.

NOVEALS, NOVEL, NOVELE, NOVELES, NOVELS, *adj.* new, 2852; 184, 340; 2184, 2320; 1068, 1341; 1267, 2908.

NOVELEMENT, *adv.* anew, newly, 2220.

NOZ, *pron.* we, us, 1982, 637; *poss. adj.* our, 284, 874.

NUE, NUES, *adj.* naked, 2506; 1947.

NUESCE, *sf.* nakedness, 2264.

NUIRE, NUISIR, *vb.*, NUIST, *pr.* 3, harm, hurt, 1166; 2347; 952, 1566.

NUIT, NUIZ, *sf.* night, 1355, 1965; 1181 1566.

NUL, NULE, NULS, *adj.* and *pron.* any, anyone, 258, 277, 871; 359, 878; 20, 22.

NULLUI, *pron.* anyone, 1922, 2602.

NUMBRES, *sm.* number, 3360, 3361.

NUVELE, *adj.* new, 2640.

NUZ, *adj.* naked, bereft, 1152.

O, *conj.* or, 28, 594.

O, *adv.* where, whither, 157, 222.

O, *prep.* with, 214, 648.

OANZ, *sm.* hearers, 2294.

OBLIE, *pr.* 3, OBLIENT, *pr.* 6, OBLIEZ, *imper. pl.*, OBLIER, *vb.* forget, 1914; 2323, 2634; 2642.

OCCULTEMENT, *adv.* in a hidden manner, 3289.

OCIRRE, *vb.*, OCIS, *past part.*, kill, 3262; 1772.

OD, *prep.* with, 53, 682.

ODEUR, ODEURS, ODOR, ODORS, *sf.* scent, smell, perfume, 168, 171; 2301, 2314; 257, 505; 256.

OEIL, *sm.* eyes, 569.

OEVRE, *sf.* work, toil, 1452, 1467.

OFFENDRE, *vb.* attack, offend, 3430.

OFFERT, *past part.*, OFFRIRENT, *pft.* 6, OFFRIR, *vb.* offer, 3013; 3015; 2009.

OÏ, *pr.* 1 and *past part.*, OÏE, *past part.* and *pr. subj.* 3, OÏEZ, *imper. pl.*, OÏR, *vb.* hear, 220, 1040; 1607, 2262; 972; 2276; 317, 1588; 1035.

OI, *pft.* 1, AVEIR, *vb.* have, 361, 1201.

OÏE, *sf.* hearing, 1143.

OILES, *sf.* oil, 1507.

OINDRE, *vb.*, OINT, *pr.* 3, anoint, 2019; 217.

OISEALS, OISEL, OISELS, *sm.* bird, 2759, 2911; 571; 2778, 2836.

OLIE, *sf.* oil, 1428.

OLTRAGE, *sm.* excess, 1805.

OLTRE, *adv.* beyond, 583.

OM, *indef. pron.* one, 212, 301.

OM, OME, OMES, OMME, *sm.* man, 599, 2767; 90, 397; 784, 1649; 3519.

OMANITÉ, *sf.* humanity, the quality of being human, 3161, 3441.

OMBRE, *sf.* shade, 735.

ON, *indef. pron.* one, 1930, 2472.

ONDE, *sf.* flow, flood, 1012.

ONE, *num.* one, 1529.

ONESTÉ, ONESTEIZ, *sf.* honesty, 3339; 3282.

ONEUR, ONOR, *sm.* honour, 2126, 2561; 235, 320.

ONKES, ONQUES, *adv.* ever, 1330, 1882; 3178.

OOÏT, *impf.* 3, OÏR, *vb.* hear, 2370.

OR, *adv.* now, 40, 43.

OR, *sm.* gold, 452, 476.

ORDENEE, *past part.*, ORDENE, *pr.* 3, ORDENENT, *pr.* 6, ORDENEIR, *vb.* order, arrange, 2295; 1538; 3158.

ORDENEMENT, *sm.* ordering, arrangement, 1653.

ORE, *adv.* now, 414, 485.

OREISON, OREISONS, *sf.* prayer, 1072, 1423; 347, 1582.

ORGUEIL, ORGUELS, *sm.* pride, 3077; 409, 416.

ORGUEILLOS, *adj.* proud, 3062.

ORIE, ORIES, *adj.* of gold, golden, 1389, 1480; 478, 3401.

ORISON, *sf.* prayer, 1928.

ORRA, *fut.* 3, ORREIZ, ORREZ, *fut.* 5, OÏR, *vb.* hear, 2644; 3504; 44.

ORS, *sm.* gold, 298, 486.

ORT, ORZ, *adj.* dirty, filthy, p. 97, l. 16; 1585.

ORZ, *sm.* gold, 2821.

OS, *pr. subj.* 3, OSAI, *pft.* 1, OSE, *pr.* 1 and 3, OSENT, *pr.* 6, OSONS, *pr.* 4, OST, *pr. subj.* 3, OSER, *vb.* dare, 864; 3024; 124, 693; 1054; 3207; 454, 818.

OSCUR, OSCURE, *adj.* hidden, obscure, 829; 46, 1798.

OST, *sm.* army, 3029.

OSTA, *pft.* 3, OSTE, *pr.* 3, OSTER, *vb.* take away, remove, 2599; 1371, 2418; 969.

OSTE, *sm.* army, 1372.

OSTOIRS, *sm.* goshawk, 2926.

OT, *pft.* 3, AVEIR, *vb.* have, 599, 1475.

OT, *pft.* 3, OÏR, *vb.* hear, 1083, 1295.

OTROI, *pr.* 1, OTROIER, *vb.* grant, 2440.

OUT, *pft.* 3, AVEIR, *vb.* have, 472, 1638.

OUT, *pft.* 3, OÏR, *vb.* hear, 982.

OUVRER, *vb.* work, toil, 938.

OUVRIR, *vb.* open, interpret, 3402.

OV, *prep.* with, 3030.

OVERRUNT, *fut.* 3, OVRER, work, 482.

OVERZ, *past part.*, OVRIR, *vb.* open, 3291.

OVRA, *pft.* 3, OVRER, *vb.* work, 2675.

OVRAGE, *sm.* work, 483, 723.

OVRE, *pr.* 3, OVRENT, *pr.* 6, OVREIR, OVRER, *vb.* work, 1300; 488; 3107; 823, 1207.

OVRE, *sf.* work, 514, 999.

OVRES, *sf.* works, 782, 980.

OVRI, *pft.* 3, OVRIR, *vb.* open, 2517, 2597.

OVRIER, *sm.* worker, workman, 473, 479.

OVRIR, *vb.* open, 1029.

PACIENCE, *sf.* patience, 1818, 3131.

PAIE, *sf.* payment, 2280.

PAIENS, *sm.* pagans, 1513.

PAILLE, *sf.* chaff, straw, 357.

PAINENT, *pr.* 6, PAINER, *vb.* take pains, 1198.

PAIS, *sf.* peace, 102, 140.

PAIS, *imper. sing.*, PAISCENT, *pr.* 6, PAISCHANT, *pres. part.*, PAIST, *pr.* 3, PAISTRUNT, *fut.* 6, PAISTRE, *vb.* feed, graze, pasture, 413; 383, 2041; 1975; 2294; 363, 364; 2055.

PAISIBLEMENT, *adv.* tranquilly, 3097.

PALEUR, PALOUR, *sf.* pallor, 1629; 1894.

PALTONIER, *sm.* wretch, beggar, 1054.

PANSEZ, *sf.* thoughts, 1027.

PAR, *prep.* through, by, 8, 24; *adv.* very, 70.

PARA, *pft.* 3, PARER, *vb.* adorn, 2627.

PARAGE, *sm.* birth, lineage, 1646.

PARCHONERS, PARCHONIERE, *sm.* sharer, partner, 2031; 1222.

PARDONEZ, *past part.*, PARDONER, *vb.* pardon, 85.

PAREIL, *adj.* equal, like, 472.

PARFIN, *sf.* end, the very end, 1967.

PARFONDE, PARFONT, PARFUNDE, *adj.* deep, profound, 1011; 2212, 3326; 2330.

PARLÉ, *past part.*, PARLERA, *fut.* 3, PARLOIT, *impf.* 3, PARLOMS, *pr.* 4, PAROL, *pr.* 1, PAROLE, *pr.* 3, PAROLENT, *pr.* 6, PARLEIR, PARLER, *vb.* speak, say, talk, 809, 1089; 48, 3373; 2612; 2253; 197; 11, 26; 3379; 2761, 3130; 45, 124.

PARLERS, *sm.* speech, 1848.

PARMANABLE, PARMANABLES, *adj.* everlasting, permanent, 2732, 2848; 3176.

PARMANOIR, *vb.* live for ever, 2157.

PAROIT, PAROIZ, *sf.* wall, 896; 903, 1512.

PAROLE, PAROLES, PAROLEZ, spoken word, speech, 25, 205; 493, 679; 1452.

PARS, PART, *sf.* direction, way, side, 949, 3341; 17, 444.

PARTI, *pft.* 3, PARTIE, *past part.*, PARTIR, *vb.* depart, separate from, 94; 37, 2531; 718, 994.

PARTOT, *adv.* everywhere, throughout, 26, 2887, 2968.

PARVIENT, *pr.* 3, PARVENIR, *vb.* reach, 489.

PARZ, *sf.* part, 2736.

PASMER, *inf.* used as *sm.* swoon, faint, 3515.

PASSAGE, *sm.* narrow way, passage, p. 97, l. 12.

PASSE, *pr.* 3, PASSEES, *past part.*, PASSENT, *pr.* 6, PASSER, *vb.* pass, surpass, 455, 1970; 2051; 167; 3382.

PASSION, PASSIONS, *sf.* the Passion, suffering, torment, 535, 881; 386, 2814.

PASTURE, *sf.* nourishment, food, 1154, 2044.

PECHEOR, PECHEUR, *sm.* sinner, 1782; 303.

PECHIÉ, PECHIEZ, *sm.* sin, 38, 92; 339, 874.

PEIRE, *sf.* stone, gem, 3147.

PEIRRE, PEIRRES, *sm.* father, 2825; 2559.

PEL, PELS, *sf.* skin, 2542; 1262, 1268.

PENEANZ, *sm.* penitent, 2735.

PENERUNT, *fut.* 6, PENEZ, *past part.*, PENOI-

ENT, *impf.* 6, PENER, *vb.* torment, torture, toil, take trouble, 480; 534; 950.

PENNES, *sf.* feathers, plumage, 2804.

PENS, *pr.* 1, PENSAST, *impf. subj.* 3, PENSEROIT, *cond.* 3, PENSER, *vb.* think, 460, 699; 1238; 2672.

PENSE, PENSEE, PENSEES, PENSEZ, *sf.* thought, 432; 73, 245; 688, 1068; 3262.

PER, *sm.* equal, like, peer, 440.

PER, *prep.* by, 2399.

PERCHIERENT, *pft.* 6, PERCIE, PERCIEZ, *past part.*, PERCIER, *vb.* pierce, 1015; 2789; 1008.

PERDENT, *pr.* 6, PERDERA, *fut.* 3, PERDI, *pft.* 1, PERDU, PERDUE, *past part.*, PERDRE, *vb.* lose, waste, 244; 674; 2535; 1141, 2628; 3452.

PERE, *sm.* father, 715, 865.

PERECEUSE, *adj.* idle, lazy, slothful, 2273.

PERESCE, *sf.* sloth, idleness, 2535.

PERIRAI, *fut.* 1, PERIRENT, *pft.* 6, PERIST, *pr.* 3, PERIR, *vb.* perish, 130; 425; 436, 1075.

PERNEZ, *imper. pl.*, PRENDRE, *vb.* take, 1043.

PERS, *adj.* and *sf.* equal, like, peer, 1308, 2283.

PERSONE, PERSONES, *sf.* person, 530, 2018; 54.

PERT, *pr.* 3, PAREIR, *vb.* appear, be apparent, 560, 1214.

PERTUIS, *sm.* hole, tunnel, 1003.

PESLE, *sm.* latch, 2599.

PET, *pr.* 3, POOIR, *vb.* be able, 1414.

PETICIONS, *sf.* plea, prayer, petition, 3053.

PETIT, PETITE, PETITES, PETIZ, *adj.* small, 193, 294; 323; 3203; 185, 204.

PEURENT, *pres.* 6, PEUS, *past part.*, PAISTRE , *vb.* feed, 2459; 636.

PEUST, *impf. subj.* 3, PEUT, *pr.* 3, POOIR, *vb.* be able, 3075; 85, 95.

PIÉ, PIES, PIEZ, *sm.* foot, feet, 2790; 2503; 1007, 1535.

PIERE, PIERRE, PIERRES, *sf.* stone, 1003; 2990, 2993; 1329, 1377.

PIETÉ, PIETEZ, *sf.* piety, 118, 514; 597, 2001.

PIUS, *adj.* merciful, gentle, pious, 2241, 2411.

PIVE, *adj.* merciful, gentle, pious, 1532.

PLAIE, PLAIES, *sf.* wound, 21, 1010; 2622.

PLAIERENT, *pft.* 6, PLAIER, *vb.* wound, insult, 2540.

PLAIGNE, *pr. subj.* 3, PLAING, *pr.* 1, PLAINT,

*pr.* 3, PLAINDRE, *vb.* complain, lament, 2918; 2677; 20; 2107, 2268.

PLAIN, PLAINE, PLAINES, PLAINS, *adj.* full, 953, 1314; 1001, 1992; 1972; 516, 707.

PLAINEMENT, *adv.* completely, 2147.

PLAIRA, *fut.* 3, PLAIROIT, *impf.* 3, PLAISANT, PLAISANZ, *pres. part.*, PLAIST, *pr.* 3, PLAISIR, *vb.* please, 3374; 2366; 3333; 980; 137, 230; 309, 1456.

PLAISIR, *sm.* pleasure, 310, 1439.

PLAIT, PLAIZ, *sm.* pleading, 84, 2428; 3364.

PLANTÉ, PLANTEIZ, PLENTE, PLENTEZ, *sf.* abundance, 227, 2345; 2403, 2404; 998, 2356; 434, 1034.

PLENIEREMENT, *adv.* abundantly, plentifully, 966.

PLEST, *pr.* 3, PLAISIR, *vb.* please, 2136.

PLEUR, *pr.* 1, PLEURENT, *pr.* 6, PLORANZ, *pres. part.*, PLOROIT, *impf.* 3, PLORER, *vb.* weep, 158, 2710; 3045; 677; 2613; 3003.

PLEUT, *pft.* 3, PLAISIR, *vb.* please, 1216.

PLOREMENT, *sm.* weeping, lamentation, 59.

PLOSORS, PLUISEUR, PLUISOR, PLUSORS, *adj.* and *pron.* several, 192; 2992, 3377; 382, 1203; 1117.

PLUME, *sf.* plumage, 2836.

POESTÉ, *sf.* power, 3404.

POESTIS, *adj.* powerful, 2685.

POET, *pr.* 3, POEZ, *pr.* 5, POI, *pft.* 3, POOIR, *vb.* be able, 1805; 2643; 2529.

POI, *sm.* little, 932.

POINTURE, POINTURES, *sf.* prick, sting, 696; 691, 838.

POIS, *sm.* pea, worthless object, 409.

POIS, *sm.* weight, 3020.

POISSANZ, *adj.* powerful, 1125.

POISSONS, *pres. subj.* 4, POOIR, *vb.* be able, 1165.

POME, POMES, *sf.* apple, fruit, 89, 91; 773, 783.

POMIERS, *sm.* apple-tree, 705.

POOIE, *impf.* 1, POOIR, *vb.* be able, 1344.

POOIR, *sm.* power, ability, 354.

POOIT, *impf.* 3, PÖOMS, PÖONS, *pr.* 4, POOIR, *vb.* be able, 33, 39; 1298, 1581;1065.

POPLE, *sm.* people, 2733.

POR, *prep.* for, because of, 29, 38.

PORCEL, *sm.* piglet, 2019.

PORCERKIER, *vb.* search through, 2056.

PORCHACE, *pr.* 3, PORCHACEIR, *vb.* procure, 320.

PORFIT, *sm.* profit, 1701, 3382.

PORMAINE, *pr.* 3, PORMENER, *vb.* lead, 415.

POROINT, *pr.* 3, POROINDRE, *vb.* anoint, 2921.

PORPENS, *pr.* 1, PORPENSE, *pr.* 3, PORPENSÉ, PORPENSEE, *past part.*, PORPENSER, *vb.* reflect, meditate, 544, 3480; 2079; 2592; 2485; 913.

PORPENSEMENZ, *sm.* thought, meditation, 2263, 3272.

PORPRE, PORPRINS, *adj.* purple, crimson (Song of Songs 3: 10: 'purple').

PORRAI, *fut.* 1, POOIR, *vb.* be able, 2654.

PORRETURE, *sf.* putrefaction, decomposition, 3246.

PORREZ, *fut.* 5, POOIR, *vb.* be able, 1175.

PORRI, *pft.* 3, PORRIR, *vb.* rot, decompose, 3303; 1470.

PORRIEMES, *cond.* 4, PORROIE, *cond.* 1, PORROIT, *cond.* 3, PORRUNT, *fut.* 6, POOIR, *vb.* be able, 3424; 920; 448, 824; 2353.

PORSIVRE, *vb.* follow, pursue, 821.

PORT, *sm.* port, harbour, 1236, 2946.

PORT, *imper. sing*, PORTA, *pft.* 3, PORTANT, *pres. part.*, PORTE, *pr.* 3, PORTEE, PORTEIZ, *past part.*, PORTENT, *pr.* 6, PORTERAI, *fut.* 1, PORTES, *pr.* 2, PORTEIR, PORTER, *vb.* carry, bear, 77; 2710; 1596, 1605; 3443; 3308; 1795, 2722; 766; 438; 2915; 140, 338.

PORTE, PORTES, *sf.* 2549, 2557.

PORTRAIT, *pr.* 3, PORTRAIRE, *vb.* portray, depict, 1368.

PORVOIT, *pr.* 3, PORVOIR, *vb.* provide, 2229.

POSA, *adv.* for a short time, 426.

POSE, *sf.* space of time, 3493; POSE A, after a short time, 1226.

POSE, *pr.* 3, POSÉ, POSEES, *past part.*, POSER, *vb.* place, 2906; 1432.

POUMS, *pr.* 4, POUT, *pr.* 3, POOIR, *vb.* be able, 2014, 2893, 3083; 1648.

POVERTÉ, *sf.* poverty, 2265.

POVRE, POVRES, *adj.* poor, 323, 557; 992, 2233.

POVRETÉ, *sf.* poverty, 869, 2881.

PRAMESSE, *sf.* promise, 2165, 2184.

PRAMET, *pr.* 3, PRAMETENT, *pr.* 6, PRAMIS, *past part.*, PRAMIST, *pft.* 3, PRAMETRE, *vb.* promise, 2203, 2471; 3284; 2796, 2818; 2065, 3499.

PRECHIER, *vb.* preach, 1616.

PRECIEUS, PRECIEUSES, PRECIOS, PRECIOSES, *adj.* precious, 2218; 1632; 31, 709; 1612.

PREDICATION, PREDICATIONS, *sf.* preaching, 1424, 1927; 1723.

PREECHE, *pr.* 3, PREECHIÉ, *past part.*, PREECHIER, *vb.* preach, 1834; 195; 189.

PREECHEUR, *sm.* preacher, 1400.

PRELAT, PRELAZ, *sm.* prelate, 2942; 2913, 2927.

PREMERAINE, *adj.* first, 113, 1657.

PREMERAINETÉ, *sf.* first fruits, priority, 3299.

PREMIER, PREMIERE, PREMIERES, PREMIERS, *adj.* first, 865; 3391; 3218; 826, 2231.

PRENDRA, *fut.* 1, PRENNENT, *pr.* 6, PRENT, *pr.* 3, PRENZ, *pr.* 2, PRENDRE, *vb.* take, 3470; 1884, 2976; 702, 1281; 714; 695, 1066.

PRESENT, *pr.* 1, PRESENTE, *pr.* 3, PRESENZ, *pres. part.*, PRESENTER, *vb.* offer, give, present, 3497; 2396; 1040; 2422.

PRESENT, *adj.* present, 3498.

PRESENZ, *sm.* gift, offering, present, 1586.

PREST, PRESTE, *adj.* ready, 2707, 2877; 188.

PRESTENT, *pr.* 6, PRESTER, *vb.* lend, 3469.

PRESTRE, *sm.* priest, 1038, 2597.

PREU, *sm.* profit, advantage, 1358.

PREUZ, *adj.* prudent, wise, 209.

PRI, *pr.* 1, PRIE, *pr.* 3, PRIENT, *pr.* 6, PRIERENT, *pft.* 6, PRIEROIT, *impf.* 3, PRIER, *vb.* pray, 528; 2632; 253; 3447; 3500; 1438.

PRIMES, PRIMEZ, *adv.* in the first place, 100, 1167; 3476.

PRIS, *pr.* 1, PRISA, *pft.* 3, PRISE, *pr.* 3, PRISEIR, *vb.* value, prize, 408; 2695; 179, 449.

PRIS, *sm.* value, worth, 1352.

PRIS, PRISES, *past part.*, PRIST, *pft.* 3, PRENDRE, *vb.* take, 532; 1056; 90, 1646.

PRISONS, *sf.* imprisonment, 1447.

PRIVE, PRIVEE, *adj.* familiar, intimate, 381; 1814.

PROCHAINEMENT, *adv.* shortly, 769.

PROFECIES, *sf.* prophecies, 3082.

PROI, *pr.* 1, PROIER, *vb.* plead, pray, 65, 276; 790.

PROIE, *sf.* prey, booty, 2904.

PROIS, *pr.* 1, PRISEIR, *vb.* value, prize, 1826.

PROISME, PROISMES, *adj.* and *sm.* nearest, near relative, 752, 755; 1824, 2560.

PROPRE, *adj.* proper, appropriate, 2980.

PROPREMENT, *adv.* properly, appropriately, 2197.

PROVIGNE, *sf.* poor widow (Mark 12: 43; Luke 12: 2), 3012.

PRUDENCE, *sf.* prudence (*prudentia*), 1658, 1667, 1679.

PUCELE, PUCELES, *sf.* maiden, 1307; 52, 251.

PUEENT, PUENT, *pr.* 6, POOIR, *vb.* be able, 429; 1855, 3200.

PUENT, *pr.* 6, PUÏR, *vb.* stink, 1788.

PUEPLES, *sm.* people, 435.

PUET, *pr.* 3, PUEZ, *pr.* 5, POOIR, *vb.* be able, 124, 140; 610.

PUEUR, *sf.* stench, 1783, 1852.

PUINT, *sm.* point, 2106; *adv.* not, 575.

PUIS, *adv.* then, since, 49, 213.

PUIS, *pr.* 1, POOIR, *vb.* be able, 64, 67.

PUISCENT, *pr. subj.* 6, PUISCHONS, *pr. subj.* 4, PUISSE, *pr. subj.* 1, PUISSENT, *pr. subj.* 6, PUISSOMS, PUISSONS, *pr. subj.* 4, PUIST, *pr. subj.* 3, POOIR, *vb.* be able, 2984; 1980, 2856; 781, 3387; 360; 174; 1876; 658, 1448.

PUIZ, *adv.* since, 1102.

PULCELE, *sf.* maiden, 1989, 2875.

PULES, PUPLE, PUPLES, *sm.* people, 2189; 2030, 2970; 2617, 2943.

PUR, *prep.* for, 1097.

PUR, PURE, PURES, *adj.* 414, 1379; 588, 626; 1096.

PUREMENT, *adv.* purely, 1834, 3462.

PURETURE, *sf.* decomposition, rotting, 624.

PURREIZ, *pr.* 5, PUREIR, *vb.* purify, 3051.

PURTÉ, *sf.* purity, 1786, 2815.

PUTIE, *sf.* filth, dirt, 2142.

PUZ, *sm.* well, spring, source, 2357.

Q', *prep.* than, that, 2836, 3470.

QE, *conj.* that, 2191, 2224.

QE, *pron.* what, that, 2177, 2424.

QU', *conj.* that, 3, 652.

QU', *pron.* what, that, 24, 843.

QUAISCENT, *pr.* 6, QUAISEIZ, *past part.*, QUAISEIR, *vb.* calm, quieten, rest, 687; 2057.

QUAN, *neut. pron.* whatever, whatsoever, 2090.

QUAN, *adv.* when, 2998.

QUANQUE, QUANQUES, *neut. pron.* whatever, whatsoever, 139, 574; 2768, 3144.

QUANT, *adv.* when, 44, 72.

QUANT, *adj.* so much, 1808.

QUAR, *conj.* for, 5, 7.

QUARANTISME, *adj.* fortieth, 3306.

QUARTE, *adj.* fourth.

QUATRE, *num.* four, 786, 1653.

QUE, *conj.* that, 96, 104.

QUE, *rel. pron.* what, which, 129, 353, 450, 2476.

QUEL, QUELE, QUELS, *rel. adj.* which, 83, 136; 853, 2329; 591, 786.

QUEU, *pron.* which, 3494.

QUEROIT, *impf.* 3, QUIERENT, *pr.* 6, QUIERS, *pr.* 2, QUIERT, *pr.* 3, QUIS, *past part.*, QUIST, *pft.* 3, QUERRE, *vb.* seek, 2676; 2044, 3371; 651; 648, 856; 1173, 1179; 3453; 98, 262.

QUI, *rel. pron.* who, whom, 300, 358.

QUIETE, *sf.* tranquillity, 3210.

QUISES, *sf.* thighs, 1431.

RACORDEE, *past part.*, RACORDER, *vb.* reconcile, 74.

RADRECE, *pr.* 3, RADRECIÉ, *past part.*, RADRECEIR, *vb.* ascend, apply oneself, 2120; 2726.

RAFERMEE, *past part.*, RAFERMER, *vb.* strengthen, 2124.

RAINS, *sm.* branch, shoot, 341, 515, 539.

RAIS, *sm.* ray, beam, 1328.

RALEIR, *vb.* go back, 2700.

RAMAINE, *pr.* 3, RAMAINDRE, *vb.* remain, 1829, 1840.

RAMEMBREZ, *pr.* 5, RAMEMBRE, *pr.* 3, RAMEMBRER, *vb.* recall to mind, 812; 958.

RAMENTOIT, *pr.* 3, RAMENTEVOIR, *vb.* mention, 314.

RAMISSEL, *sm.* branch, sprig, 503.

RANDRE, *vb.* render up, convey, 271, 1224.

RAPAIE, *pr.* 3, RAPAIEIR, *vb.* calm, appease, 294.

RAPAISE, *pr.* 3, RAPAIST, *pr. subj.* 3, RAPAISEIR, *vb.* pacify, 80; 148.

RAVIE, *past part.*, RAVIST, *pr.* 3, RAVIR, *vb.* enrapture, seize, 1324; 2903.

RAVOIE, *pr.* 3, RAVOIER, *vb.* return to the true road, 512.

RECELEE, *sf.*, A RECELEE, covertly, secretly, 374.

RECEUZ, *past part.*, RECHUT, *pft.* 3, RECEVOIR, *vb.* receive, 889, 3168.

RECLAIM, *pr.* I, RECLAIME, *pr.* 3, RECLAMER, *vb.* invoke, implore, 136; 333; 270.

RECLINATORIE, *sf.* seat of a couch (Song of Songs 3: 9–10: bottom of a chariot).

RECOMENCEMENZ, *sm.* new beginning, 2222.

RECONEISANCE, *sf.* sign, symbol, 3188.

RECONEUZ, *past part.*, RECONOISTRE, *vb.* recognize, 3194.

RECONFORTE, *pr.* 3, RECONFORTEE, *past part.*, RECONFORTER, *vb.* comfort, 1085; 792.

RECONFORTEMENZ, *sm.* comfort, consolation, 2194.

RECONICHABLES, *adj.* recognisable, 3175.

RECONISANCE, *sf.* sign, recognition, 3198.

RECONTE, *pr.* 3, RECONTER, *vb.* recount, tell, 2487.

RECOVRA, *pft.* 3, RECOVRER, *vb.* recover, retrieve, regain, 3451; 824, 2530.

REDEMPCION, REDEMPCIONS, *sf.* redemption, 536, 882; 2798.

REDIRAI, *fut.* I, REDIRE, *vb.* say for a second time, 2252, 3273.

REDOT, *pr.* I, REDOTA, *pft.* 3, REDOTE, *pr.* 3, REDOUTENT, *pr.* 6, REDOTER, *vb.* fear, 388; 2783; 2106; 1940; 680, 936.

REE, *sf.* (honey)comb, 2284, 2285.

REFAIT, *pr.* 3, REFAIRE, *vb.* remake, make new, 170, 220.

REFUIENT, *pr.* 6, REFUIRE, *vb.* flee, retreat, 1145.

REGARDENT, *pr.* 6, REGARDONS, *pr.* 4, REGARDER, *vb.* have regard to, look at, 1561; 3439.

REGEHISANT, *pres. part.*, REGEHIR, *vb.* confess, 2960.

REGNE, REGNES, *sm.* kingdom, 2158, 2705; 2704.

REGNE, *pr.* 3, REGNER, *vb.* reign, rule, dominate, 1885, 2706; 2409.

REGUARD, *sm.* attention, regard, 238.

REGUARDE, *pr.* 3, REGUARDER, *vb.* look at, SE REGUARDER, *vb.* look round, 908; 197; 2880.

REGUARDEMENT, *sm.* looking, contemplation, 916.

REGUART, *sm.* look, glance, 443, 923.

REISIN, *sm.* grape, 349.

REISNABLE, *adj.* reasonable, fair, 3268.

RELEVAILLES, *sf.* churching of women after childbirth, 2810.

REMAIGNE, REMAINE, *pr. subj.* 3, REMAINT, *pr.* 3, REMANRA, *fut.* 3, REMAINDRE, *vb.* stay, remain, 247, 2950; 1417; 952, 1301; 2158.

REMANTANT, *sm.* remainder, 3018.

REMBEER, *vb.* redeem, 2581.

REMUOIT, *impf.* 3, REMUER, *vb.* change, i.e. sell, p. 97, l. 13.

RENDE, *pr. subj.* 3, RENDENT, *pr.* 6, RENDIST, *pft.* 3, RENDOIENT, *impf.* 6, RENDOIT, *impf.* 3, RENDRA, *fut.* 3, RENDRAS, *fut.* 2, RENDUE, *past part.*, RENDRE, *vb.* render up, give back, convey, 2130; 350, 620; 886; 3192; 1332, 2611; 3471; 1006; 2801; 174, 351.

RENOIÉ, *past part.*, RENIER, *vb.* renounce, deny, 3001.

RENONS, *sm.* renown, fame, 2300.

RENOVELE, *pr.* 3, RENOVELER, *vb.* renew, 1260, 1276.

RENT, *pr.* 3, RENDRE, *vb.* render up, give back, convey, 172, 252.

REPAIRE, *pr.* 3, REPAIRONS, *pr.* 4, REPAIRS, *imper. sing.*, REPAIRIER, *vb.* abide, return, 643, 1115; 1981; 75; 1437.

REPAIS, *pr.* 2, REPAIST, *pr.* 3, REPAISTRE, *vb.* feed, nourish, 2290; 1094, 1097; 3316.

REPAROLE, *pr.* 3, REPARLER, *vb.* speak again, 1825, 2281.

REPENTANCE, REPENTENCE, *sf.* repentance, 61; 1579.

REPLENIST, *pr.* 3, REPLENIR, *vb.* replenish, 160, 1310.

REPONT, *pr.* 3, REPONDRE, *vb.* hide, 2178.

REPOS, *pr.* 1, REPOSE, *pr.* 3, REPOSEE, *past part.*, REPOSES, *pr.* 2, REPOSOIE, *impf.* 1, REPOST, *pr. subj.* 3, REPOZE, *pr.* 3, REPOSER, *vb.* repose, rest, 652; 1398, 1544; 373; 1178; 1478; 817; 1369; 1466.

REPUS, *adj.* hidden, secret, 1866.

REQUIER, *pr.* 1, REQUIERT, *pr.* 3, REQUERRE, *vb.* implore, plead, 3505; 5, 1113.

RESAMBLENT, RESANBLENT, *pr.* 6, RESEMBLE, *pr.* 3, RESEMBLER, *vb.* resemble, 2851, 2849; 855; 426.

RESCEALS, *sm.* streams (Song of Songs 5: 12: 'rivers of waters'), 2851.

RESGUART, *pr.* 1, REGUARDER, *vb.* look at, 2214.

RESOIGNE, *pr.* 3, RESOIGNIER, *vb.* give great care to, 692.

RESPLENDIENT, *pr.* 6, RESPLENDIES, *pr.* 2, RESPLENDIR, *vb.* shine, 3438; 451.

RESPLENDORS, *sf.* brilliance, 3147.

RESPONDENT, *pr.* 6, RESPONT, *pr.* 3, RESPONDRE, *vb.* reply, 2646; 394, 577.

REST, *pr.* 3, ESTRE with prefix RE-, is for his part, 861.

RESTUNT, *pr.* 6, RESTER, *vb.* stay, stop, 1142.

RESUCITA, *pft.* 3, RESUCITANT, *pres. part.*, RESUCITER, *vb.* rise up again, 1764; 3463.

RETARDIER, *vb.* hold back, 2122.

RETENIR, *vb.*, RETENOIT, *impf.* 3, retain, 2914; 1477.

RETRAIRE, RETRERE, *vb.* draw towards, draw from, draw back, 29, 1844; 404.

REVELACION, *sf.* revelation, 3313.

REVENIR, *vb.*, REVENONS, *pr.* 4, REVENRA, *fut.* 3, come back, 40, 827; 1287; 823.

REVESTUE, *past part.*, REVESTIR, *vb.* clothe again, 2505.

REVIVRE, *vb.* live again, 3202.

REVOLRA, *fut.* 3, REVUEIL, *pr.* 1, REVOLOIR, *vb.* wish again, wish for my part, 1587; 2113, 3213.

REZ, *sf.* series, rows, 3230.

RIEN, RIENS, *sf.* thing, 470, 727; 358, 1360.

RIU, *sm.* stream, 2865.

RODOTE, *pr.* 3, RODOTER, *vb.* fear, 2584.

ROGE, ROGES, *adj.* red, 425, 1883; 2655, 2683.

ROGEUR, ROGEURS, *sf.* redness, 2669; 1885, 2681.

ROGIRENT, *pft.* 3, ROGIR, *vb.* grow red, 2673.

ROI, ROIS, *sm.* king, 51, 175; 265, 501.

ROINE, *sf.* queen, 1716, 1910.

ROISANT, *sm.* coolness, freshness, 1976.

ROISIN, ROISINS, *sm.* grapes, bunch (of grapes), (see notes), 547, 549.

ROMANS, *sm.* romance, book, 3505.

ROSE, ROSES, *sf.* rose, 1391; 368, 601.

ROSEE, *sf.* dew, 2498.

ROVA, *pft.* 3, ROVÉ, *past part.*, ROVEIR, *vb.* ask, 2606; 1061; 2479.

ROVENT, *adj.* red, 1212.

RUBIN, *sm.* ruby, 1623.

RUGEUR, *sf.* redness, 2709.

RUISCELET, *sm.* rivulet, 2865.

RUISCLES, RUISELS, *sm.* stream, 3099; 2941.

RUSCELET, *sm.* rivulet, 2862.

s', *refl. pron.* himself, herself, itself, themselves, 20, 37.

s', *cond. conj.* if, 22, 63.

s', *poss. adj.* his, her, its, 98, 122.

s, *enclitic form of pron.* LES, them, 1152, 3429.

# GLOSSARY

SA, *poss. adj.* his, her, its, 23, 77.

SABAT, *sm.* sabbath, 3107.

SACES, *imper. sing.*, SACHE, *pr. subj.* 1 and 3, SACHES, *pr. subj.* 2, SACHIEZ, *imper. pl.* SAVOIR, *vb.* know, 3092; 377, 1038; 3140; 177, 1237; 109.

SACRAMENT, SACRAMENZ, SACREMENT, SACREMENZ, *sm.* sacrament, 1833; 797, 3319; 1053; 2800.

SACRARIE, *sm.* sanctuary, 2292.

SAFIR, *sm.* sapphire, 1379.

SAGE, SAGES, *adj.* wise, 35, 58; 9, 232.

SAI, *pr.* 1, SAVOIR, *vb.* know, 142, 329; 1922, 2038.

SAICHIER, *vb.* shake, 2894.

SAIETE, *sf.* arrow, 2260.

SAILI, *pft.* 3, SAILLANT, *pres. part.*, SAILLI, *pft.* 3, SAILLIR, *vb.* leap, jump, 867; 1136; 879.

SAIN, *sm.* bosom, 453, 865.

SAINE, SAINS, *adj.* whole, healthy, 1938; 342.

SAINS, *prep.* without, 1120, 1312.

SAINS, SAINT, SAINTE, SAINTES, SAINZ, *adj.* saintly, holy, 2145, 2559; 1, 15; 13, 27; 1631, 3447; 2891, 3061.

SAINT, SAINZ, *sm.* saint, 2452, 2837; 2983.

SAINTEÉ, *sf.* sanctity, holiness, 1958.

SAISIE, *past part.*, SAISIR, *vb.* seize, take possession of, 360.

SALLI, *pft.* 3, SAILLIR, *vb.* leap, jump, 875.

SALS, *adj.* unmarked, whole, 2446.

SALT, SALZ, *sm.* leap, 872, 884; 862, 864.

SALT, *pr. subj.* 3, SAILLIR, *vb.* leap, jump, 1916.

SALVAGES, *adj.* wild, uncultivated, 708.

SAMBLANT, *sm.* aspect, appearance, 617.

SANC, SANCS, *sm.* blood, 31, 1012; 1784, 3223.

SANGUINE, *adj.* red, crimson, 1846.

SANS, *prep.* without, 978, 1016.

SAPHIR, *sm.* sapphire, 1333.

SAPIENCE, *sf.* wisdom, learning, 186, 487.

SARDINES, *sm.* sard, a red-coloured gemstone, 1623.

SAVANT, *pres. part.*, SAVEIZ, *pr.* 5, SAVEZ, *pr.* 5, SAVOIE, *impf.* 1, SAVOIENT, *impf.* 6, SAVOIT, *impf.* 3, SAVROIT, *cond.* 3, SAVOIR, *vb.* know, 3464; 2795; 321, 864; 355; 1779, 3516; 2625, 3002; 2374; 3259, 3381.

SAVEREUS, *adj.* tasty, 267.

SAVOR, *sf.* taste, flavour, 726.

SCIENCE, *sf.* knowledge, 185, 3005.

SE, *cond. conj.* if, 80, 86; *sub. conj.* so, 127, 2512.

SE, *refl. pron.* himself, herself, itself, themselves, 93, 381.

SE, *poss. adj.* his, her, its, 674, 1232.

SECONDE, SECONT, *adj.* second, 1659, 3394; 1446.

SECORS, *sm.* help, succour, 769.

SECREZ, *sm.* secrets, 2307.

SEENT, *pr.* 6, SEIR, *vb.* sit, be situated, 2889.

SEIGNIER, *vb.* mark with a sign (of the Cross), 1074.

SEIGNEUR, SEIGNOR, SEIGNORS, *sm.* lord, 2698, 2986; 1172, 1420; 173.

SEIGNORIE, *sf.* dominion, lordship, 1699.

SEIN, *adj.* whole, healthy, 6.

SEINT, *sm.* saint, 3225.

SEINTE, *adj.* holy, 45.

SEIR, *vb.* sit, be situated, 732, 2981.

SEIT, *pr.* 3, SEIVENT, *pr.* 6, SEIZ, *pr.* 2, SAVOIR, *vb.* know, 22, 41; 3157; 442.

SEJOR, SEJORS, SEJUR, *sm.* stay, sojourn, resting place, 2932, 3305; 1132; 304.

SELON, SELONC, *prep.* according to, by the side of, 3403; 501, 1633.

SELS, *adj.* alone, sole, 2679.

SEMBLANCE, *sf.* appearance, aspect, 2024, 3197.

SEMBLANT, *sm.* aspect, appearance, 927, 930.

SEMBLANT, SEMBLANZ, *pres. part.*, SEMBLE, *pr.* 3, SEMBLENT, *pr.* 6, SEMBLOIT, *impf.* 3, SEMBLER, *vb.* resemble, seem, be like, 1137, 1163; 861, 1160; 223, 1788; 1793, 1828; 1340.

SEMEE, SEMEZ, *past part.*, SEMER, *vb.* sow, 2302; 780.

SEMENCE, *sf.* seed, 1812.

SEMONS, *pr.* 2, SEMONT, *pr.* 3, SEMONDRE, *vb.* invite, call, summon, 1730; 1445.

SEN, *poss. adj.* his, her, its, 37, 38.

SENARIE, *adj.* senary, 3355.

SENBLANCE, *sf.* aspect, appearance, 2758.

SENBLANT, *sm.* aspect, appearance, 2760.

SENEFIANCE, *sf.* meaning, significance, 1270.

SENEFIE, *pr.* 3, SENEFIENT, *pr.* 6, SENEFIER, *vb.* mean, signify, 625, 1271; 1381, 2324; 1784, 3362.

SENESTRE, *sf.* left hand, 793, 799.

SENS, *sm.* meaning, significance, sense, 8, 117, 1410.

SENS, *prep.* without, 110, 331.
SENT, *pr.* 1 and 3, SENTI, *pft.* 3, SENTIRA, *fut.* 3, SENTOIENT, *impf.* 6, SENTIR, *vb.* feel, sense, smell, 143, 171; 238, 399; 505, 3296; 1104; 949; 149, 698.
SENTENCE, *sf.* saying, aphorism, 113, 1278.
SENTIERS, *sm.* path, 1395.
SEPULCRE, *sm.* sepulchre, 3254, 3305.
SERA, *fut.* 3, SERONT, *fut.* 6, ESTRE, *vb.* be, 2444; 3359.
SERAPHIN, *adj.* seraphic, 268.
SERMONS, *sm.* speech, 1729, 3380.
SERPENS, SERPENTS, SERPENZ, *sm.*, snake, serpent, 1261; 622; 833, 838.
SERRE, *sf.* bolt, bar, 1450.
SERS, *sm.* serf, servant, 1726, 3344.
SERS, *pr.* 2, SERT, *pr.* 3, SERVEZ, *pr.* 5, SERVIZ, *past part.*, SERVIR, *vb.* serve, 1725; 154; 274; 748; 270, 3481.
SERVICE, SERVIGE, *sm.* service, 1762; 2209.
SES, *poss. adj.* his, her, its, 80, 311.
SET, *pr.* 1, SEIR, *vb.* be suitable, 549.
SET, *pr.* 3, SAVOIR, *vb.* know, 586, 853.
SET, *num.* seven, 2290, 2291.
SEU, *ind. pron.* this, that, 76.
SEUL, SEULE, *adj.* alone, sole, 3003, 3107; 593, 1603.
SEUR, *prep.* above, 2306.
SEUR, SEURE, *adj.* sure, secure, 435, 3080; 103, 640.
SEURENT, *pft.* 6, SEVENT, *pr.* 6, SEVRONT, *fut.* 6, SAVOIR, *vb.* know, 2460, 3116; 188, 233; 2058.
SEVERAIN, *adj.* sovereign, 3220.
SEXANTE, *num.* sixty, 1352, 1403.
SEZ, *poss. adj.* his, 1817.
SI, *conj.* and *adv.* so, 19, 50, 16, 62.
SI, *poss. adj.* his, 424, 2591.
SIECLE, SIECLES, *sm.* the world, things mundane, 3, 12, 94, 1100.
SIEGE, SIEGES, *sm.* seat, 1462, 1465; 1503, 1517.
SIEN, SIENS, *poss. pron.* his, hers, its, 498, 1399; 1514, 1696.
SIET, *pr.* 3, SEIR, *vb.* sit, be situated, 1537, 1669.
SIGNE, SIGNES, *sm.* sign, 1988, 2771; 101, 3339.
SIGNE, *pr.* 3, SIGNENT, *pr.* 6, SIGNER, *vb.* signify, mean, 2372; 1386.
SIMPLE, SIMPLES, *adj.* simple, 323, 570; 1733.
SIMPLESCE, *sf.* simplicity, 2857.

SIMPLICITE, *sf.* simplicity, 3093.
SIRE, SIRES, *sm.* lord, 30, 187; 393, 873.
SIS, *pft.* 1, SEIR, *vb.* sit, 733.
SIS, *num.* six, 3323, 3347.
SIU, *imper. sing.*, SIVONS, *imper. pl.* 4, SIVRAI, *fut.* 1, SIVRE, *vb.* follow, 1017; 1789; 3022.
SOCORRE, *pr.* 3, SOCORRE, *vb.* help, succour, 2522.
SODEMENT, *adv.* suddenly, 841.
SOEF, SOEFS, SOES, *adj.* gentle, soft, 596, 737; 1977; 2717.
SOEFMENT, *adv.* gently, 1085.
SOFFRANCE, SOFRANCE, *sf.* suffering, 1672; 3187.
SOFERTE, *past part.*, SOFFRI, *pft.* 3, SOFRE, *pr.* 1, SOFRENT, *pr.* 6, SOFRI, *pft.* 3, SOFRIRENT, *pft.* 6, SOFROIE, *cond.* 1, SOFFRIR, SOFRIR, *vb.* suffer, 3501; 535, 3179; 300; 628, 2838; 305, 880; 2447, 3225; 327; 2511; 68, 161.
SOFIST, *pr.* 3, SOFFIR, *vb.* suffice, 2069.
SOFLE, *pr.* 3, SOFLER, *vb.* blow, 2402.
SOGIT, *adj.* subject, 3370.
SOI, *refl. pron.* himself, herself, itself, 29, 120.
SOIE, *pr. subj.* 1, ESTRE, *vb.* be, 69, 591.
SOIELS, *sm.* seal, 2307.
SOIENT, *pr. subj.* 6, SOIES, *imper. sing.*, SOIEZ, *imper. pl.*, ESTRE, *vb.* be, 1740, 2186; 2496; 1246.
SOIG, SOIGN, *sm.* care, 412; 2012.
SOIGNEUR, *adj.* careful, 2018, 3473.
SOIN, SOING, *sm.* care, 445, 1542; 194, 2470.
SOIS, *sf.* thirst, 2839.
SOIT, *pr. subj.* 3, ESTRE, *vb.* be, 4, 46.
SOJORS, *sm.* sojourn, stay, 604.
SOL, SOLE, *adj.* alone, 141, 148; 1026, 1056.
SOLAUS, SOLAUSZ, SOLEUS, *sm.* sun, 371; 1045; 1328, 1336.
SOLEZ, *pr.* 5, SOLOIR, *vb.* be accustomed to, 821.
SOLONC, *prep.* according to, by the side of, 190, 230, 2785.
SOM, *sm.* top, summit, 1740.
SOME, *sf.* whole, sum, 1031, 3010.
SOMEILLIER, *vb.* doze, sleep, 937.
SOMELS, *sm.* sleep, 2493.
SOMME, *sf.* whole, sum, 590, 956.
SOMONT, *pr.* 3, SEMONDRE, *vb.* call, invite, summon, 2564.
SON, *poss. adj.* his, her, its, 31, 36.

SONE, *pr.* 3, SONER, *vb.* sound, utter, denote, 222, 805; 3006.

SONT, *pr.* 6, ESTRE, *vb.* be, 238, 369.

SOPRIS, SOPRISE, *past part.*, SOPRENDRE, *vb.* take by surprise, 2650; 2096, 2394.

SOR, *prep.* on, over, above, 462, 549.

SORMONTA, *pft.* 3, SORMONTER, *vb.* overcome, 878, 3131; 659.

SORT, *pr.* 3, SORTIST, *pft.* 3, SORTIR, *vb.* come out of, 458; 1644.

SORT, *pr.* 3, SORDRE, *vb.* spring from, well out of, 1991.

SUS, *adv.* up, 796.

SOSKE, *pr.* 3, SOSKEIR, *vb.* graft, 470.

SOSPIR, *pr.* 1, SOSPIRER, *vb.* sigh, 158.

SOSTENIR, *vb.*, SOSTIENENT, *pr.* 6, uphold, support, sustain, 3482; 347.

SOTILS, *adj.* subtle, 2752.

SOVENT, *adv.* frequently, often, 48, 51.

SOVERAIN, SOVERAINS, *adj.* sovereign, 275, 1636; 363, 1746.

SOVIEGNE, *pr. subj.* 3, SOVIENT, *pr.* 1, SOVINT, *pft.* 3, SOVENIR, *vb. impers.* remind, p. 97, l. 1; 281; 529; 2609.

SOVRAIN, SOVRAINS, SOVRAN, *adj.* sovereign, supreme, 1438, 2243; 1543, 1704; 3090.

SOZ, *adv.* beneath, under, 2305.

'ST, *enclitic form of* EST, *pr.* 3, ESTRE, *vb.* be, 1504, 1513.

SUBTILE, SUBTILS, SUCCILS, *adj.* subtle, 1728; 2117; 1311.

SUBTILMENT, *adv.* with subtlety, 3050.

SUDDUIENT, *pr.* 6, SUDDUIRE, *vb.* deceive, subvert, 1049.

SUE, *poss adj.* and *pron.* his, her, its, 24, 545.

SUEF, *adj.* gentle, soft, 3043.

SUEIL, *pr.* 1, SUELENT, *pr.* 6, SUELS, *pr.* 2, SUELT, *pr.* 3, SOLOIR, *vb.* be accustomed, be wont, 2214; 176; 642; 507.

SUEN, SUENS, *poss. adj.* and *pron.* his, her, its, 320, 2368; 2822.

SUER, *sf.* sister, beloved, 2211, 2286.

SUES, *poss. adj.* his, her, 1190.

SUFLE, *imper. sing.*, SUFLER, *vb.* blow, 2351.

SUFLE, *sm.* blowing, 2352.

SUFRIR, *vb.* suffer, 2595.

SUI, *pr.* 1, SUMES, *pr.* 4, SUNT, *pr.* 6, ESTRE, *vb.* be, 138, 198; 2147, 2862; 166, 241.

SUR, *prep.* on, 2851, 3099.

SURE, *adj.* certain, sure, 3245.

SURRECTION, *sf.* resurrection, 545.

SUS, *prep.* above, 800, 888.

SUSCITE, *pr.* 3, SUSCITER, *vb.* raise up, 3251.

SUSTANCE, *sf.* substance, 455.

SUSTENANCE, *sf.* sustenance, nourishment, 2233.

SUTCILMENT, *adv.* with subtlety, 1869.

SUZ, *prep.* above, 2283, 2388.

SYNAGOGE, *sf.* synagogue, 55.

T', *pron.* thou, thee, 231, 287.

T', *poss. adj.* thy, 166, 1966.

TA, *poss. adj.* thy, 932, 1033.

TABERNACLE, *sm.* shrine, tabernacle, 1362.

TAILLE, *sf.* tax roll, 2151.

TAISENT, *pr.* 6, TAIST, *pr.* 3, TAISIR, *vb.* be silent, 3310; 1969, 2068; 124, 125.

TALENT, *sm.* wish, inclination, 1370.

TANS, *sm.* time, 71, 823.

TANT, *adv.* and *adj.* so much, so many, 60, 69, 100, 145.

TANTES, *adj.* so many, 2652.

TANTZ, *sm.* times, 3470.

TARGE, *pr.* 3, TARGENT, *pr.* 6, TARGIER, *vb.* delay, be slow, 1264; 1144; 1169, 2162.

TE, *pron.* thee, 230, 276.

TEIL, TEL, TELE, TELS, TELZ, *adj.* such, 2044, 2669; 5, 238; 412; 319, 375; 1356.

TEMPLE, *sm.* temple, 3013.

TEMPRIUS, *adj.* moderate, 991.

TEMTACIONS, *sf.* temptation, 385.

TEMPTÉS, *past part.*, TEMTER, *vb.* tempt, 1759.

TEN, *poss. adj.* thy, 449, 1037.

TENCE, *pr.* 3, TENCER, *vb.* quarrel, argue, torment, 1392, 2097.

TENDENT, *pr.* 6, TENDEZ, *pr.* 5, TENDOIE, *impf.* 1, TENDRE, *vb.* lead towards, 1785, 2848; 811; 519; 272.

TENDRE, *adj.* tender, 508, 694.

TENDRA, *fut.* 3, TENEZ, *pr.* 5 and *imper. pl.*, TENOIE, *impf.* 1, TENOIENT, *impf.* 6, TENRA, *fut.* 3, TENRAI, *fut.* 1, TENIR, *vb.* hold, 793; 774, 3089; 517; 3232; 1232; 1217; 828, 892.

TENPRIU, *adj.* moderate, 986.

TENRE, *adj.* tender, 2394.

TENS, *sm.* time, 349, 2018.

TENT, *pr.* 3, TENTE, *pr. subj.* 3, TENDRE, *vb.* lead towards, stretch out, 321, 647, 706, 1081; 3266.

TENTA, *pft.* 3, TENTER, *vb.* tempt, 877.

TENUE, TENUZ, *past part.*, TENIR, *vb.* hold, 976, 3364; 1108, 1150.

TERIENETEZ, *sf.* earthly things, 2934.

TERNARIE, *adj.* ternary, 3357.

TERTRE, TERTRES, *sm.* hill, 2073, 2114; 848, 1136.

TES, *poss. adj.* thy, 165, 214.

TESMOIGN, *sm.* witness, 1753, 1769.

TESMOIGNAGE, *sm.* testifying, witness, evidence, 1748.

TESMOIGNS, TESMOING, *sm.* witness, 1768; 2994.

TESTE, *sf.* head, 1183, 1815.

TEUS, *adj.* such, 1987, 1900.

TI, *poss. adj.* thy, 713, 1793.

TIEGN, *pr. subj.* 1, TIEN, *imper. sing.* and *pr.* 3, TIENENT, *pr.* 6, TIENG, *pr.* 1, TIENGNE, *pr. subj.* 3, TIENT, *pr.* 3, TENIR, *vb.* hold, 574; 964; 2082; 168, 3286; 1217, 2492; 1206; 557, 755.

TIENS, *poss. adj.* thy, 727, 1729.

TIERCE, TIERS, TIERZ, *adj.* third, 1661, 2736; 1765; 755, 757.

TINT, *pft.* 3, TENIR, *vb.* hold, 2493, 2608.

TIRE, *pr.* 3, TIRER, *vb.* be attracted, 1172.

TOCHE, *pr.* 3, TOCHEIR, *vb.* touch, 119.

TOI, *pron.* thou, thee, 212, 234.

TOILLE, *pr. subj.* 3, TOLIR, *vb.* take, 3409.

TOISON, *sf.* fleece, 1820.

TOIT, *pron.* thee, 1966.

TOLEZ, *imper. pl.*, TOLI, *pft.* 3, TOLIRENT, *pft.* 6, TOLRONT, *fut.* 6, TOLT, *pr.* 3, TOLTE, *pr. subj.* 3, TOLUE, *past part.*, TOLIR, *vb.* take, 822; 735; 2541, 2624; 1055; 543, 1243; 2917; 1324, 2802; 2919, 3273.

TON, *poss. adj.* thy, 543, 560.

TONDUES, *past part.*, TONDRE, *vb.* shear, 1793.

TOPACE, *sf.* topaz, 1628, 1630.

TOR, *sf.* tower, 1915, 1951.

TOR, *sm.* turning, 3428, 3471.

TORBE, *sf.* crowd, 2188.

TORETES, *sf.* turrets, 1613.

TORMENZ, *sm.* tortures, torments, 1568.

TORNE, *pr.* 3, TORNEE, TORNEES, TORNÉS, TORNEZ, *past part.*, TORNENT, *pr.* 6, TORNERENT, *pft.* 6, TORT, *pr. subj.* 3, TORNER, *vb.* turn, 17, 1458; 496, 2486; 3399, 3484; 2210; 406; 2539, 3418; 3222; 1410, 3471.

TORNEICES, *adj.* turning, revolving, 3415.

TORS, *sf.* towers, 1617, 1621.

TORT, *sm.* wrong, 1013, 1526.

TORTERELE, TORTORELE, *sf.* turtle-dove, 439, 971, 982.

TORTRE, *sf.* turtle-dove, 445.

TOS, *adj.* and *pron.* all, 1696, 2150, 2272.

TOST, *adv.* soon, 400, 416.

TOT, TOTE, TOTES, TOZ, *adj.* all, 2, 17; 150, 170; 255, 419; 4, 94.

TRACE, TRACES, TRACHE, *sf.* track, 1017; 1190; 378.

TRAI, *imper. sing.*, TRAIENT, *pr.* 6, TRAIRA, *fut.* 3, TRAIST, *pft.* 3, TRAIT, *pr.* 3, TRAITE, *past part.*, TRAIRE, *vb.* draw, drag, pull, 245; 247; 1811; 1514; 1809; 666; 1200, 2189.

TRAIRES, *sm.* pulling, attracting, 250.

TRAMBLE, *pr.* 3, TRAMBLER, *vb.* tremble, 2997.

TRAVAIL, *sm.* work, toil, pain, 387, 654.

TRAVAILLE, *pr.* 3, TRAVEILLIEZ, *imper. pl.*, TRAVAILLIER, TRAVEILLIER, *vb.* work, toil, torment, 358; 816; 3129; 1064.

TRAVALS, TRAVALZ, *sm.* work, toil, torment, 1082, 2057, 2838; 1556, 2057.

TREBUCHIÉ, *past part.*, TREBUCHIER, *vb.* overthrow, 430.

TREILLE, TREILLES, *sf.* grill, trellis, 911; 899.

TREMBLAI, *pft.* 1, TREMBLER, *vb.* tremble, 2510.

TRENCHIER, *vb.* cut out, 1435.

TRES, *adv.* very, up to, 41, 89, 143.

TRESELS, *sm.* small barrel, 3051, 3055.

TRESHAUT, *adj.* highest, 2829.

TRESOR, TRESORS, *sm.* treasure, 493, 1386; 1484, 1499.

TRESPAS, *sm.* crossing, 435.

TRESPASSE, *pr.* 3, TRESPASSEZ, *past part.*, TRESPAST, *pr. subj.* 3, TRESPASSERUNT, *fut.* 6, TRESPASSERENT, *pft.* 6, TRESPASSER, *vb.* pass through, pass by, 461; 951; 939; 1205; 632; 995.

TRESSAILLE, *pr.* 3, TRESSAILLER, *vb.* shiver, tremble, 852.

TRESSALT, *pr.* 3, TRESSAILLIR, *vb.* leap over, 832, 848, 857.

TRESTOT, TRESTOZ, *pron.* all, 711, 1040; 799.

TRIBULACION, *sf.* tribulation, 2779.

TRIBULS, *sm.* torment, affliction, 693.

TRICHE, *sf.* trickery, deceit, 346.

TRISTECE, *sf.* grief, sadness, 1025, 1664.

TROBLA, *pft.* 3, TROBLE, *pr.* 3, TROBLER, *vb.* disturb, 3178, 1994; 818.

TROBLEMENT, *sm.* disturbance, upset, 3098.

TROI, TROIS, *num.* three, 3356; 786, 877.

TROP, *adv.* very, 70, 144.

TROVA, *pft.* 3, TROVAI, *pft.* 1, TROVÉ, TROVEE, *past part.,* TROVERENT, *pft.* 6, TROVEROIE, *cond.* 1, TROVEZ, *past part.,* TROVONS, *pr.* 4, TRUEVE, *pr.* 3, TRUE-VENT, *pr.* 6, TRUIS, *pr.* 1 and 2, TRUIST, *pft.* 3, TROVER, *vb.* find, 2605, 2676; 733, 1180; 152, 2067; 2546; 2537, 2619; 356; 2812; 2877; 464, 1209; 1812; 234, 248; 1152, 3414; 2272; 1184, 1208.

TU, *pron.* thou, 213, 229.

TUE, *poss. adj.* thy, 256, 1018.

TUIT, *adj.* all, 3073.

TUR, *sf.* tower, 3073.

U, *adv.* where, in which, 248, 2202.

U, *conj.* or, 2247, 3196.

UEIL, UELS, UELZ, *sm.* eye, 568, 1364; 1930, 2099; 3092.

UES, *sm.* need, use, 2662.

UEUVRE, UEVRE, UEVRES, *sf.* work, works, 3431; 486, 640; 2598, 3180.

UEVRE, *pr.* 3, UEVRER, *vb.* work, 1406, 3409.

UIL, *sm.* eye, 2223.

UINZ, *past part.,* UINDRE, *vb.* anoint, 258.

UIS, *sm.* door, 2512, 2517.

UIT, *num.* eight, 1663.

ULTRAGE, *sm.* intemperate behaviour, 36.

ULTRE, *prep.* beyond, 2398.

UMAINE, *adj.* human, 2749.

UMANITÉ, *sf.* humanity, 3123.

UMBRE, UMBRES, *sf.* shade, 1101; 1978, 2051.

UMILITÉ, *sf.* humility, 2385, 3079.

UMLES, *adj.* humble, 677.

UN, UNE, UNS, UNZ, *art.* and *num.* a, one, 19, 142, 3107; 17, 112; 155, 289, 290, 595; 1344.

UNCIONS, *sf.* unction, anointing, 1052.

UNGEMENT, UNGEMENZ, *sm.* unguent, salve, 257; 2218, 2221.

UNIE, *past part.,* UNIR, *vb.* unite, 3352.

UNITÉ, UNITEZ, *sf.* unity, unit, 1059, 1756; 3356.

UNKES, UNQUES, *adv.* ever, 1328, 1347; 472, 2384.

UNT, *pr.* 6, AVOIR, *vb.* have, 257, 287.

USAGES, *sm.* use, 252.

USERIER, *sm.* moneylender, usurer, 3468.

UVRE, *sf.* work, 1488.

VA, *pr.* 3, ALEIR, *vb.* go, 411, 765.

VAIER, *vb.* wander, travel, 391.

VAIL, *pr.* 1, VAILLANS, VAILLANT, VAILLANZ, *pres. part.,* VAILLENT, *pr.* 6, VALOIR, *vb.* be worth, be worthy, 2368; 1592; 2756; 203, 1555; 3370.

VAINCRE, *vb.,* VAINT, *pr.* 3, 1014; 127, 156.

VAIN, VAINE, VAINES, VAINS, *adj.* vain, empty, 871; 360, 1312; 837; 2100.

VAIRELEES, *adj.* particoloured, variegated, 1974, 2033.

VAISSEAUS, *sm.* vessel, 1585.

VAL, *adv.* below, 1317.

VALEES, *sf.* valleys, 675.

VALOR, *sf.* worth, 236, 243.

VALT, *pr. subj.* 3, VALUT, *pft.* 3, VALOIR, *vb.* be worth, be worthy, 620, 768; 3033.

VANITÉS, *sf.* vanity, emptiness, 3456.

VANTA, *pft.* 3, VANTER, *vb.* boast, 2382.

VARIELEES, *adj.* particoloured, variegated, 491.

VARIETÉ, *sf.* variety, 2037.

VASTENT, *pr.* 6, VASTER, *vb.* devastate, lay waste, 1061.

VAT, *pr.* 5, VALOIR, *vb.* be worth, be worthy, 1865.

VEEZ, *pr.* 5, VEIR, *vb.* see, 107, 497.

VEIL, *pr.* 1, VOLOIR, *vb.* wish, 1437, 1441.

VEILLES, *sf.* watch, waking, vigil, 1523.

VEILLA, *pft.* 3, VEILLE, *pr.* 3, VEILLIER, *vb.* wake, keep vigil, 3072; 1291, 2489; 1063, 3130.

VEIR, *vb.* see, 1036, 2006.

VEIR, VEIRS, *sm.* sight, 2005; 1777.

VEL, *pr.* 1, VELS, *pr.* 2, VELT, *pr.* 3, VOLOIR, *vb.* wish, 1032; 1124, 3125; 645, 649.

VENIM, VENIMS, VENINS, *sm.* poison, 628; 629; 1264.

VENIST, *impf. subj.* 3, VENIR, *vb.,* come, 846, 898.

VENJANCE, *sf.* vengeance, 1016, 3112.

VENQUEEUR, VENQUERRE, *sm.* victor, conqueror, 2827, 2830; 2772.

VENRA, *fut.* 3, VENIR, *vb.* come, 966, 1034.

VENT, *pr.* 1, VANTER, praise, vaunt, 362.

VENTÉ, *past part.,* VENTE, *pr.* 3, VENTER, blow, 2355; 2395.

VENTRE, *sm.* belly, womb, 1212, 2243.

VENUE, VENUZ, *past part.,* VENIR, *vb.* come, 922, 1236; 213, 606.

VEOIE, *impf.* 1, VEOMMES, *pr.* 4, VEOIR, *vb.* see, 1337, 1343; 3144; 1962, 2805.

VER, *sm.* worm, 624.

VERAI, VERAIE, VERAIS, *adj.* true, 2343; 603, 2287; 1507, 1893.
VERAIMENT, *adv.* truly, 1168.
VERGELE, VERGELES, *sf.* wand, 1303, 1308; 3330, 3331.
VERGELETE, *sf.* small wand, 3325.
VERITÉ, VERITÉS, VERITEZ, *sf.* truth, 1188, 1768; 3375; 598, 3457.
VERMEIL, VERMEILLE, *adj.* red, crimson, 267, 1562; 1830.
VERRIEZ, *cond.* 5, VEIR, *vb.* see, 1941.
VERS, *prep.* towards, 290, 428.
VERS, *sm.* worms, 3246.
VERTU, VERTUS, VERTUZ, *sf.* virtue, 3288; 1651, 1655; 565, 605.
VESQUIRENT, *pft.* 6, VIVRE, *vb.* live, 2448.
VESTE, *past part.*, VESTIR, *vb.* clothe, dress, 2708.
VESTEMENT, VESTEMENZ, *sm.* clothing, clothes, robe, 2299, 2696; 2297.
VESTEURE, VESTEURES, *sf.* clothing, 3475; 2839.
VESTIR, *vb.* VESTUZ, *past part.*, clothe, put on clothes, 2696; 638, 1896.
VEU, *past part.*, VEOIR, *vb.* see, 571, 2986.
VEUE, *sf.* sight, 921, 2869.
VEULT, *pr.* 3, VOLOIR, *vb.* wish, 2187.
VI, *pft.* 1, VEOIR, *vb.* see, 1327.
VIANDE, VIANDES, *sf.* food, 1098, 2012; 365.
VICES, *sm.* vice, 659, 837.
VICTORIE, *sf.* victory, 653, 672.
VIE, *sf.* life, 24, 262.
VIEGNE, *imper. sing.*, VIEGNES, *pr. subj.* 2, VENIR, *vb.* come, 147, 2423; 1156, 1727.
VIEL, *adj.* old, 241.
VIELLARD, *sm.* old man, 237.
VIELS, *adj.* old, 1575.
VIEN, *pr.* 3 and *imper. sing.*, VIENENT, *pr.* 6, VIENGNE, *imper. sing.* and *pr. subj.* 3, VIENS, *pr.* 2, VIENT, *pr.* 3, VENIR, *vb.* come, 409, 916; 931, 2159; 53, 253; 75; 665; 586, 606, 642, 643; 14, 282.
VIEX, VIEZ, *adj.* old, 340; 199, 2628.
VIF, *sm.* living state, 3118.
VIGNE, VIGNES, *sf.* vine, 334, 335; 330, 554.
VIL, VILS, *adj.* wretched, 1856; 992, 1260.
VILAIN, VILAINS, *sm.* peasant, person of low birth, p. 97, ll. 1, 9.
VILE, *sf.* town, 2538.
VILTE, *sf.* wretchedness, 2265.
VIN, VINS, *sm.* wine, 167, 208; 200, 2961.
VING, *pft.* 1, VINT, *pft.* 3, VENIR, *vb.* come, 1195; 98, 206.

VIRGELE, *sf.* slender column, wand, 1301.
VIRGES, *sf.* virgins, 1631.
VIRGINAL, *adj.* virginal, 2243.
VIRGINITÉ, *sf.* virginity, 3064, 3073.
VIRGNE, *sf.* and *adj.* virgin, 1643, 1703, 1758.
VIS, *sm.* face, 1212, 1864.
VISION, *sf.* vision, 2740.
VISITAST, *impf. subj.* 3, VISITE, *pr.* 3, VISITENT, *pr.* 6, VISITER, *vb.* visit, examine, 2066; 3252; 3477.
VIT, *pft.* 3, VEOIR, *vb.* see, 1882.
VIVANT, VIVANZ, *pres. part.*, VIVRONT, *fut.* 6, VIVRE, *vb.* live, 2337; 3044; 973; 429, 770.
VIVE, *adj.* living, 2337.
VOI, *pr.* 1, VOIANZ, *pres. part.*, VOIENT, *pr.* 6, VOIES, *pr. subj.* 2, VOIEZ, *pr.* 5, VOIOMS, *imper. pl.* 4, VEOIR, *vb.* see, 763, 765; 1766; 1780, 2633; 1007, 1010; 1594; 1867.
VOIE, *sf.* way, road, 42, 828.
VOIR, VOIRE, VOIRS, *adj.* true, 175, 1961; 105, 1484; 1489, 1859.
VOIREMENT, *adv.* truly, 1005, 3233.
VOIS, *sf.* voice, 1128.
VOISINES, VOISINS, *sm.* and *sf.* neighbour, 689, 1090; 550.
VOIT, *pr.* 3, VEOIR, *vb.* see, 132, 161.
VOIZ, *sf.* voice, 844, 972.
VOLDROIE, *cond.* 1, VOLOIR, *vb.* wish, 391.
VOLE, *pr.* 3, VOLER, *vb.* fly, 2909.
VOLENTÉ, VOLENTEZ, *sf.* desire, wish, will, 2882, 3412; 1026, 1028.
VOLENTIERS, *adv.* willingly, 908, 1396.
VOLEZ, *pr.* 5, VOLIST, *impf. subj.* 3, VOLOIE, *impf.* 1, VOLOIT, *impf.* 3, VOLOMS, VOLONS, *pr.* 4, VOLRA, *fut.* 3, VOLRENT, *fut.* 6, VOLROIE, *cond.* 1, VOLROIT, *cond.* 3, VOLRONT, *fut.* 6, VOLT, *pft.* 3, VOLUNS, *pr.* 4, VOLOIR, *vb.* wish, desire, 273, 827; 3076; 504; 2481, 3023; 2987; 2762, 3026; 698, 1498; 994; 1131; 695, 1107; 881, 1761; 2902; 72.
VOLOIR, *sm.* desire, 72.
VOLONTÉ, *sf.* wish, desire, 870.
VOLPISELES, *sf.* female fox cubs (Song of Songs 2: 15: 'little foxes'), 1043.
VOLUNTEZ, *sf.* wishes, 433.
VONT, *pr.* 6, ALEIR, *vb.* go, 53, 814.
VOS, *pron.* you, 44, 46.
VOSTRE, *poss. adj.* your, 2352.

VOZ, *pron.* you, 1338.
VRAIEMENT, VRAIMENT, *adv.* truly, 615; 212.
VRAIS, *adj.* true, 1365, 2783.
VUEIL, *pr.* 1, VUILLE, *pr. subj.* 3, VUELENT, *pr.* 6, VUELS, *pr.* 2, VUELSZ, *pr.* 2, VUELT, *pr.* 3, VOLOIR, *vb.* wish, desire, will, 128, 306; 42, 2602; 3138; 447, 3381; 3091; 2, 40.
VUEL, *sm.* wish, desire, 2586.
VUIDE, VUIT, VUIZ, *adj.* empty, void, 1183; 3414; 4, 2315.
VULPILLES, *sf.* female foxes, 1055.
VULT, *pft.* 3, VOLOIR, *vb.* wish, desire, 1170.

VUOLPISELES, *sf.* female fox cubs, 1067, 1073, 1123.

WAEGNIER, *vb.* gain, earn, p. 97, l. 2.
WAGEURE, *sf.* promise, guarantee, 2939.
WAPE, *adj.* weak, lacking in strength, 223.
WARDE, *pr.* 3, WARDER, *vb.* look forward to, 3104.
WARIST, *pr.* 3, WARIR, *vb.* provision, 2907.
WUIZ, *adj.* empty, void, 2776.

YPOCRESIE, YPRECRESIE *sf.* hypocrisy, 359; 1948.